STAR WARS®
AGENT OF THE EMPIRE

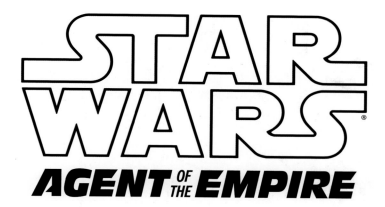

Illustration by » STÉPHANE ROUX

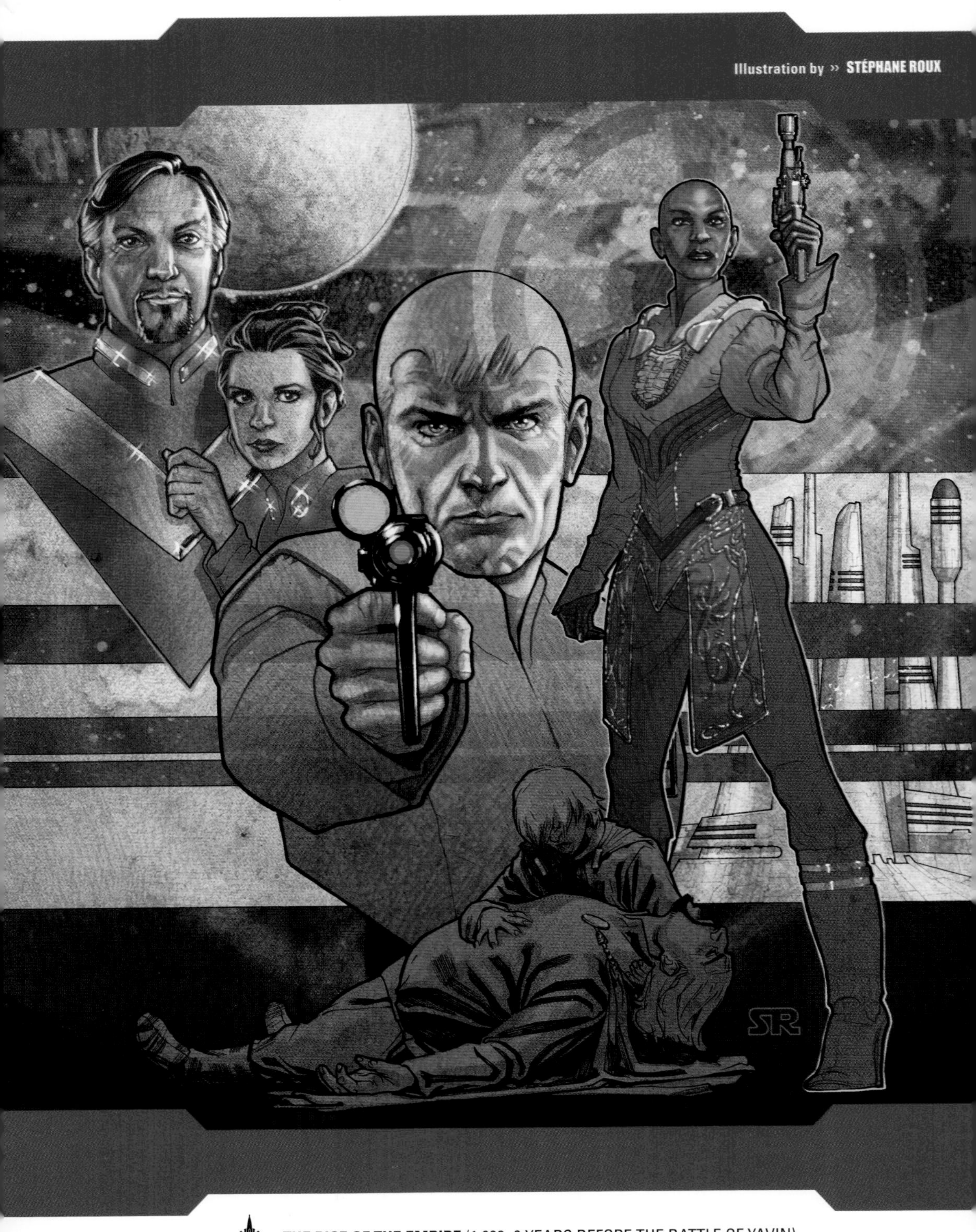

THE RISE OF THE EMPIRE (1,000–0 YEARS BEFORE THE BATTLE OF YAVIN)

After the seeming final defeat of the Sith, the Republic enters a state of complacency. In the waning years of the Republic, the Senate rife with corruption, the ambitious Senator Palpatine causes himself to be elected Supreme Chancellor. This is the era of the prequel trilogy.

The events in this story take place approximately three years before the events in Star Wars: *Episode IV*—A New Hope.

STAR WARS®
AGENT OF THE EMPIRE

VOLUME TWO

HARD TARGETS

Script
JOHN OSTRANDER

Pencils
DAVIDÉ FABBRI

Inks
CHRISTIAN DALLA VECCHIA

Colors
WES DZIOBA

Lettering
MICHAEL HEISLER

Cover Art
STÉPHANE ROUX

DARK HORSE BOOKS
LUCAS BOOKS

president and publisher
MIKE RICHARDSON

collection designer
JIMMY PRESLER

editor
RANDY STRADLEY

assistant editor
FREDDYE LINS

Special thanks to **JENNIFER HEDDLE, LELAND CHEE, TROY ALDERS, CAROL ROEDER, JANN MOORHEAD,** and **DAVID ANDERMAN** at Lucas Licensing.

NEIL HANKERSON Executive Vice President TOM WEDDLE Chief Financial Officer RANDY STRADLEY Vice President of Publishing MICHAEL MARTENS Vice President of Book Trade Sales ANITA NELSON Vice President of Business Affairs SCOTT ALLIE Editor in Chief MATT PARKINSON Vice President of Marketing DAVID SCROGGY Vice President of Product Development DALE LAFOUNTAIN Vice President of Information Technology DARLENE VOGEL Senior Director of Print, Design, and Production KEN LIZZI General Counsel DAVEY ESTRADA Editorial Director CHRIS WARNER Senior Books Editor DIANA SCHUTZ Executive Editor CARY GRAZZINI Director of Print and Development LIA RIBACCHI Art Director CARA NIECE Director of Scheduling TIM WIESCH Director of International Licensing MARK BERNARDI Director of Digital Publishing

STAR WARS®: AGENT OF THE EMPIRE Volume 2—HARD TARGETS

This volume collects issues #1–#5 of the Dark Horse comic-book series *Star Wars: Agent of the Empire—Hard Targets*.

Published by Dark Horse Books, a division of Dark Horse Comics, Inc.
10956 SE Main Street, Milwaukie, OR 97222

DarkHorse.com
StarWars.com

International Licensing: 503-905-2377
To find a comics shop in your area, call the Comic Shop Locator Service toll-free at 1-888-266-4226

LIBRARY OF CONGRESS CATALOGING-IN-PUBLICATION DATA

Ostrander, John.
Star Wars, agent of the empire. Volume 2, Hard targets / script, John Ostrander ; pencils, Davidé Fabbri ; inks, Christian Dalla Vecchia ; colors, Wes Dzioba ; lettering, Michael Heisler ; cover art, Stéphane Roux.
  pages cm
Summary: "When the current Count Dooku is assassinated and Boba Fett is framed for the murder, Imperial Agent Jahan Cross is assigned to make sure the ramifications favor the Empire"--Provided by publisher.
ISBN 978-1-61655-167-4
1. Star Wars fiction--Comic books, strips, etc. 2. Graphic novels. I. Fabbri, Davidé. II. Dalla Vecchia, Christian. III. Roux, Stéphane. IV. Title. V. Title: Hard targets.
PN6728.S730834 2013
741.5'973--dc23
                    2013010624

First edition: July 2013
ISBN 978-1-61655-167-4

10 9 8 7 6 5 4 3 2 1
Printed in China

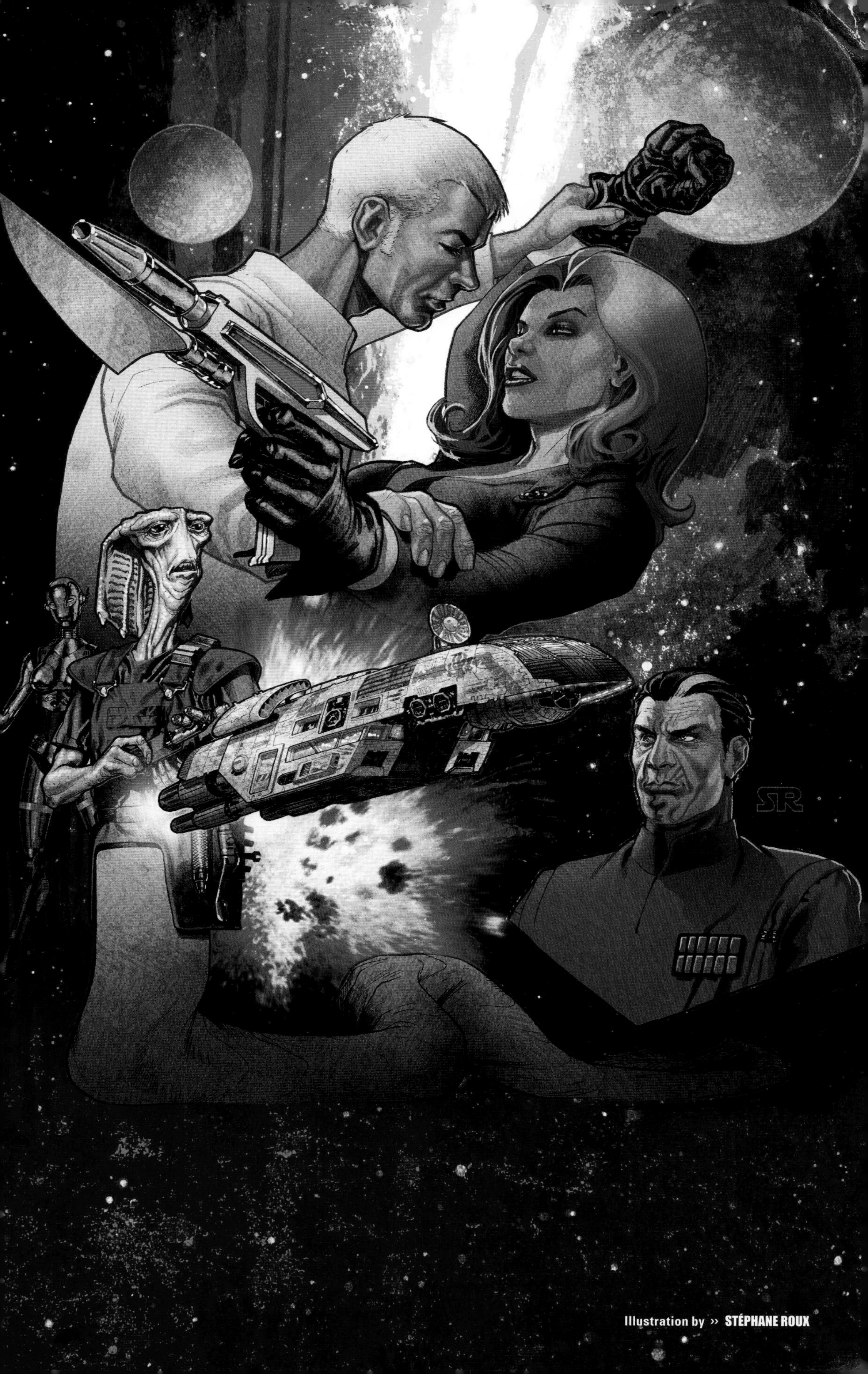

Illustration by ›› STÉPHANE ROUX

FOR THE AGENTS OF IMPERIAL INTELLIGENCE, information gathering and assessment is just a part of the job. Their ongoing mission is to further the Emperor's control in all aspects of galactic policy and politics, by whatever means necessary—overt, covert, or duplicitous.

Agent of the Empire Jahan Cross is the very best of Imperial Intelligence—a man willing and able to get any job done, no matter what it takes . . . and no matter what the cost to his own conscience. Thus far.

Quickly, quietly, and efficiently is how Cross's missions are supposed to play out. But sometimes discretion is impossible . . .

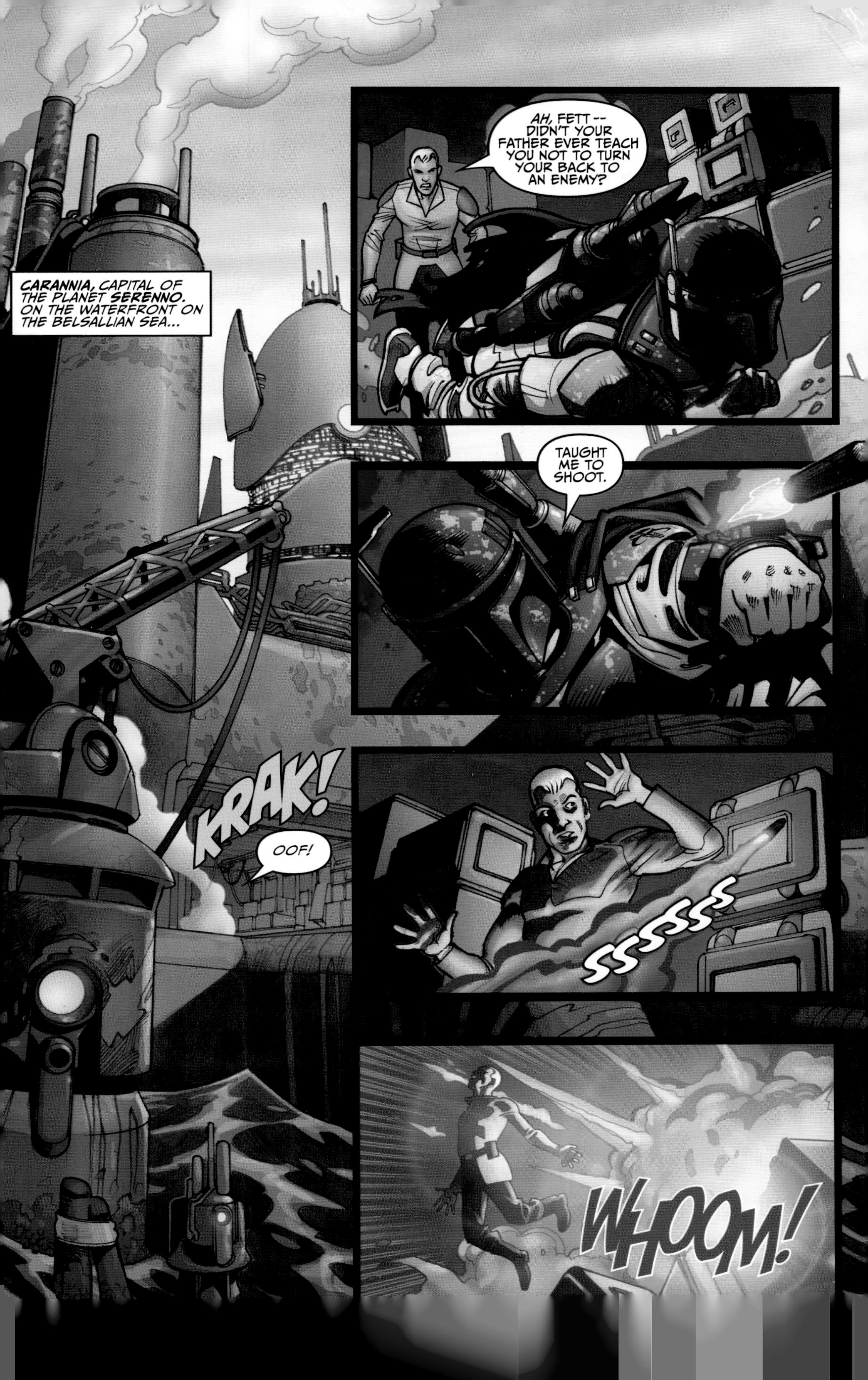
CARANNIA, CAPITAL OF THE PLANET SERENNO. ON THE WATERFRONT ON THE BELSALLIAN SEA...
AH, FETT -- DIDN'T YOUR FATHER EVER TEACH YOU NOT TO TURN YOUR BACK TO AN ENEMY?
TAUGHT ME TO SHOOT.
KRAK!
OOF!
SSSSSS
WHOOM!

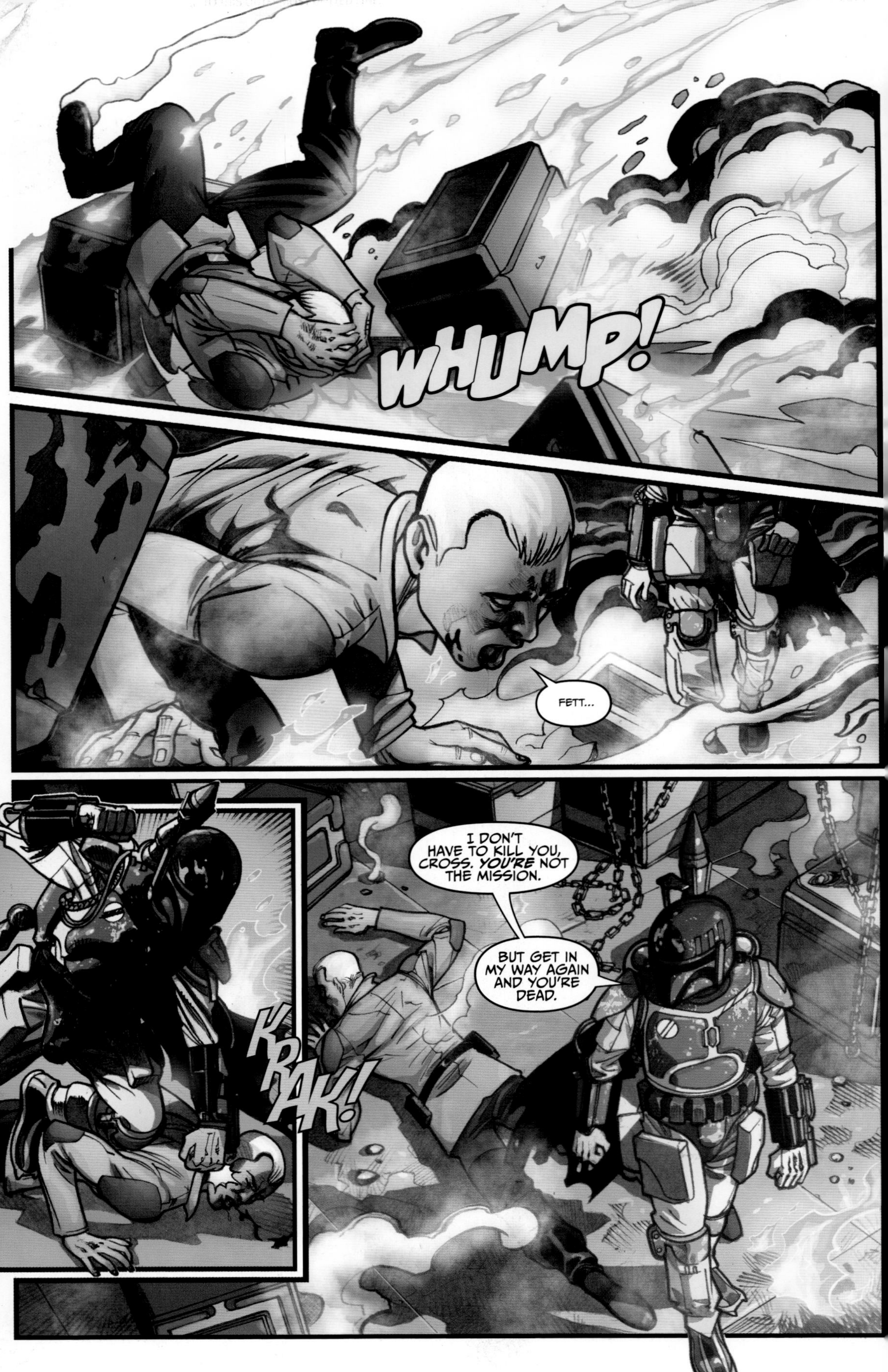
WHUMP!
FETT...
I DON'T HAVE TO KILL YOU, CROSS. YOU'RE NOT THE MISSION.
BUT GET IN MY WAY AGAIN AND YOU'RE DEAD.
KRAK!

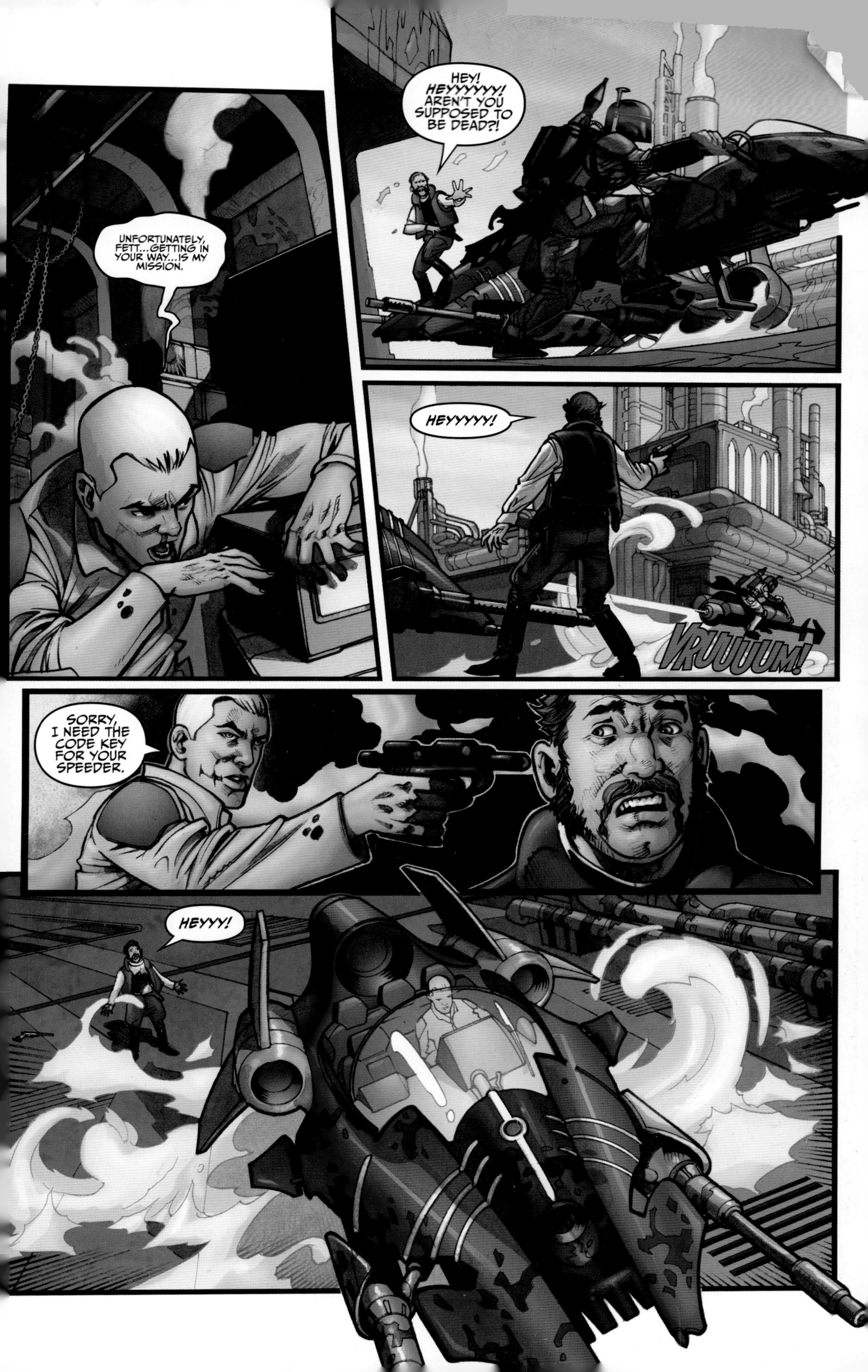
UNFORTUNATELY, FETT...GETTING IN YOUR WAY...IS MY MISSION.
HEY! *HEYYYYYY!* AREN'T YOU SUPPOSED TO BE DEAD?!
HEYYYYY!
VRUUUUM!
SORRY, I NEED THE CODE KEY FOR YOUR SPEEDER.
HEYYY!

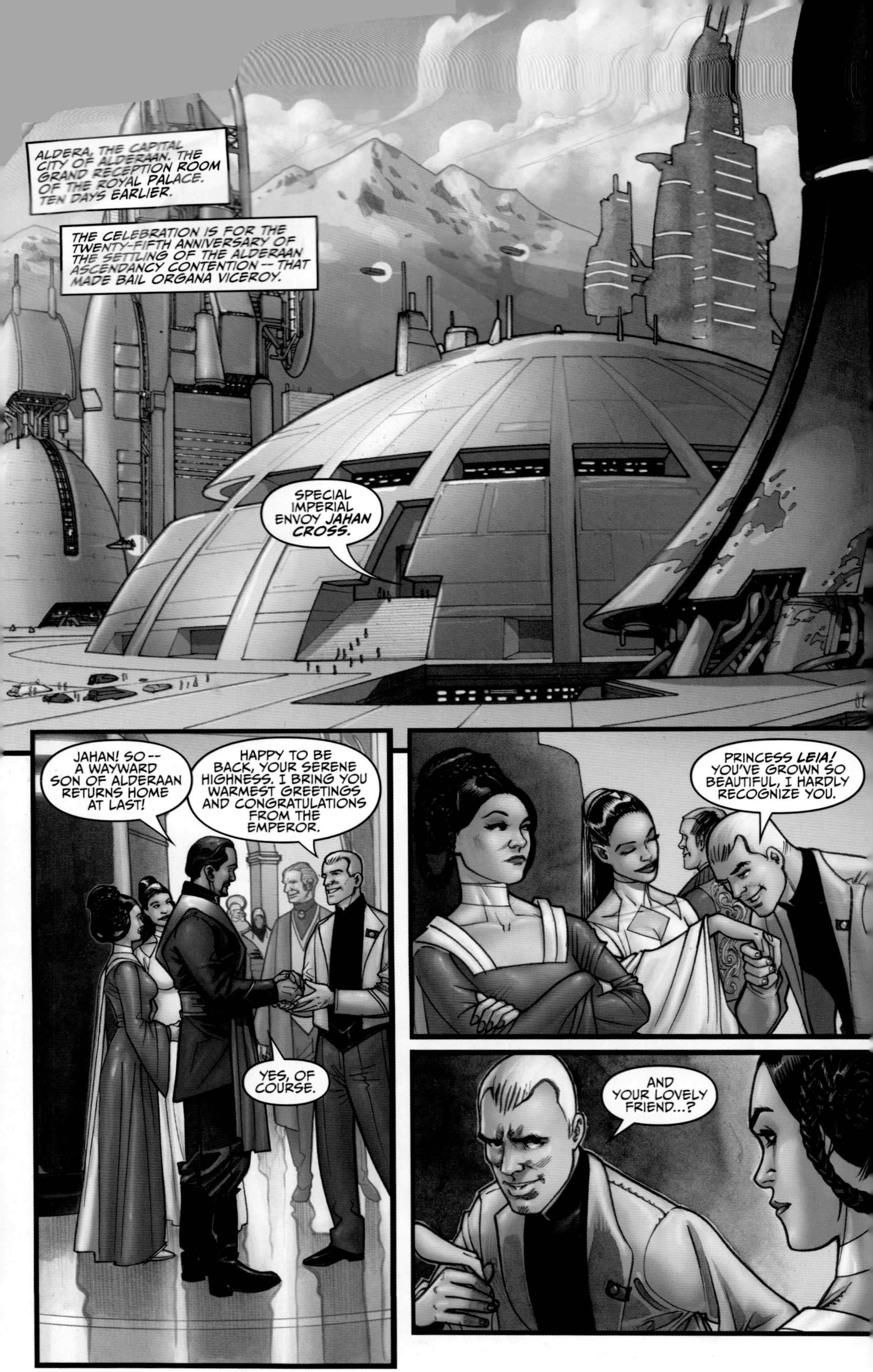
ALDERA, THE CAPITAL CITY OF ALDERAAN. THE GRAND RECEPTION ROOM OF THE ROYAL PALACE. TEN DAYS EARLIER.
THE CELEBRATION IS FOR THE TWENTY-FIFTH ANNIVERSARY OF THE SETTLING OF THE ALDERAAN ASCENDANCY CONTENTION -- THAT MADE BAIL ORGANA VICEROY.
SPECIAL IMPERIAL ENVOY JAHAN CROSS.
JAHAN! SO -- A WAYWARD SON OF ALDERAAN RETURNS HOME AT LAST!
HAPPY TO BE BACK, YOUR SERENE HIGHNESS. I BRING YOU WARMEST GREETINGS AND CONGRATULATIONS FROM THE EMPEROR.
YES, OF COURSE.
PRINCESS LEIA! YOU'VE GROWN SO BEAUTIFUL, I HARDLY RECOGNIZE YOU.
AND YOUR LOVELY FRIEND...?

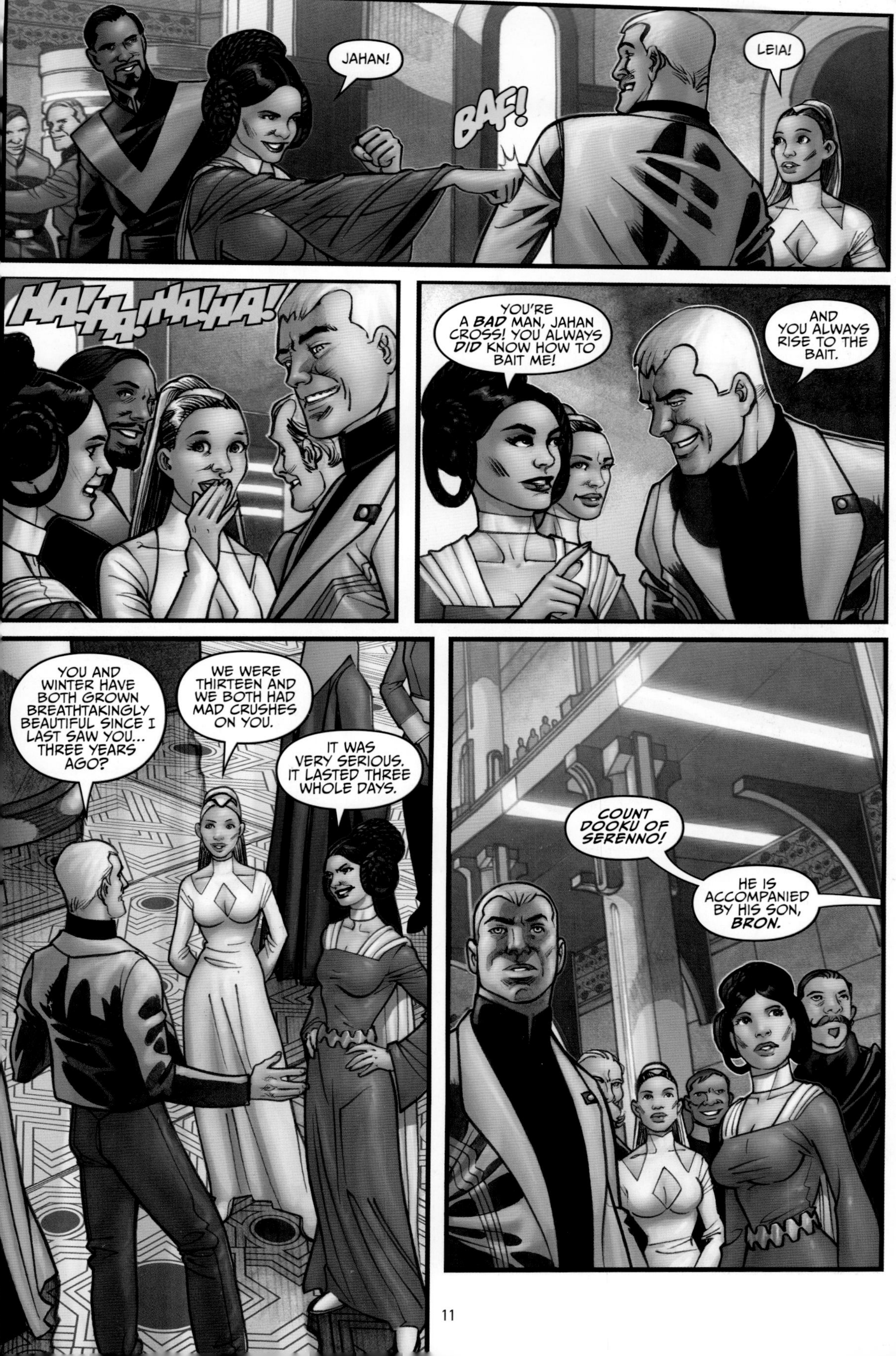
JAHAN!
BAF!
LEIA!
HA! HA! HA! HA!
YOU'RE A BAD MAN, JAHAN CROSS! YOU ALWAYS DID KNOW HOW TO BAIT ME!
AND YOU ALWAYS RISE TO THE BAIT.
YOU AND WINTER HAVE BOTH GROWN BREATHTAKINGLY BEAUTIFUL SINCE I LAST SAW YOU... THREE YEARS AGO?
WE WERE THIRTEEN AND WE BOTH HAD MAD CRUSHES ON YOU.
IT WAS VERY SERIOUS. IT LASTED THREE WHOLE DAYS.
COUNT DOOKU OF SERENNO!
HE IS ACCOMPANIED BY HIS SON, BRON.

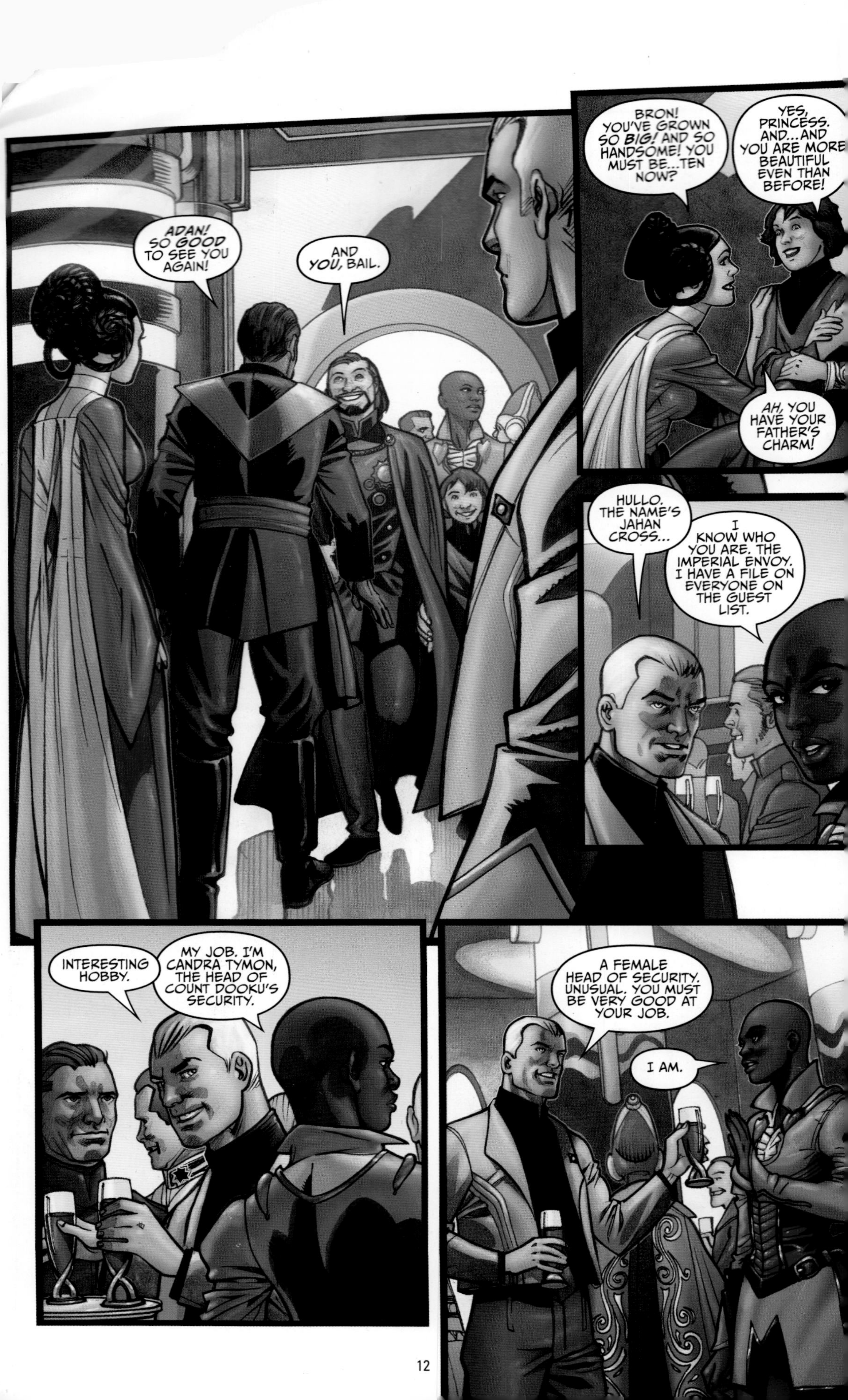
ADAN! SO GOOD TO SEE YOU AGAIN!
AND YOU, BAIL.
BRON! YOU'VE GROWN SO BIG! AND SO HANDSOME! YOU MUST BE...TEN NOW?
YES, PRINCESS. AND...AND YOU ARE MORE BEAUTIFUL EVEN THAN BEFORE!
AH, YOU HAVE YOUR FATHER'S CHARM!
HULLO. THE NAME'S JAHAN CROSS...
I KNOW WHO YOU ARE. THE IMPERIAL ENVOY. I HAVE A FILE ON EVERYONE ON THE GUEST LIST.
INTERESTING HOBBY.
MY JOB. I'M CANDRA TYMON, THE HEAD OF COUNT DOOKU'S SECURITY.
A FEMALE HEAD OF SECURITY. UNUSUAL. YOU MUST BE VERY GOOD AT YOUR JOB.
I AM.

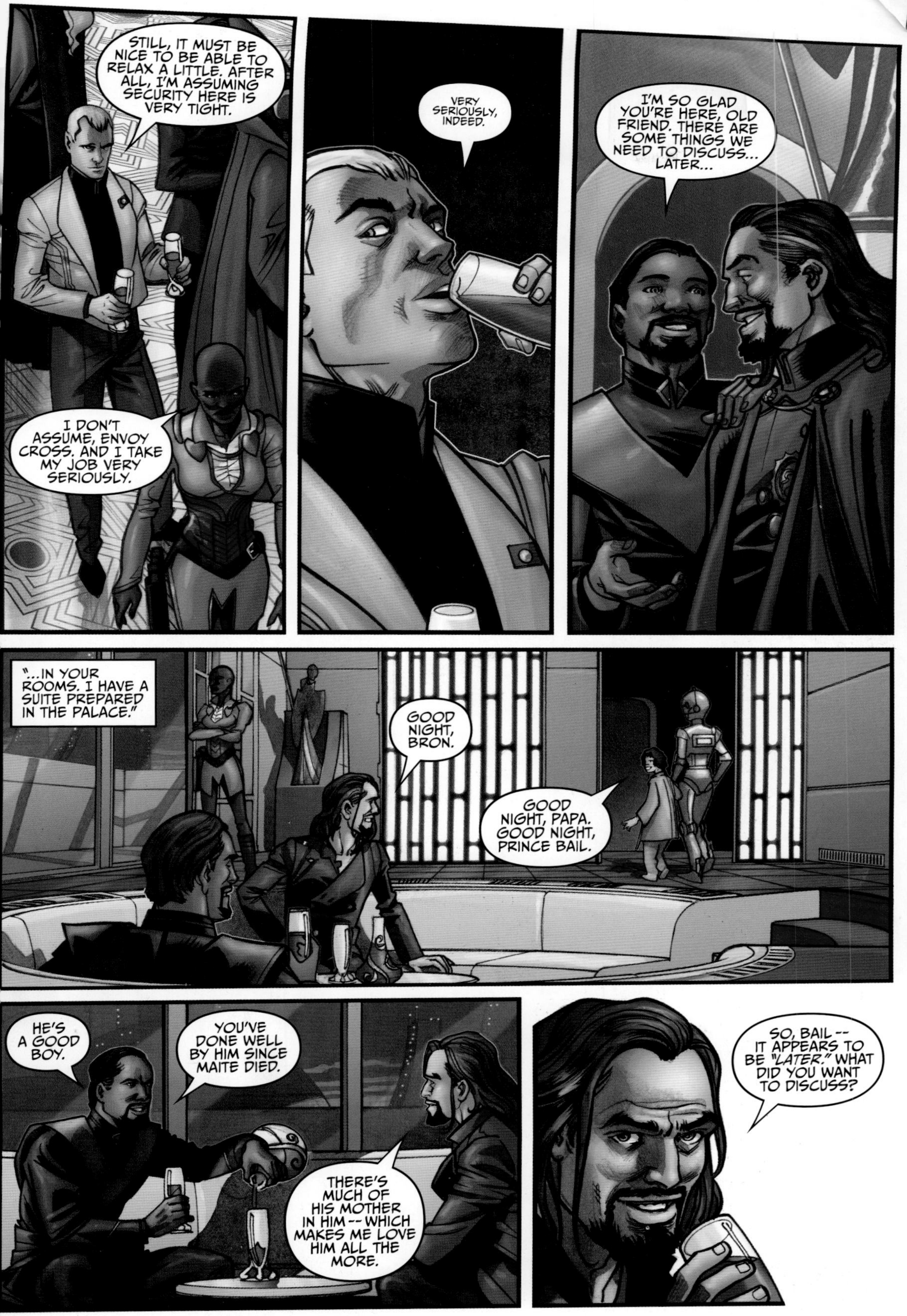
STILL, IT MUST BE NICE TO BE ABLE TO RELAX A LITTLE. AFTER ALL, I'M ASSUMING SECURITY HERE IS VERY TIGHT.
I DON'T ASSUME, ENVOY CROSS. AND I TAKE MY JOB VERY SERIOUSLY.
VERY SERIOUSLY, INDEED.
I'M SO GLAD YOU'RE HERE, OLD FRIEND. THERE ARE SOME THINGS WE NEED TO DISCUSS... LATER...
"...IN YOUR ROOMS. I HAVE A SUITE PREPARED IN THE PALACE."
GOOD NIGHT, BRON.
GOOD NIGHT, PAPA. GOOD NIGHT, PRINCE BAIL.
HE'S A GOOD BOY.
YOU'VE DONE WELL BY HIM SINCE MAITE DIED.
THERE'S MUCH OF HIS MOTHER IN HIM -- WHICH MAKES ME LOVE HIM ALL THE MORE.
SO, BAIL -- IT APPEARS TO BE "LATER." WHAT DID YOU WANT TO DISCUSS?

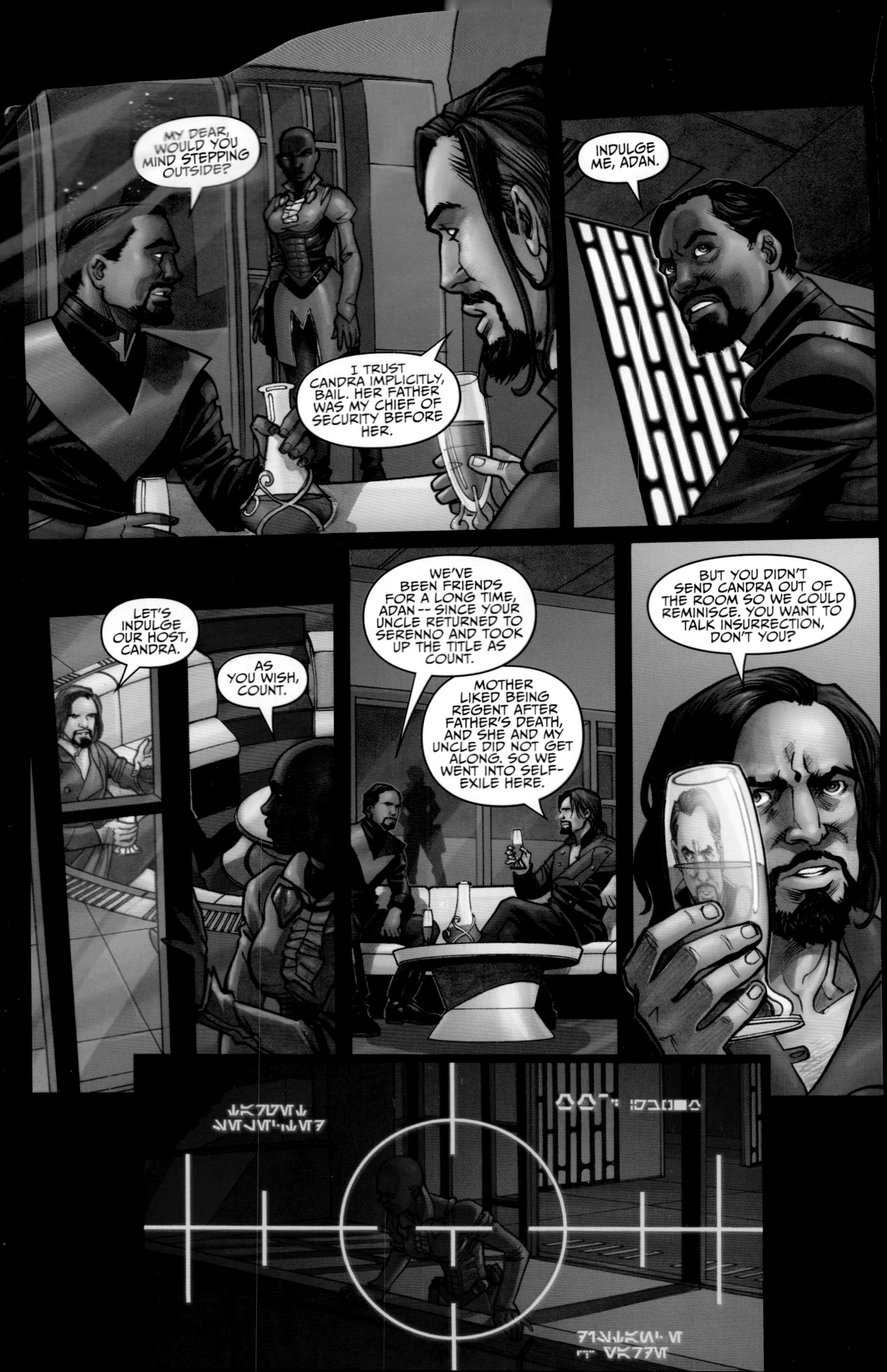
MY DEAR, WOULD YOU MIND STEPPING OUTSIDE?
I TRUST CANDRA IMPLICITLY, BAIL. HER FATHER WAS MY CHIEF OF SECURITY BEFORE HER.
INDULGE ME, ADAN.
LET'S INDULGE OUR HOST, CANDRA.
AS YOU WISH, COUNT.
WE'VE BEEN FRIENDS FOR A LONG TIME, ADAN -- SINCE YOUR UNCLE RETURNED TO SERENNO AND TOOK UP THE TITLE AS COUNT.
MOTHER LIKED BEING REGENT AFTER FATHER'S DEATH, AND SHE AND MY UNCLE DID NOT GET ALONG. SO WE WENT INTO SELF-EXILE HERE.
BUT YOU DIDN'T SEND CANDRA OUT OF THE ROOM SO WE COULD REMINISCE. YOU WANT TO TALK INSURRECTION, DON'T YOU?

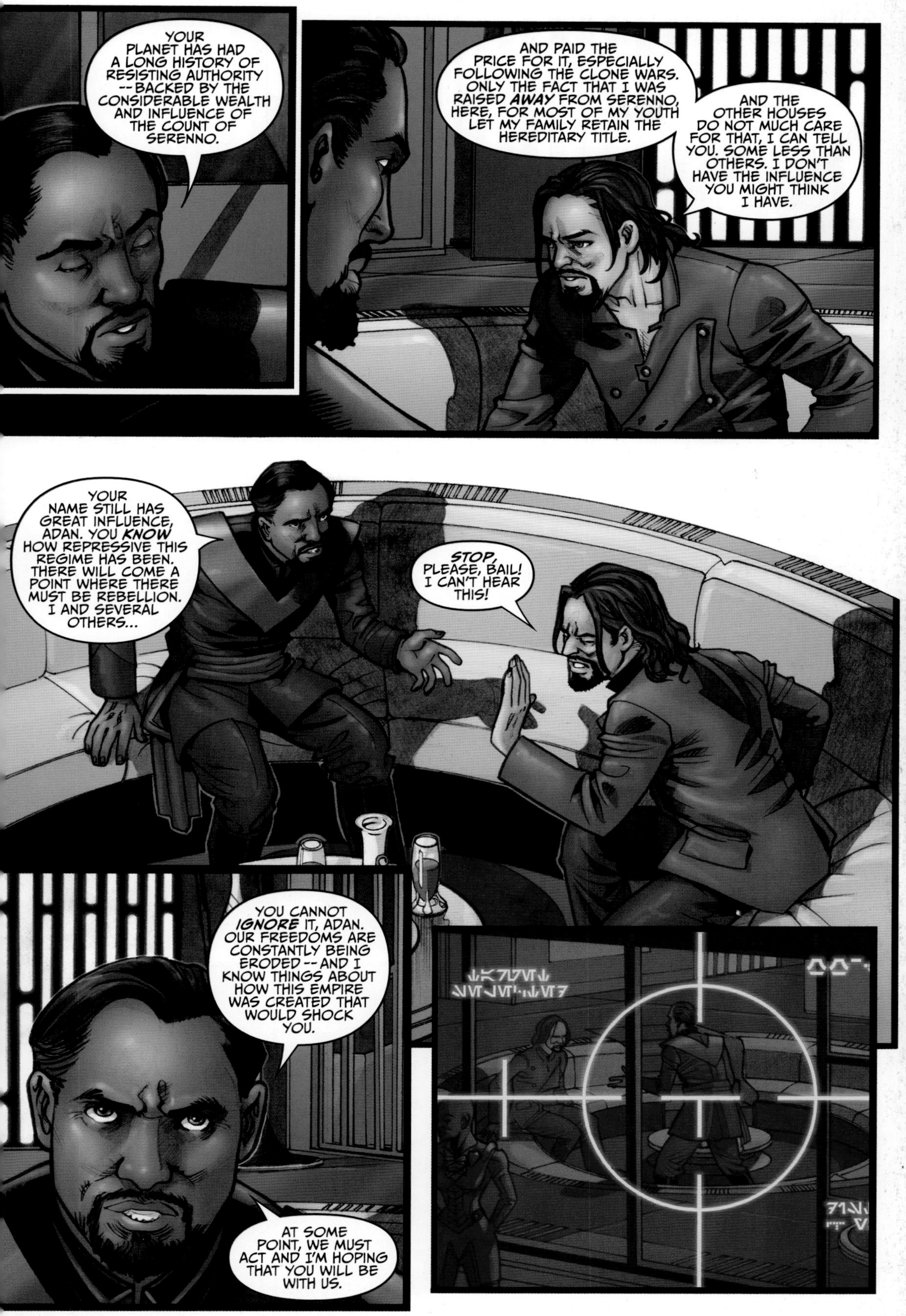
YOUR PLANET HAS HAD A LONG HISTORY OF RESISTING AUTHORITY --BACKED BY THE CONSIDERABLE WEALTH AND INFLUENCE OF THE COUNT OF SERENNO.
AND PAID THE PRICE FOR IT, ESPECIALLY FOLLOWING THE CLONE WARS. ONLY THE FACT THAT I WAS RAISED *AWAY* FROM SERENNO, HERE, FOR MOST OF MY YOUTH LET MY FAMILY RETAIN THE HEREDITARY TITLE.
AND THE OTHER HOUSES DO NOT MUCH CARE FOR THAT, I CAN TELL YOU. SOME LESS THAN OTHERS. I DON'T HAVE THE INFLUENCE YOU MIGHT THINK I HAVE.
YOUR NAME STILL HAS GREAT INFLUENCE, ADAN. YOU *KNOW* HOW REPRESSIVE THIS REGIME HAS BEEN. THERE WILL COME A POINT WHERE THERE MUST BE REBELLION. I AND SEVERAL OTHERS...
STOP, PLEASE, BAIL! I CAN'T HEAR THIS!
YOU CANNOT *IGNORE* IT, ADAN. OUR FREEDOMS ARE CONSTANTLY BEING ERODED--AND I KNOW THINGS ABOUT HOW THIS EMPIRE WAS CREATED THAT WOULD SHOCK YOU.
AT SOME POINT, WE MUST ACT AND I'M HOPING THAT YOU WILL BE WITH US.

THE EMPEROR'S POWER CONTINUES TO GROW AND SO DOES HIS AMBITION! HE WON'T BE SATISFIED UNTIL HIS WILL AND HIS WILL ALONE GOVERNS THE GALAXY!

YOU CAN'T KNOW THAT, BAIL!

I DO KNOW IT, ADAN! FAR MORE THAN YOU CAN GUESS! STARS, MAN -- ARE YOU IN DENIAL -- OR HAVE YOU SIMPLY BECOME A COWARD?!

FATHER? IS EVERYTHING ALL RIGHT? I HEARD VOICES...

IT'S FINE, BRON. EVERYTHING'S FINE. GO BACK TO BED.

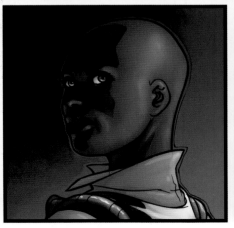

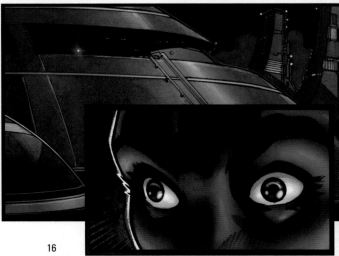

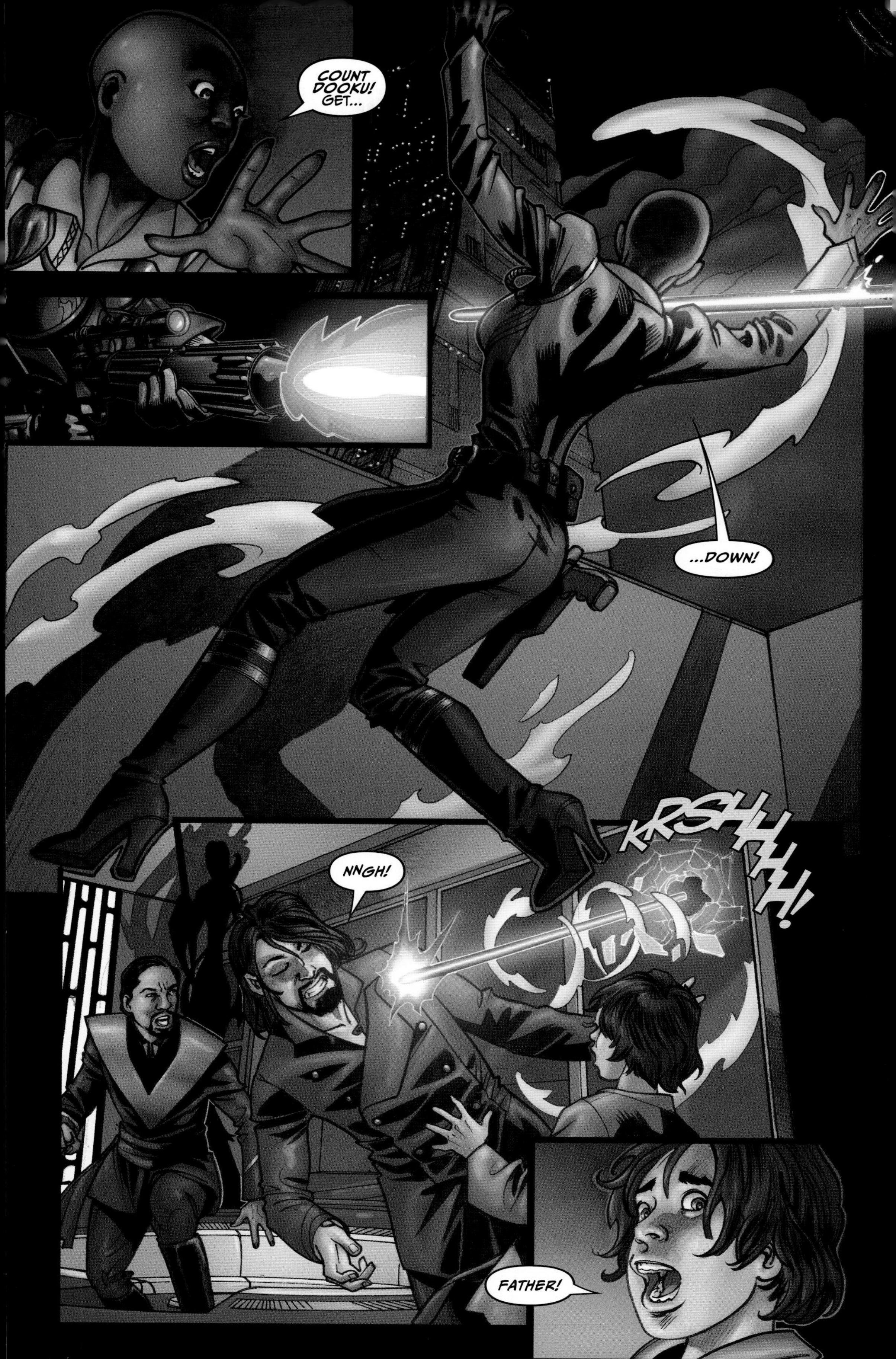
COUNT DOOKU! GET...
...DOWN!
NNGH!
KRSHHHH!
FATHER!

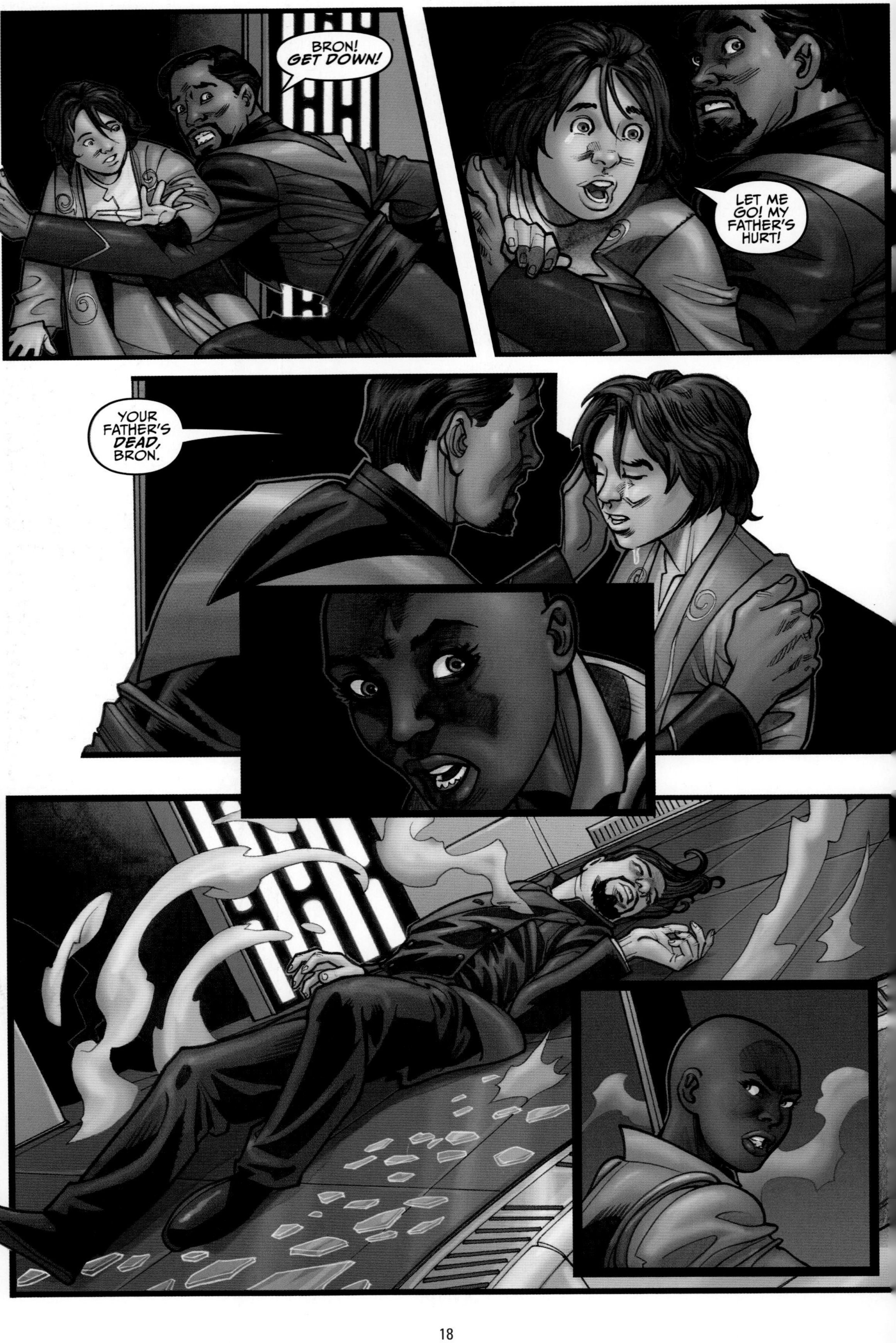
BRON! GET DOWN!
LET ME GO! MY FATHER'S HURT!
YOUR FATHER'S DEAD, BRON.

ALL UNITS! THIS IS CANDRA TYMON! COUNT DOOKU HAS BEEN SHOT! REPEAT, COUNT DOOKU IS DOWN! EMERGENCY MEDICS TO HIS SUITE IMMEDIATELY! SECURE THE PALACE!

THE SHOOTER IS ON THE ROOF OPPOSITE THE COUNT'S ROOMS, HEADING NORTHWEST! I'M IN PURSUIT!

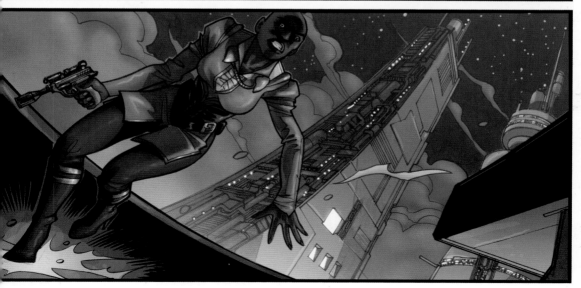

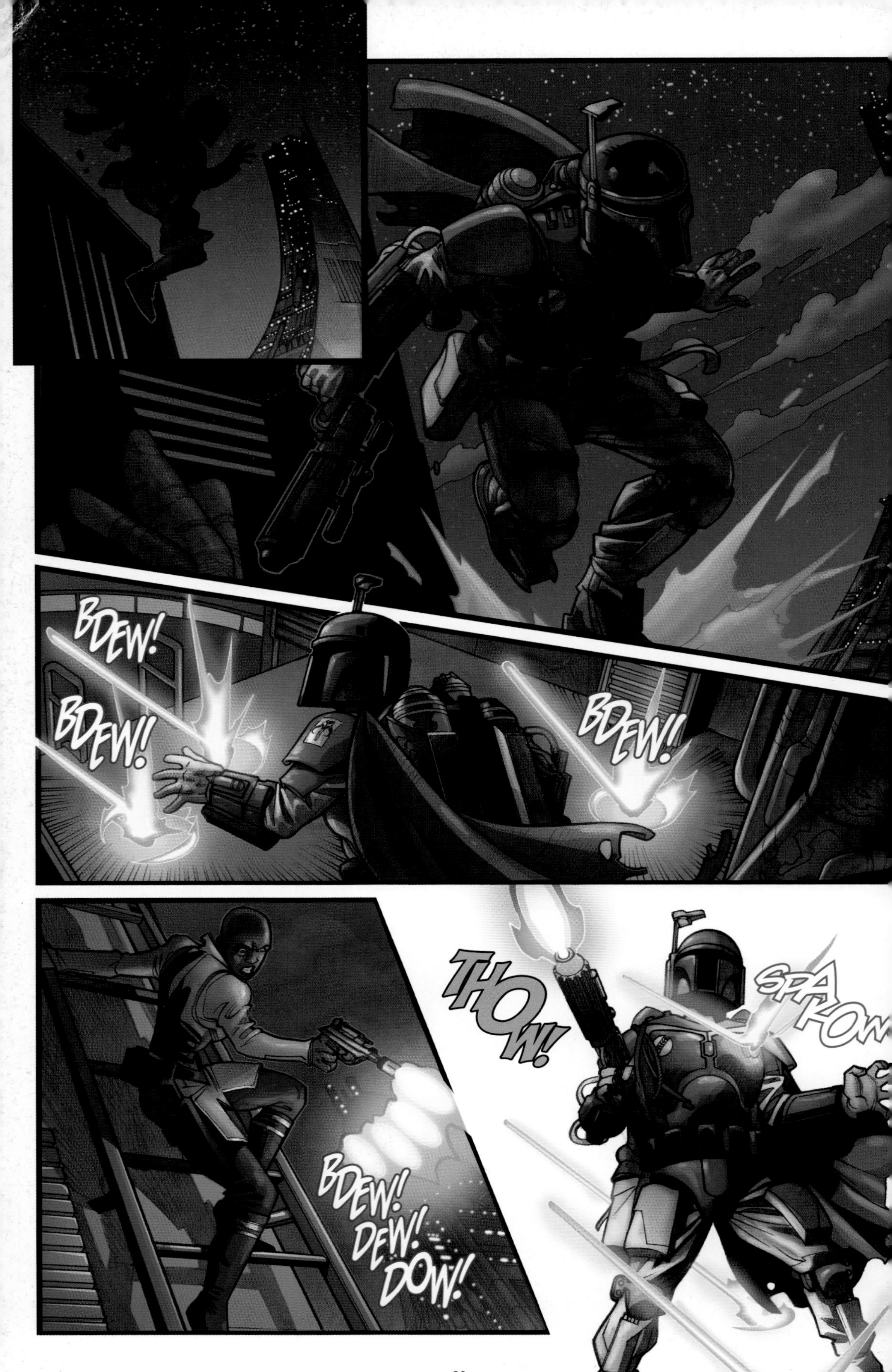
BDEW!
BDEW!
BDEW!
THOW!
SPAKOW
BDEW! DEW! DOW!

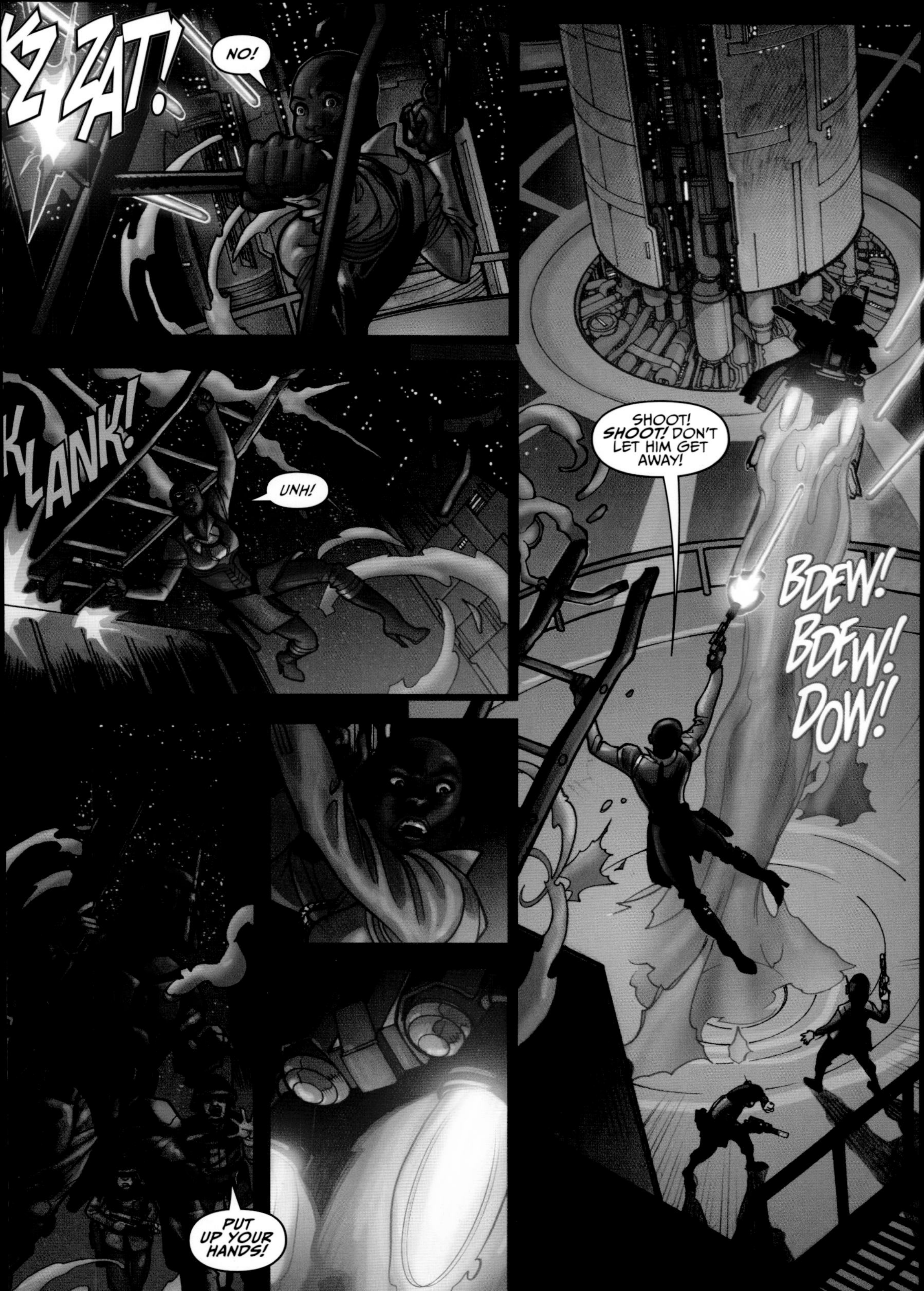
KZ ZAT!
NO!
KLANK!
UNH!
SHOOT! SHOOT! DON'T LET HIM GET AWAY!
BDEW! BDEW! DOW!
PUT UP YOUR HANDS!

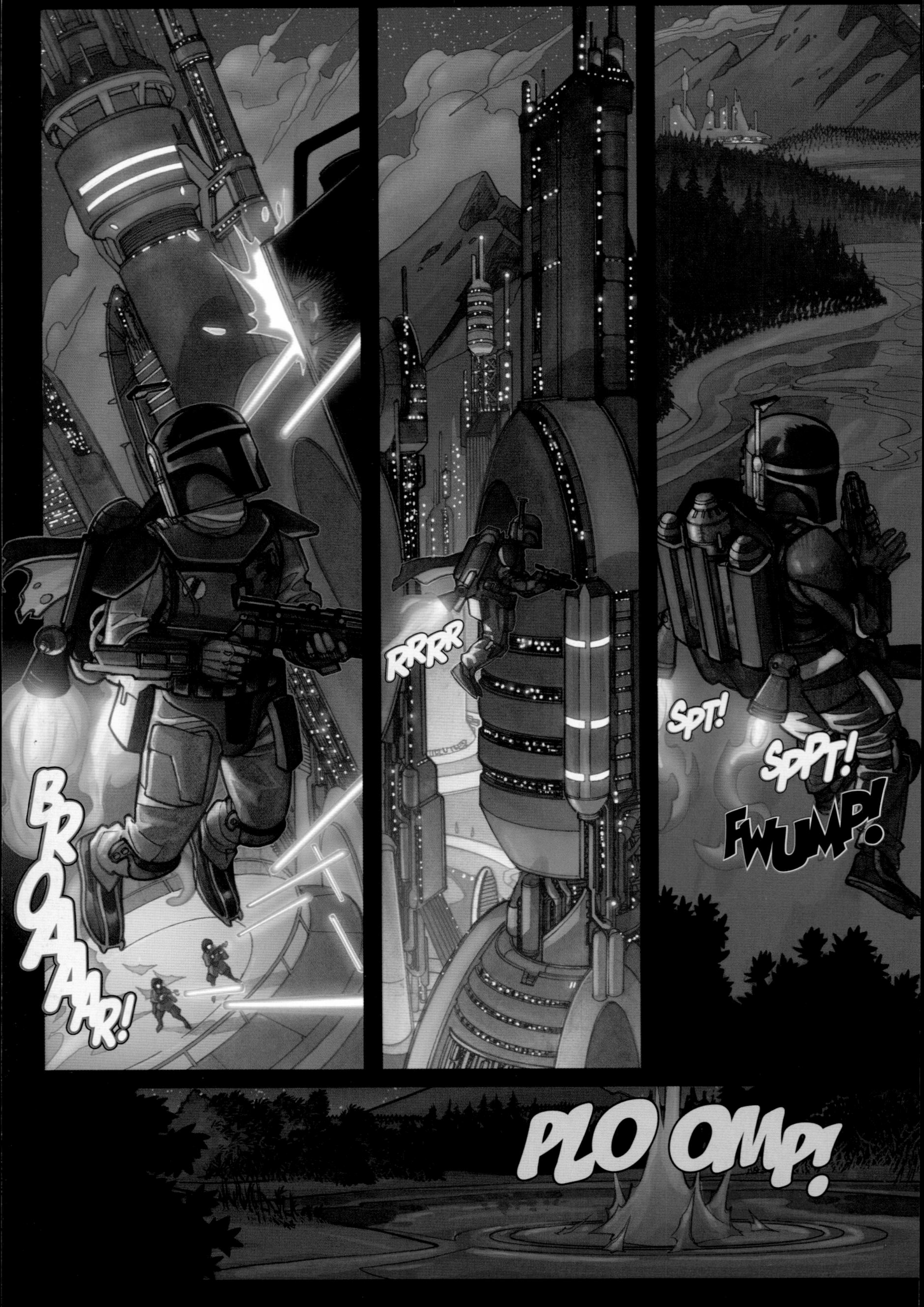
BROAAAR!
RRRR
SPT!
SPPT!
FWUMP!
PLO OMP!

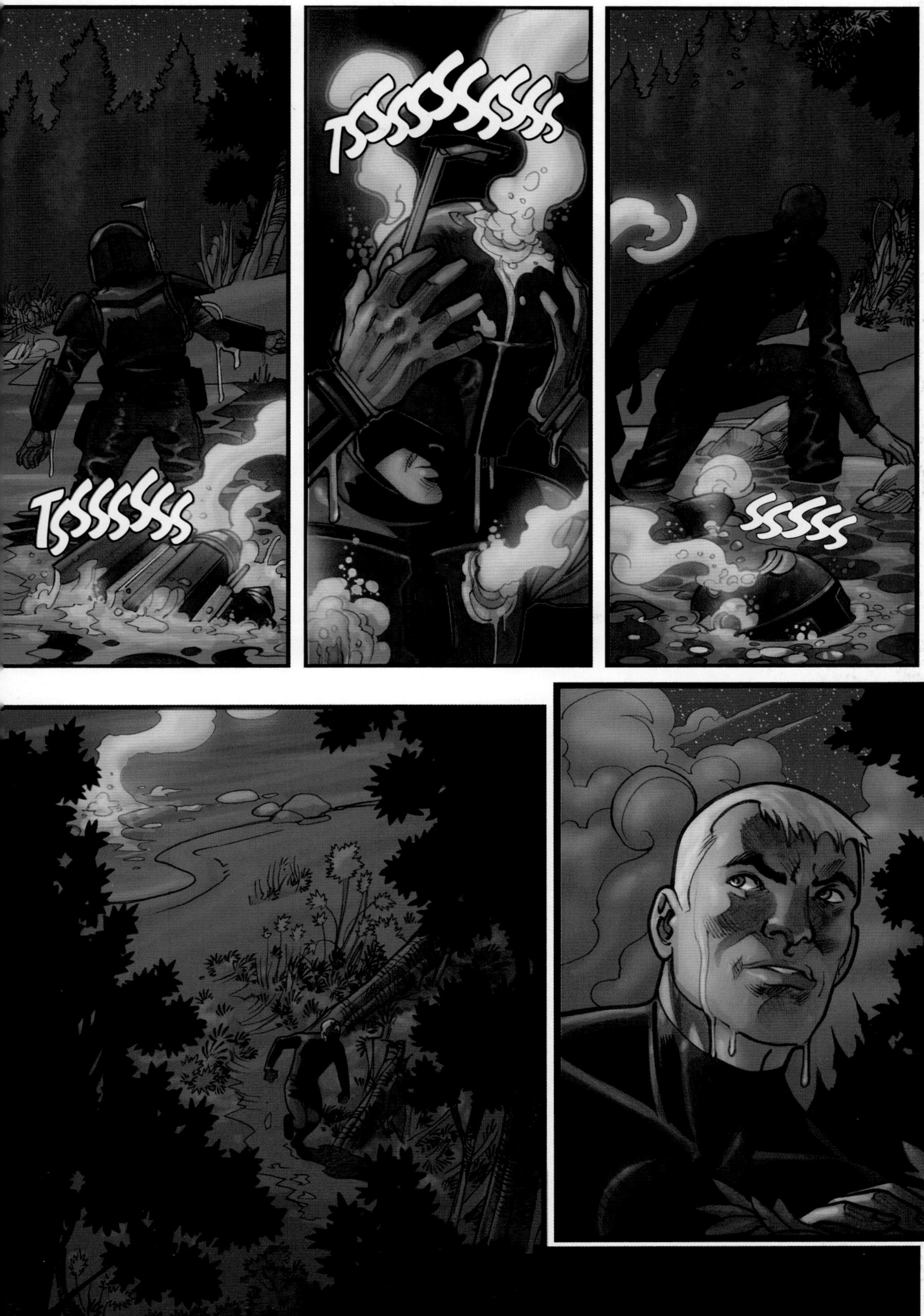
TSSSSSSS
TSSSSSSSSSSS
SSSSS

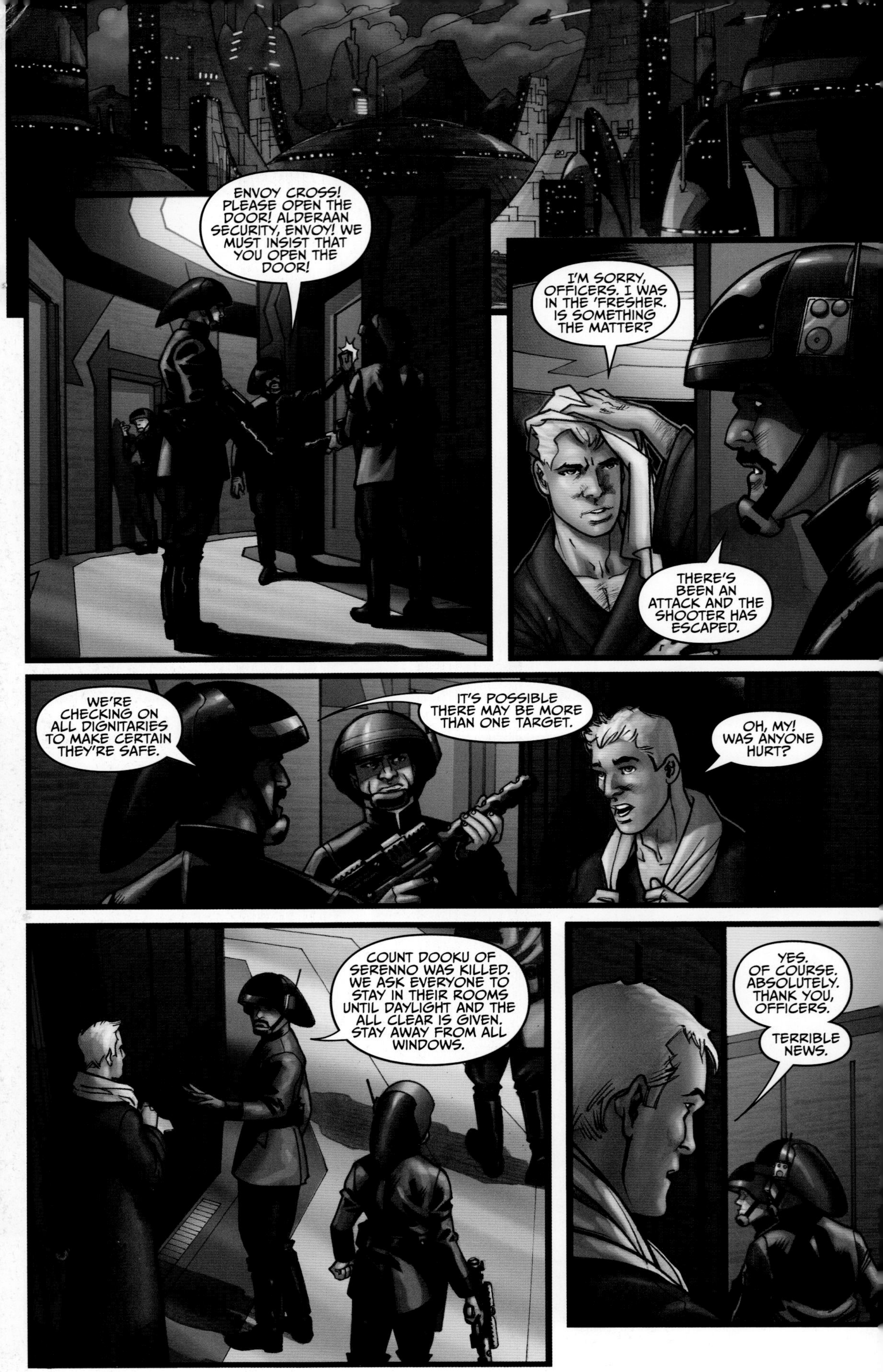

ENVOY CROSS! PLEASE OPEN THE DOOR! ALDERAAN SECURITY, ENVOY! WE MUST INSIST THAT YOU OPEN THE DOOR!
I'M SORRY, OFFICERS. I WAS IN THE 'FRESHER. IS SOMETHING THE MATTER?
THERE'S BEEN AN ATTACK AND THE SHOOTER HAS ESCAPED.
WE'RE CHECKING ON ALL DIGNITARIES TO MAKE CERTAIN THEY'RE SAFE.
IT'S POSSIBLE THERE MAY BE MORE THAN ONE TARGET.
OH, MY! WAS ANYONE HURT?
COUNT DOOKU OF SERENNO WAS KILLED. WE ASK EVERYONE TO STAY IN THEIR ROOMS UNTIL DAYLIGHT AND THE ALL CLEAR IS GIVEN. STAY AWAY FROM ALL WINDOWS.
YES. OF COURSE. ABSOLUTELY. THANK YOU, OFFICERS.
TERRIBLE NEWS.

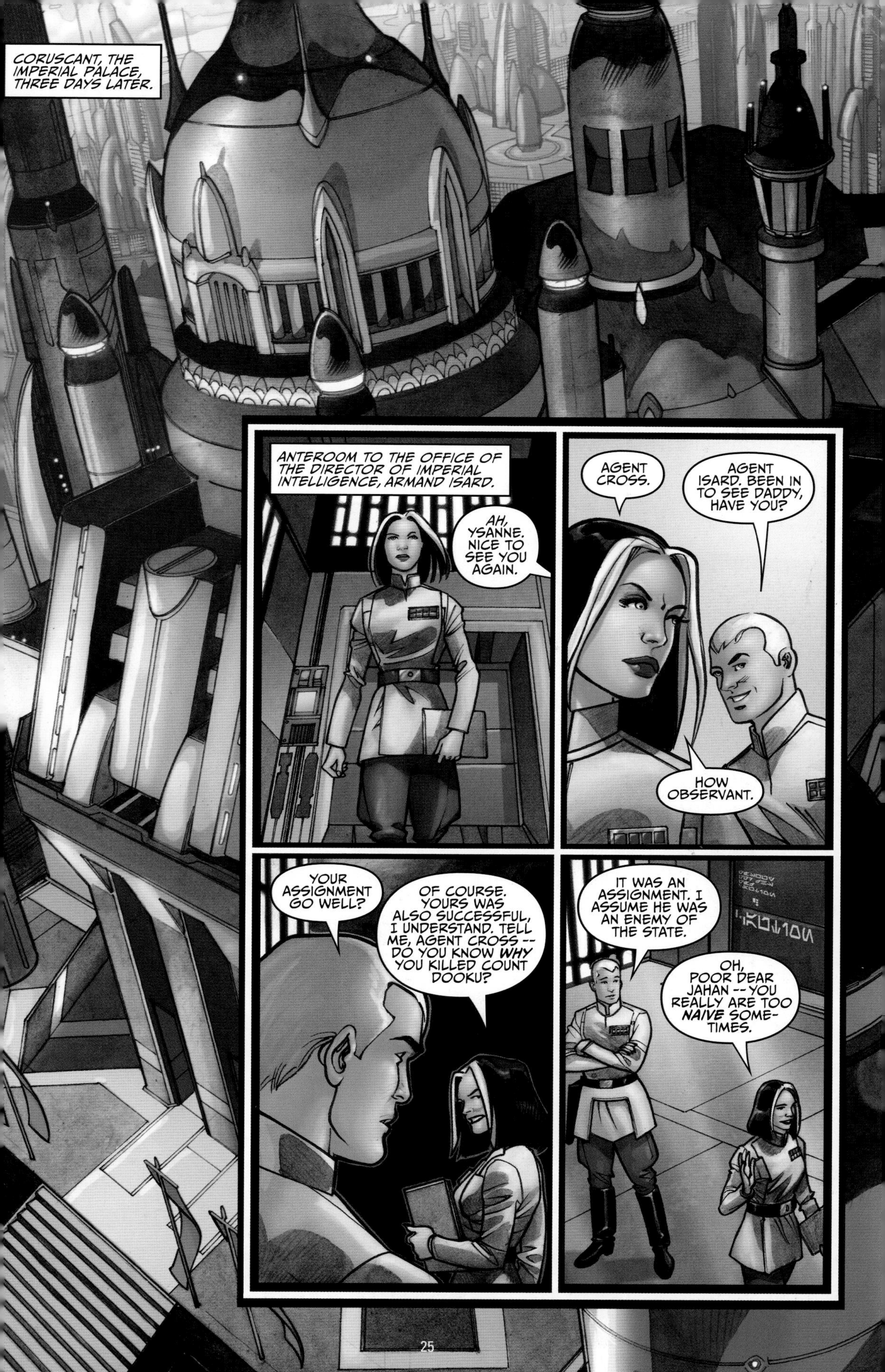
CORUSCANT, THE IMPERIAL PALACE, THREE DAYS LATER.
ANTEROOM TO THE OFFICE OF THE DIRECTOR OF IMPERIAL INTELLIGENCE, ARMAND ISARD.
AH, YSANNE. NICE TO SEE YOU AGAIN.
AGENT CROSS.
AGENT ISARD. BEEN IN TO SEE DADDY, HAVE YOU?
HOW OBSERVANT.
YOUR ASSIGNMENT GO WELL?
OF COURSE. YOURS WAS ALSO SUCCESSFUL, I UNDERSTAND. TELL ME, AGENT CROSS -- DO YOU KNOW *WHY* YOU KILLED COUNT DOOKU?
IT WAS AN ASSIGNMENT. I ASSUME HE WAS AN ENEMY OF THE STATE.
OH, POOR DEAR JAHAN -- YOU REALLY ARE TOO *NAIVE* SOME-TIMES.

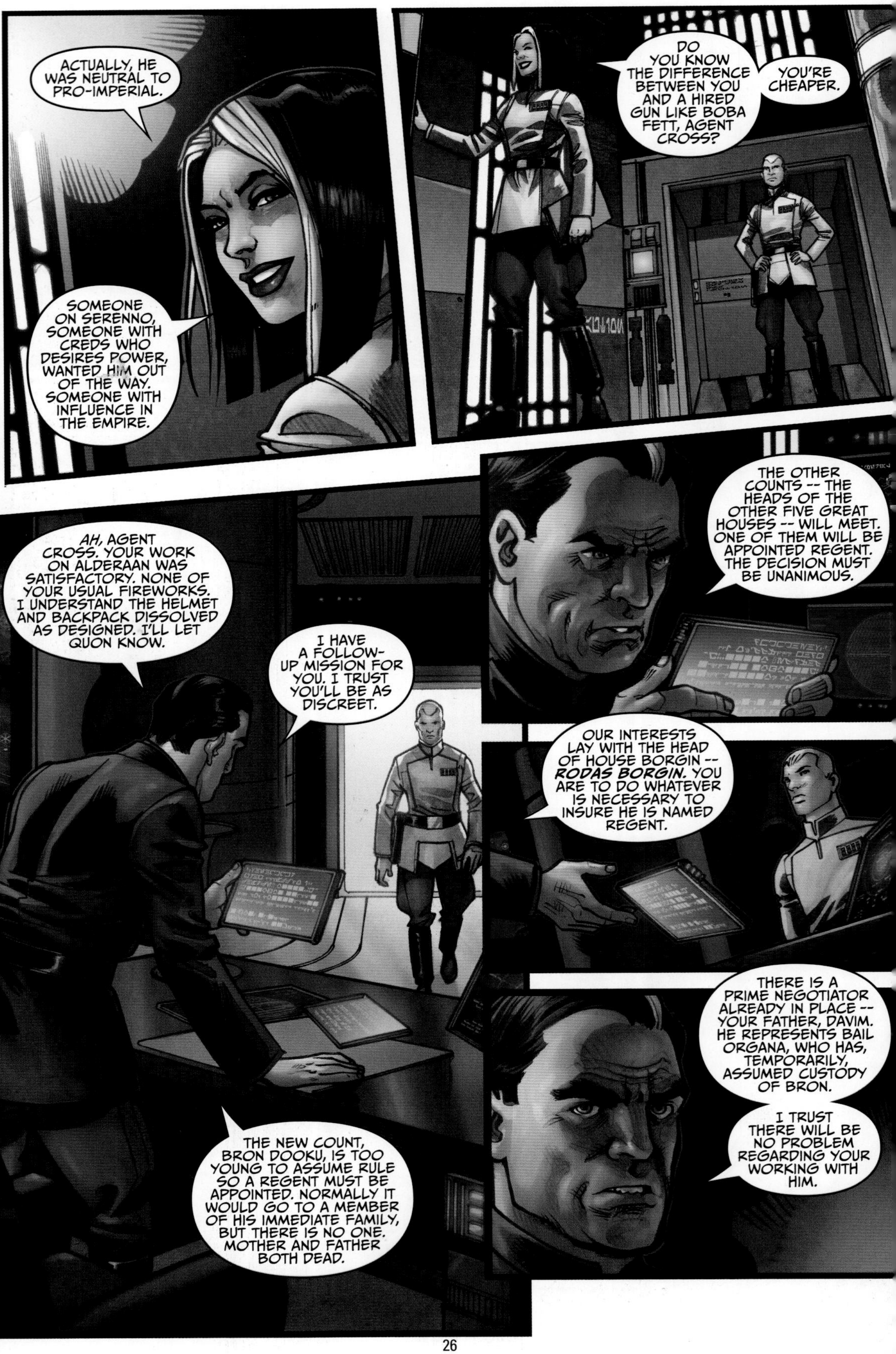
ACTUALLY, HE WAS NEUTRAL TO PRO-IMPERIAL.
SOMEONE ON SERENNO, SOMEONE WITH CREDS WHO DESIRES POWER, WANTED HIM OUT OF THE WAY. SOMEONE WITH INFLUENCE IN THE EMPIRE.
DO YOU KNOW THE DIFFERENCE BETWEEN YOU AND A HIRED GUN LIKE BOBA FETT, AGENT CROSS?
YOU'RE CHEAPER.
AH, AGENT CROSS. YOUR WORK ON ALDERAAN WAS SATISFACTORY. NONE OF YOUR USUAL FIREWORKS. I UNDERSTAND THE HELMET AND BACKPACK DISSOLVED AS DESIGNED. I'LL LET QUON KNOW.
I HAVE A FOLLOW-UP MISSION FOR YOU. I TRUST YOU'LL BE AS DISCREET.
THE NEW COUNT, BRON DOOKU, IS TOO YOUNG TO ASSUME RULE SO A REGENT MUST BE APPOINTED. NORMALLY IT WOULD GO TO A MEMBER OF HIS IMMEDIATE FAMILY, BUT THERE IS NO ONE. MOTHER AND FATHER BOTH DEAD.
THE OTHER COUNTS -- THE HEADS OF THE OTHER FIVE GREAT HOUSES -- WILL MEET. ONE OF THEM WILL BE APPOINTED REGENT. THE DECISION MUST BE UNANIMOUS.
OUR INTERESTS LAY WITH THE HEAD OF HOUSE BORGIN -- ***RODAS BORGIN.*** YOU ARE TO DO WHATEVER IS NECESSARY TO INSURE HE IS NAMED REGENT.
THERE IS A PRIME NEGOTIATOR ALREADY IN PLACE -- YOUR FATHER, DAVIM. HE REPRESENTS BAIL ORGANA, WHO HAS, TEMPORARILY, ASSUMED CUSTODY OF BRON.
I TRUST THERE WILL BE NO PROBLEM REGARDING YOUR WORKING WITH HIM.

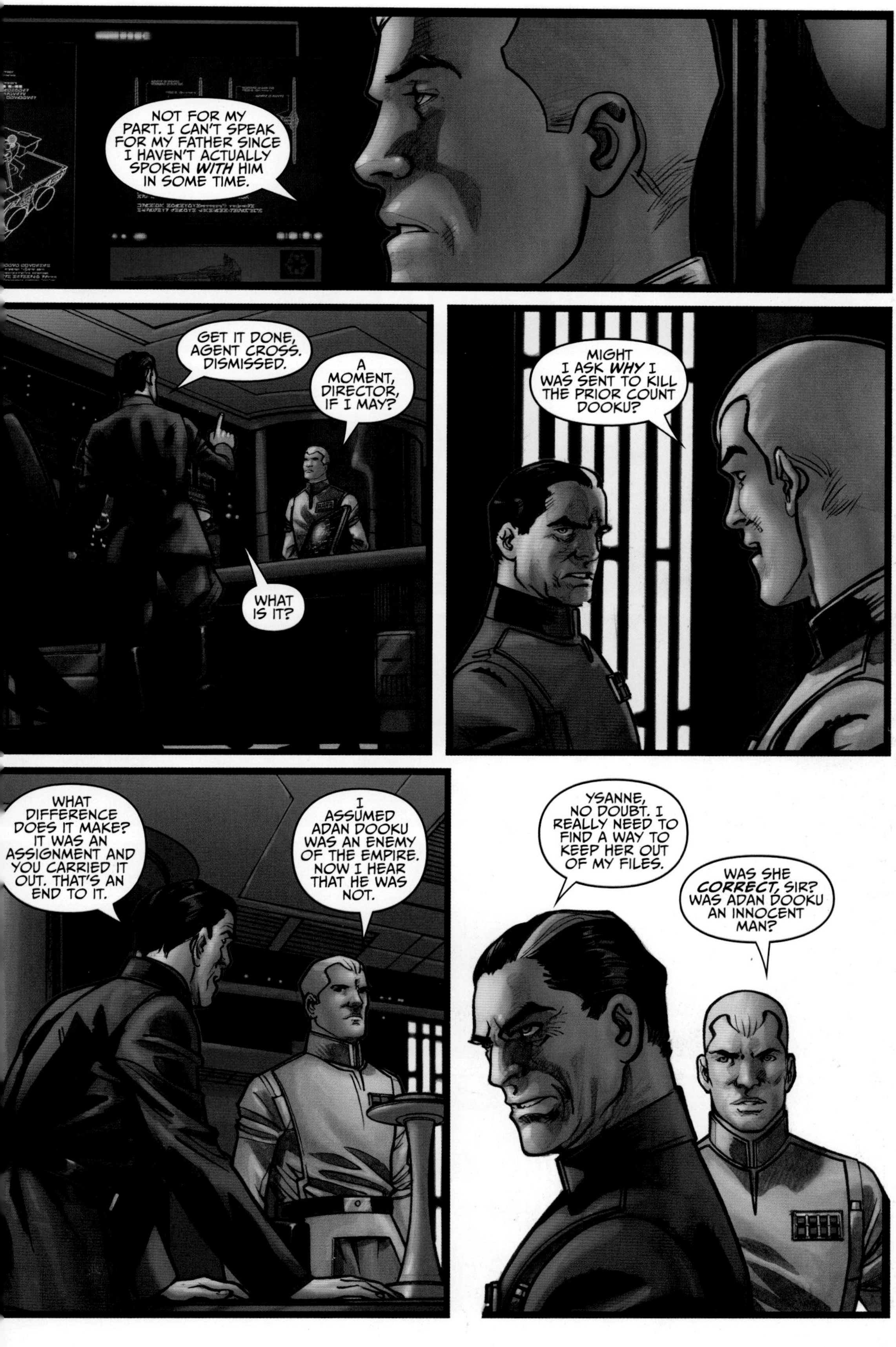
NOT FOR MY PART. I CAN'T SPEAK FOR MY FATHER SINCE I HAVEN'T ACTUALLY SPOKEN WITH HIM IN SOME TIME.
GET IT DONE, AGENT CROSS. DISMISSED.
A MOMENT, DIRECTOR, IF I MAY?
WHAT IS IT?
MIGHT I ASK WHY I WAS SENT TO KILL THE PRIOR COUNT DOOKU?
WHAT DIFFERENCE DOES IT MAKE? IT WAS AN ASSIGNMENT AND YOU CARRIED IT OUT. THAT'S AN END TO IT.
I ASSUMED ADAN DOOKU WAS AN ENEMY OF THE EMPIRE. NOW I HEAR THAT HE WAS NOT.
YSANNE, NO DOUBT. I REALLY NEED TO FIND A WAY TO KEEP HER OUT OF MY FILES.
WAS SHE CORRECT, SIR? WAS ADAN DOOKU AN INNOCENT MAN?

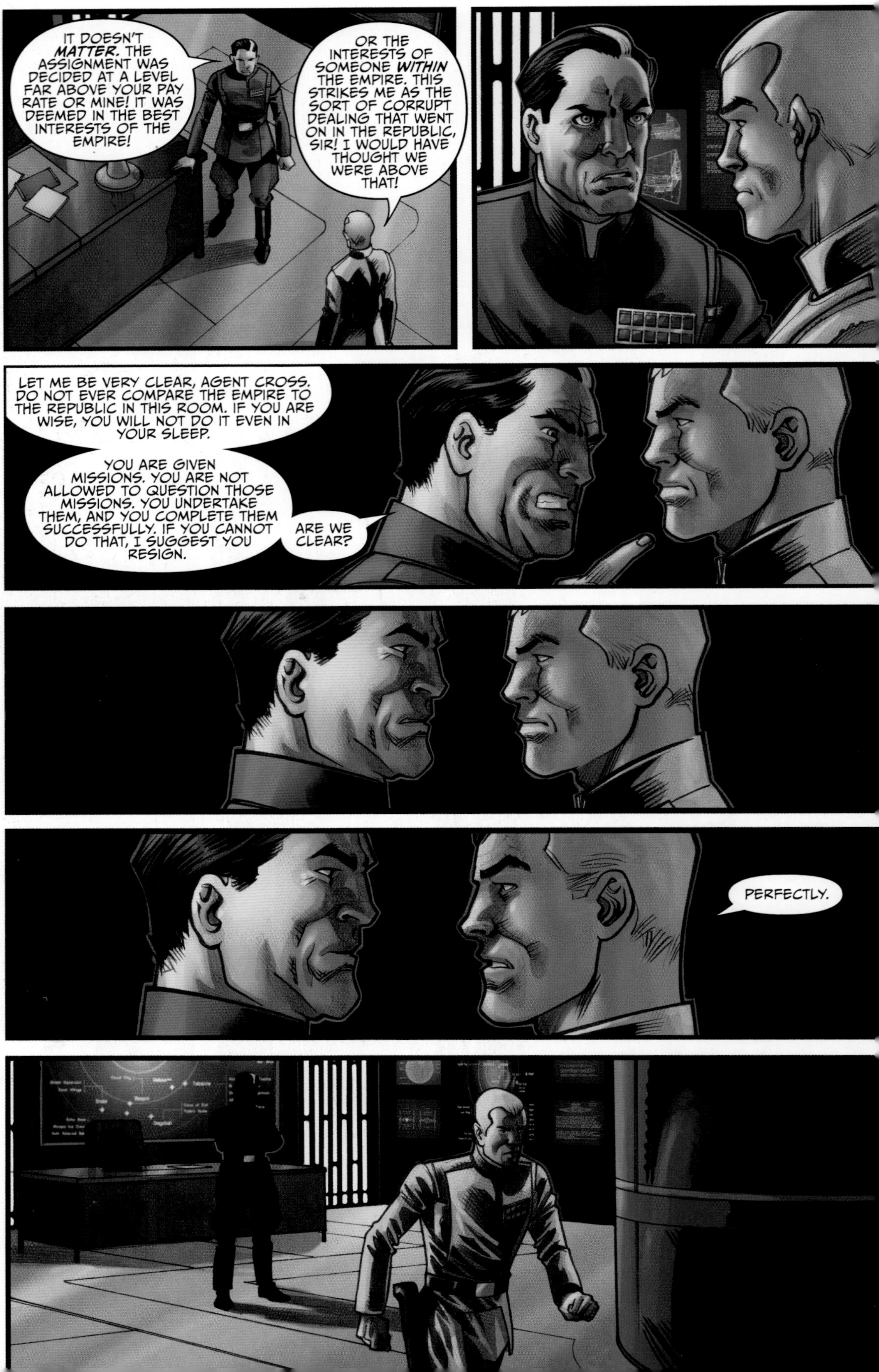
IT DOESN'T *MATTER.* THE ASSIGNMENT WAS DECIDED AT A LEVEL FAR ABOVE YOUR PAY RATE OR MINE! IT WAS DEEMED IN THE BEST INTERESTS OF THE EMPIRE!
OR THE INTERESTS OF SOMEONE *WITHIN* THE EMPIRE. THIS STRIKES ME AS THE SORT OF CORRUPT DEALING THAT WENT ON IN THE REPUBLIC, SIR! I WOULD HAVE THOUGHT WE WERE ABOVE THAT!
LET ME BE VERY CLEAR, AGENT CROSS. DO NOT EVER COMPARE THE EMPIRE TO THE REPUBLIC IN THIS ROOM. IF YOU ARE WISE, YOU WILL NOT DO IT EVEN IN YOUR SLEEP.
YOU ARE GIVEN MISSIONS. YOU ARE NOT ALLOWED TO QUESTION THOSE MISSIONS. YOU UNDERTAKE THEM, AND YOU COMPLETE THEM SUCCESSFULLY. IF YOU CANNOT DO THAT, I SUGGEST YOU RESIGN.
ARE WE CLEAR?
PERFECTLY.

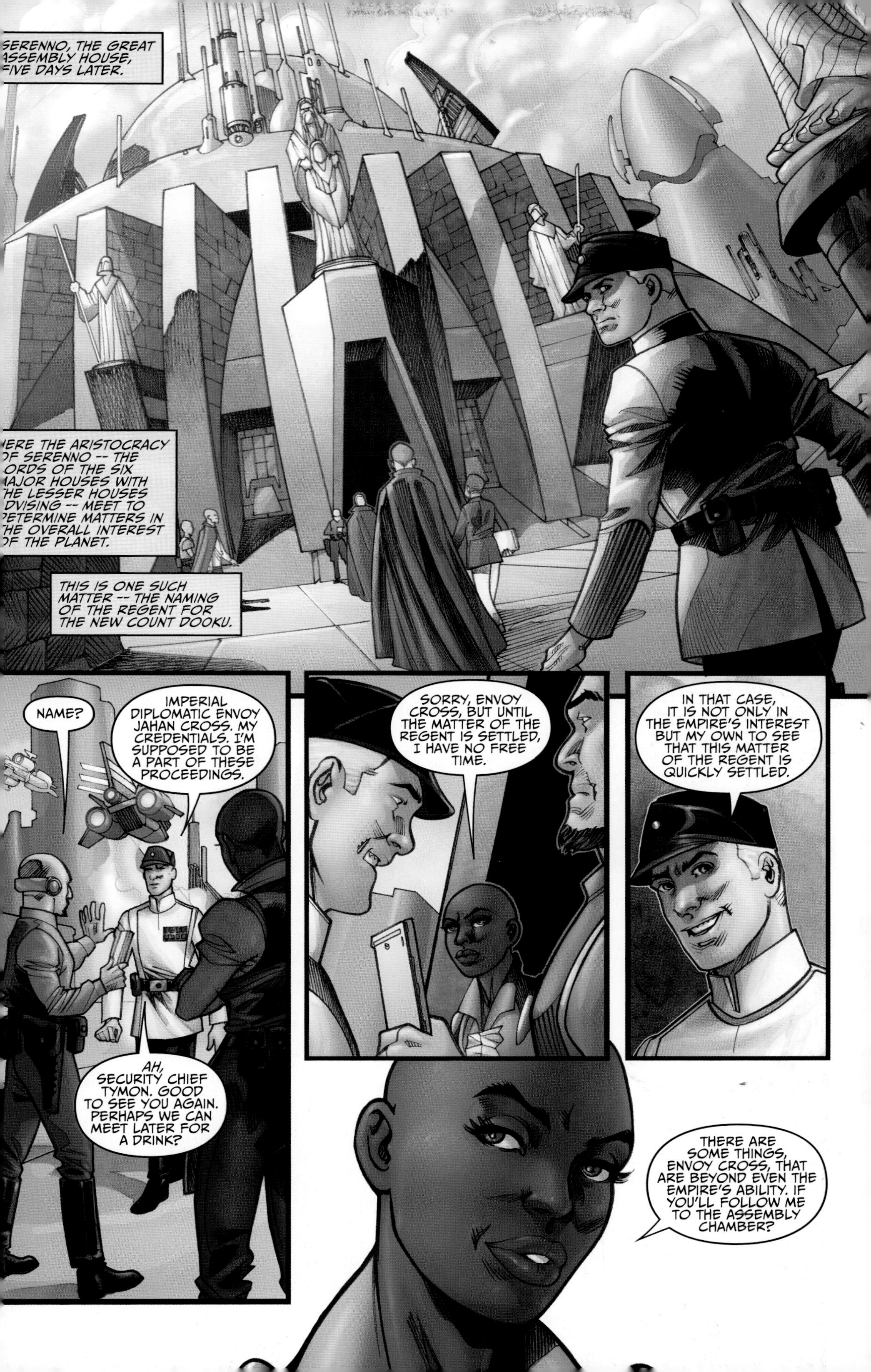
SERENNO, THE GREAT ASSEMBLY HOUSE, FIVE DAYS LATER.
ERE THE ARISTOCRACY OF SERENNO -- THE ORDS OF THE SIX MAJOR HOUSES WITH THE LESSER HOUSES DVISING -- MEET TO DETERMINE MATTERS IN THE OVERALL INTEREST OF THE PLANET.
THIS IS ONE SUCH MATTER -- THE NAMING OF THE REGENT FOR THE NEW COUNT DOOKU.
NAME?
IMPERIAL DIPLOMATIC ENVOY JAHAN CROSS. MY CREDENTIALS. I'M SUPPOSED TO BE A PART OF THESE PROCEEDINGS.
AH, SECURITY CHIEF TYMON. GOOD TO SEE YOU AGAIN. PERHAPS WE CAN MEET LATER FOR A DRINK?
SORRY, ENVOY CROSS, BUT UNTIL THE MATTER OF THE REGENT IS SETTLED, I HAVE NO FREE TIME.
IN THAT CASE, IT IS NOT ONLY IN THE EMPIRE'S INTEREST BUT MY OWN TO SEE THAT THIS MATTER OF THE REGENT IS QUICKLY SETTLED.
THERE ARE SOME THINGS, ENVOY CROSS, THAT ARE BEYOND EVEN THE EMPIRE'S ABILITY. IF YOU'LL FOLLOW ME TO THE ASSEMBLY CHAMBER?

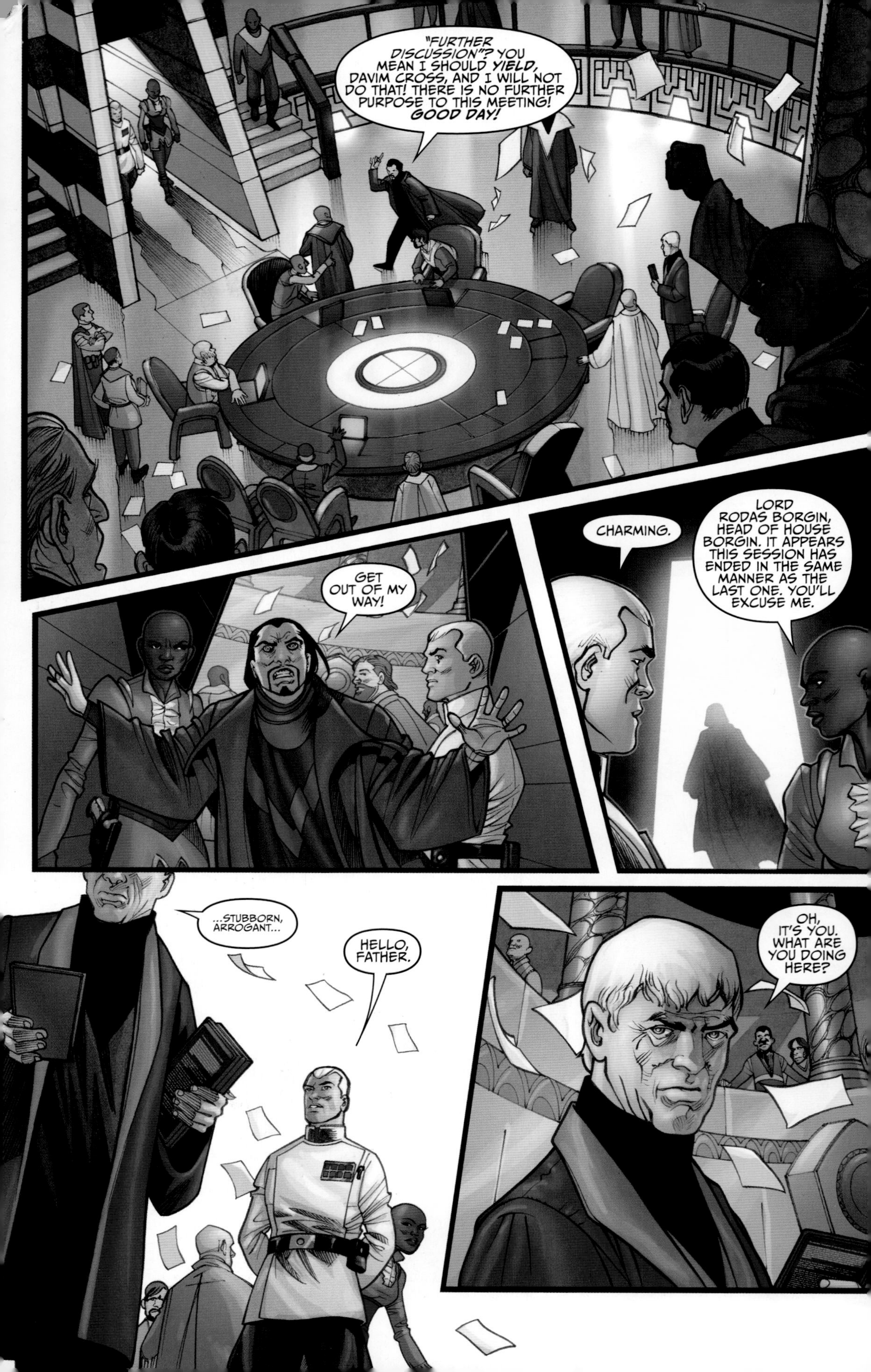
"FURTHER DISCUSSION"? YOU MEAN I SHOULD YIELD, DAVIM CROSS, AND I WILL NOT DO THAT! THERE IS NO FURTHER PURPOSE TO THIS MEETING! GOOD DAY!
GET OUT OF MY WAY!
CHARMING.
LORD RODAS BORGIN, HEAD OF HOUSE BORGIN. IT APPEARS THIS SESSION HAS ENDED IN THE SAME MANNER AS THE LAST ONE. YOU'LL EXCUSE ME.
...STUBBORN, ARROGANT...
HELLO, FATHER.
OH, IT'S YOU. WHAT ARE YOU DOING HERE?

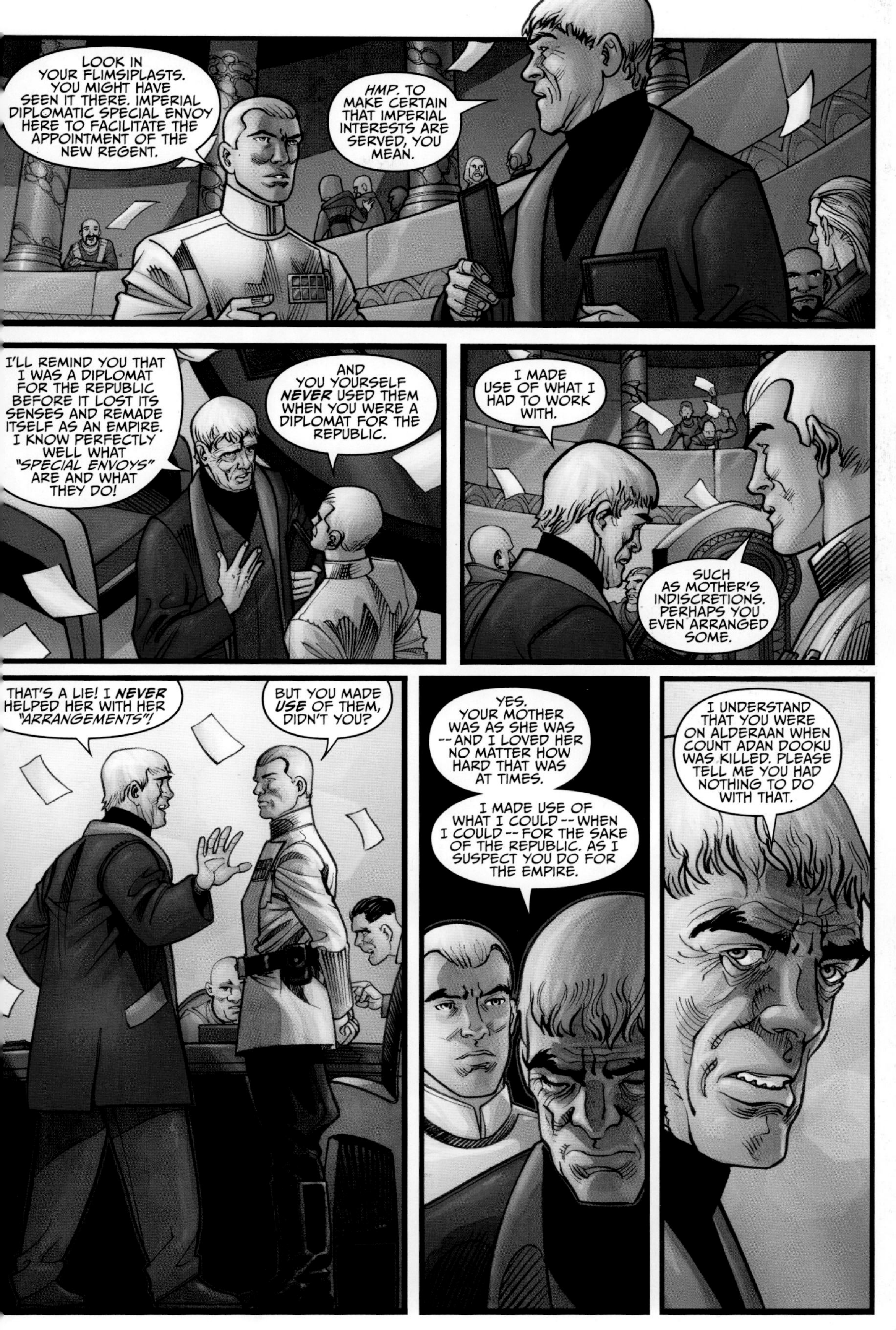
LOOK IN YOUR FLIMSIPLASTS. YOU MIGHT HAVE SEEN IT THERE. IMPERIAL DIPLOMATIC SPECIAL ENVOY HERE TO FACILITATE THE APPOINTMENT OF THE NEW REGENT.
HMP. TO MAKE CERTAIN THAT IMPERIAL INTERESTS ARE SERVED, YOU MEAN.
I'LL REMIND YOU THAT I WAS A DIPLOMAT FOR THE REPUBLIC BEFORE IT LOST ITS SENSES AND REMADE ITSELF AS AN EMPIRE. I KNOW PERFECTLY WELL WHAT "SPECIAL ENVOYS" ARE AND WHAT THEY DO!
AND YOU YOURSELF NEVER USED THEM WHEN YOU WERE A DIPLOMAT FOR THE REPUBLIC.
I MADE USE OF WHAT I HAD TO WORK WITH.
SUCH AS MOTHER'S INDISCRETIONS. PERHAPS YOU EVEN ARRANGED SOME.
THAT'S A LIE! I NEVER HELPED HER WITH HER "ARRANGEMENTS"!
BUT YOU MADE USE OF THEM, DIDN'T YOU?
YES. YOUR MOTHER WAS AS SHE WAS --AND I LOVED HER NO MATTER HOW HARD THAT WAS AT TIMES.
I MADE USE OF WHAT I COULD--WHEN I COULD--FOR THE SAKE OF THE REPUBLIC. AS I SUSPECT YOU DO FOR THE EMPIRE.
I UNDERSTAND THAT YOU WERE ON ALDERAAN WHEN COUNT ADAN DOOKU WAS KILLED. PLEASE TELL ME YOU HAD NOTHING TO DO WITH THAT.

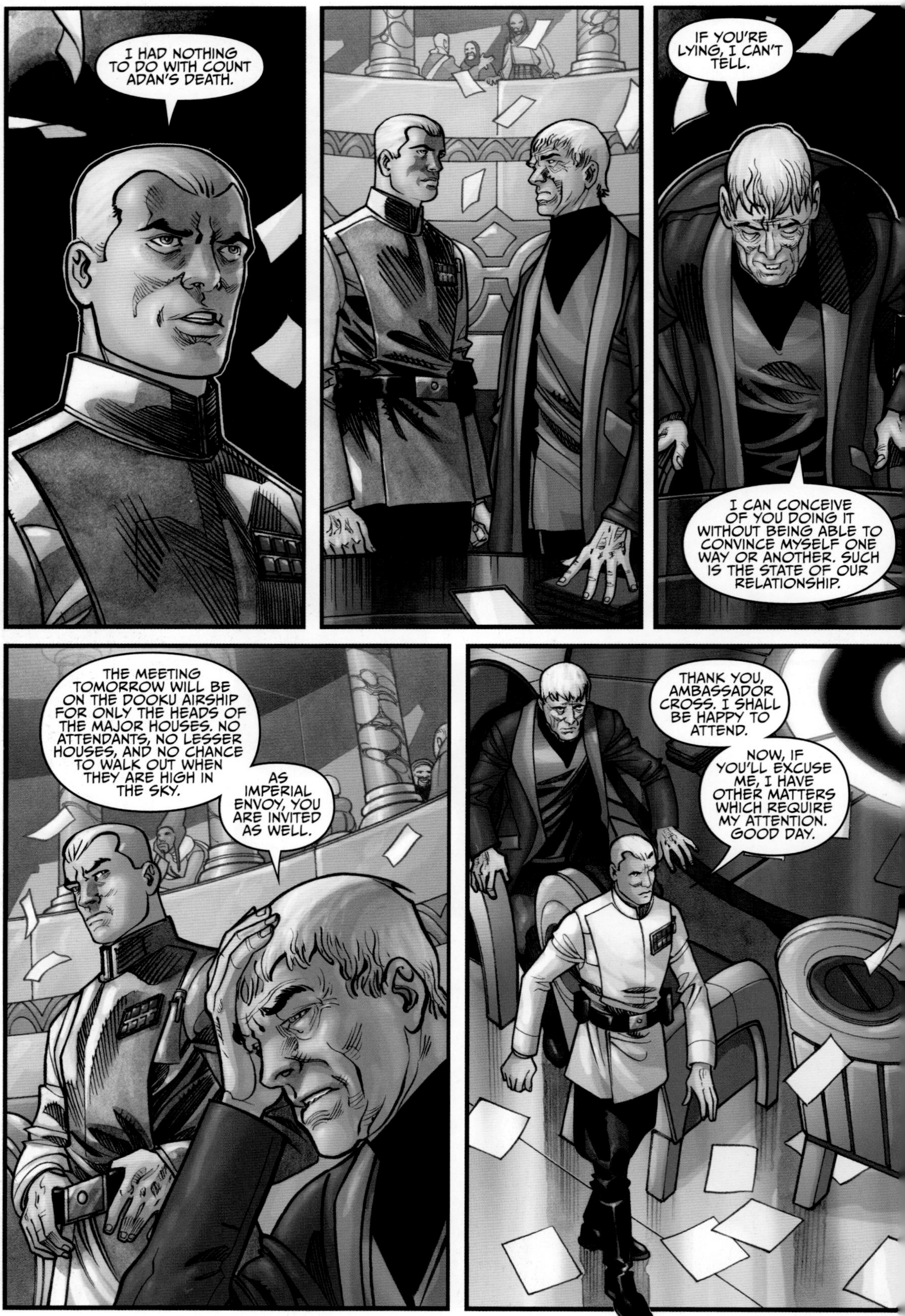
I HAD NOTHING TO DO WITH COUNT ADAN'S DEATH.
IF YOU'RE LYING, I CAN'T TELL.
I CAN CONCEIVE OF YOU DOING IT WITHOUT BEING ABLE TO CONVINCE MYSELF ONE WAY OR ANOTHER. SUCH IS THE STATE OF OUR RELATIONSHIP.
THE MEETING TOMORROW WILL BE ON THE DOOKU AIRSHIP FOR ONLY THE HEADS OF THE MAJOR HOUSES. NO ATTENDANTS, NO LESSER HOUSES, AND NO CHANCE TO WALK OUT WHEN THEY ARE HIGH IN THE SKY.
AS IMPERIAL ENVOY, YOU ARE INVITED AS WELL.
THANK YOU, AMBASSADOR CROSS. I SHALL BE HAPPY TO ATTEND.
NOW, IF YOU'LL EXCUSE ME, I HAVE OTHER MATTERS WHICH REQUIRE MY ATTENTION. GOOD DAY.

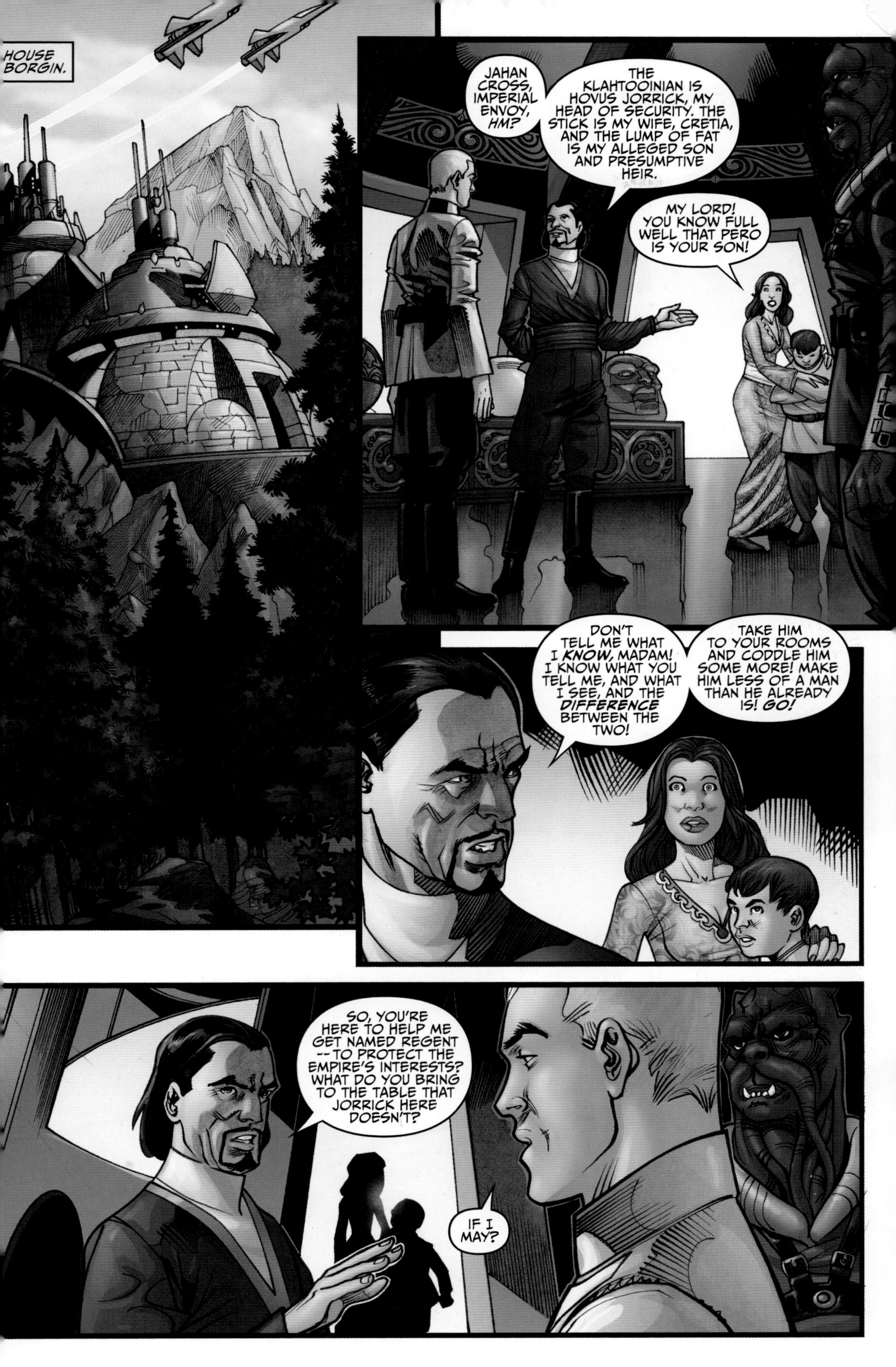
HOUSE BORGIN.
JAHAN CROSS, IMPERIAL ENVOY, HM?
THE KLAHTOOINIAN IS HOVUS JORRICK, MY HEAD OF SECURITY. THE STICK IS MY WIFE, CRETIA, AND THE LUMP OF FAT IS MY ALLEGED SON AND PRESUMPTIVE HEIR.
MY LORD! YOU KNOW FULL WELL THAT PERO IS YOUR SON!
DON'T TELL ME WHAT I KNOW, MADAM! I KNOW WHAT YOU TELL ME, AND WHAT I SEE, AND THE DIFFERENCE BETWEEN THE TWO!
TAKE HIM TO YOUR ROOMS AND CODDLE HIM SOME MORE! MAKE HIM LESS OF A MAN THAN HE ALREADY IS! GO!
SO, YOU'RE HERE TO HELP ME GET NAMED REGENT --TO PROTECT THE EMPIRE'S INTERESTS? WHAT DO YOU BRING TO THE TABLE THAT JORRICK HERE DOESN'T?
IF I MAY?

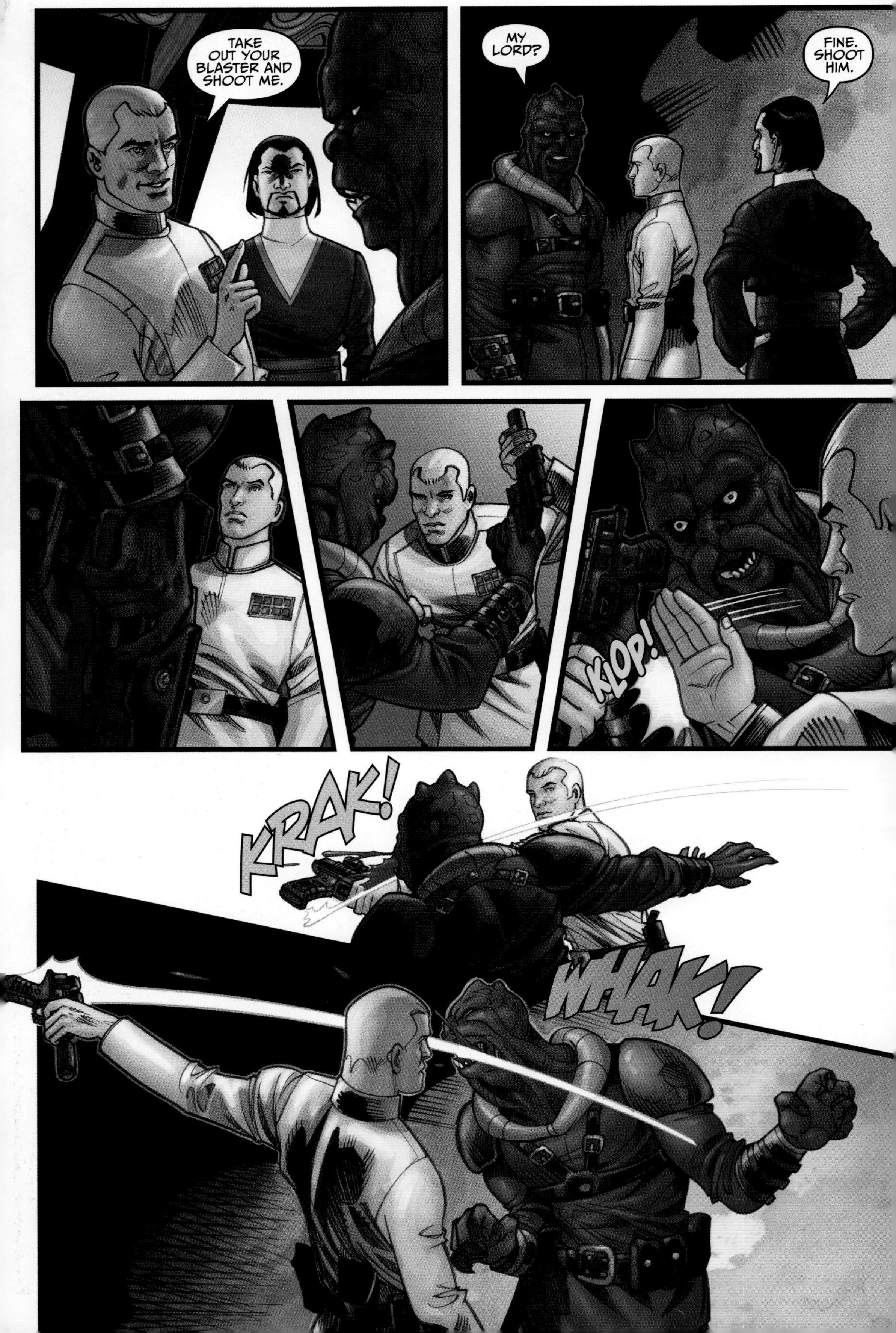
TAKE OUT YOUR BLASTER AND SHOOT ME.
MY LORD?
FINE. SHOOT HIM.
KLOP!
KRAK!
WHAK!

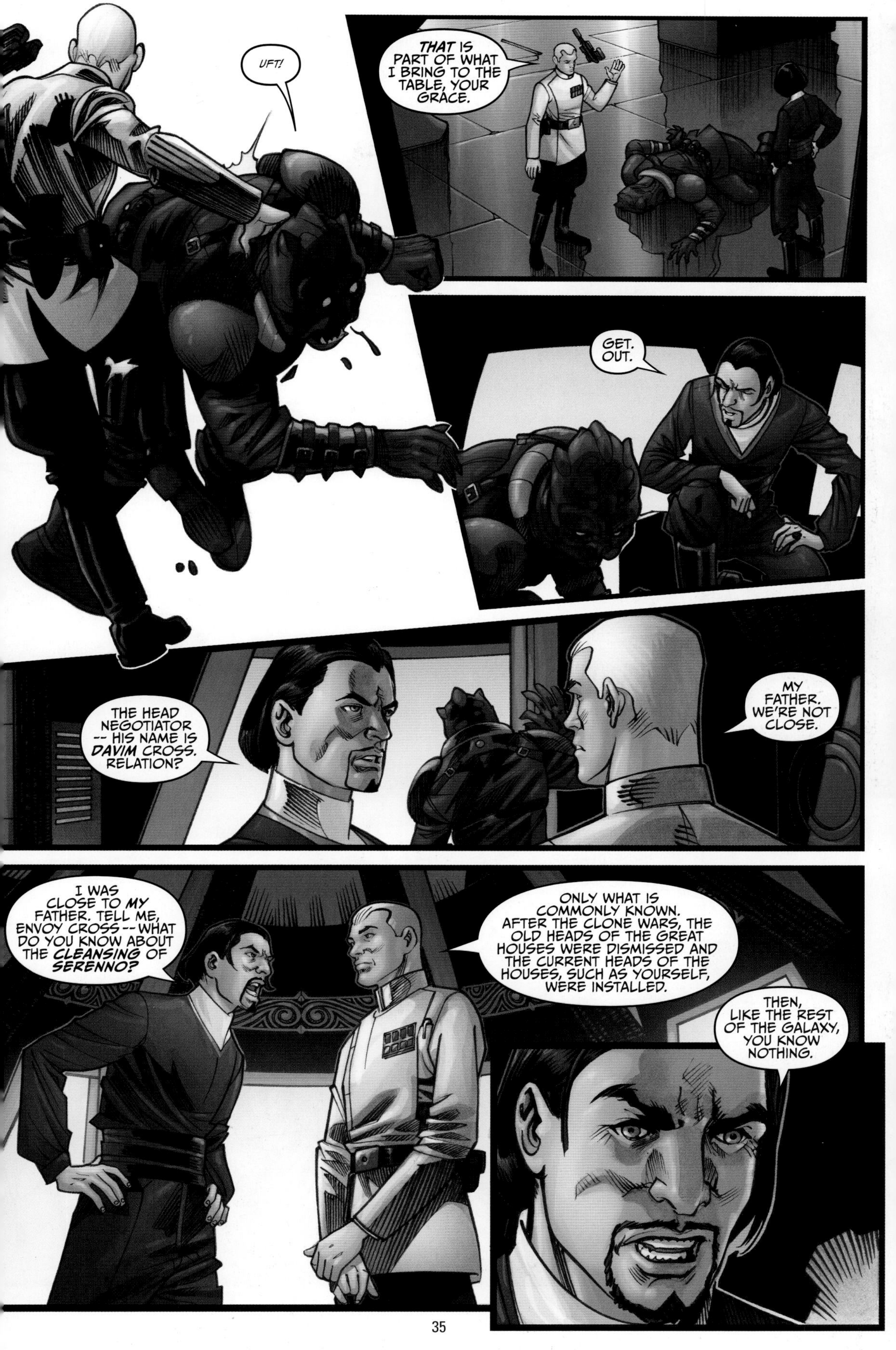
UFT!
THAT IS PART OF WHAT I BRING TO THE TABLE, YOUR GRACE.
GET. OUT.
THE HEAD NEGOTIATOR -- HIS NAME IS DAVIM CROSS. RELATION?
MY FATHER. WE'RE NOT CLOSE.
I WAS CLOSE TO MY FATHER. TELL ME, ENVOY CROSS -- WHAT DO YOU KNOW ABOUT THE CLEANSING OF SERENNO?
ONLY WHAT IS COMMONLY KNOWN. AFTER THE CLONE WARS, THE OLD HEADS OF THE GREAT HOUSES WERE DISMISSED AND THE CURRENT HEADS OF THE HOUSES, SUCH AS YOURSELF, WERE INSTALLED.
THEN, LIKE THE REST OF THE GALAXY, YOU KNOW NOTHING.

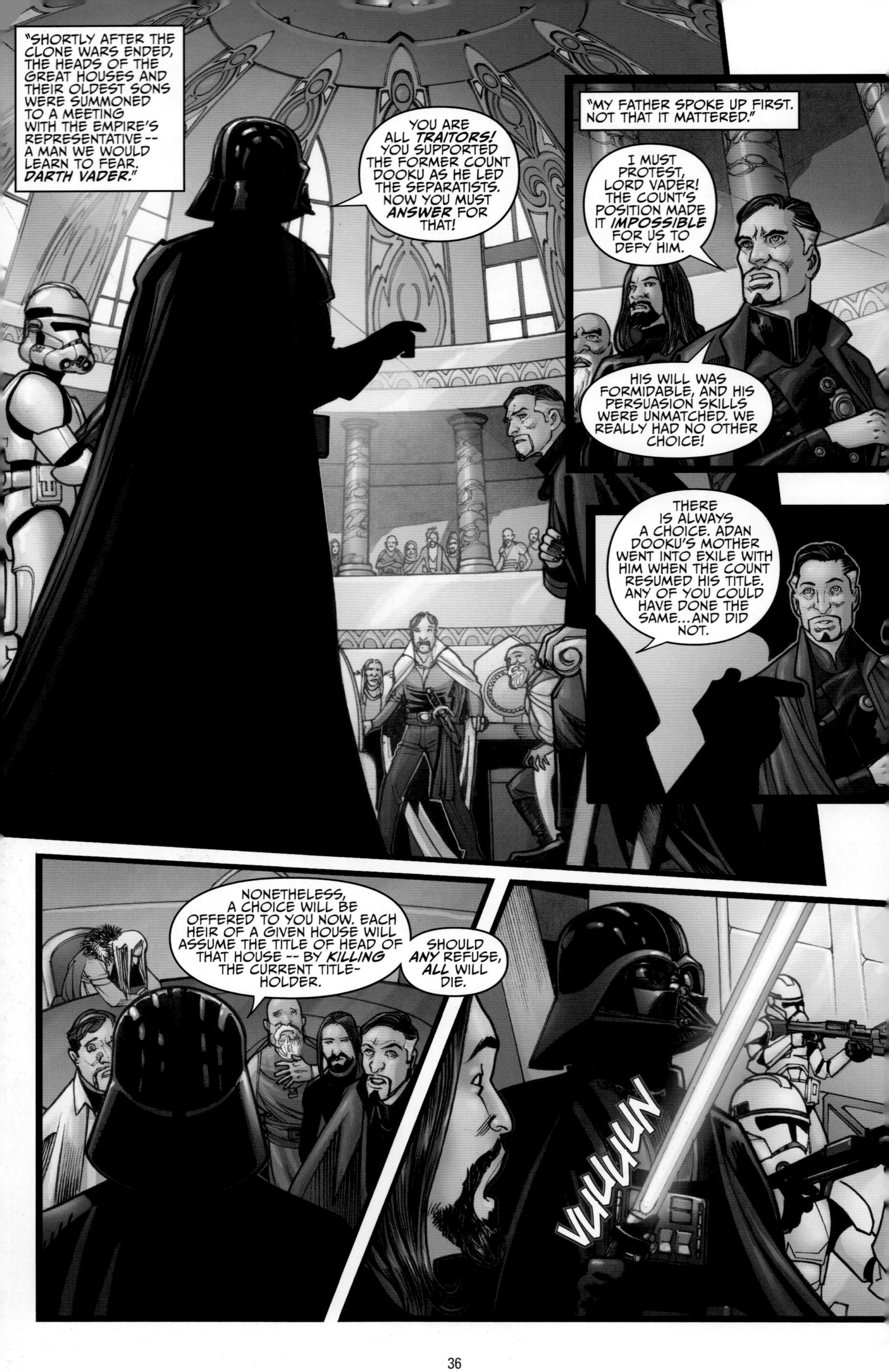
"SHORTLY AFTER THE CLONE WARS ENDED, THE HEADS OF THE GREAT HOUSES AND THEIR OLDEST SONS WERE SUMMONED TO A MEETING WITH THE EMPIRE'S REPRESENTATIVE -- A MAN WE WOULD LEARN TO FEAR. DARTH VADER."
YOU ARE ALL TRAITORS! YOU SUPPORTED THE FORMER COUNT DOOKU AS HE LED THE SEPARATISTS. NOW YOU MUST ANSWER FOR THAT!
"MY FATHER SPOKE UP FIRST. NOT THAT IT MATTERED."
I MUST PROTEST, LORD VADER! THE COUNT'S POSITION MADE IT IMPOSSIBLE FOR US TO DEFY HIM.
HIS WILL WAS FORMIDABLE, AND HIS PERSUASION SKILLS WERE UNMATCHED. WE REALLY HAD NO OTHER CHOICE!
THERE IS ALWAYS A CHOICE. ADAN DOOKU'S MOTHER WENT INTO EXILE WITH HIM WHEN THE COUNT RESUMED HIS TITLE. ANY OF YOU COULD HAVE DONE THE SAME...AND DID NOT.
NONETHELESS, A CHOICE WILL BE OFFERED TO YOU NOW. EACH HEIR OF A GIVEN HOUSE WILL ASSUME THE TITLE OF HEAD OF THAT HOUSE -- BY KILLING THE CURRENT TITLE-HOLDER.
SHOULD ANY REFUSE, ALL WILL DIE.
VUUUUN

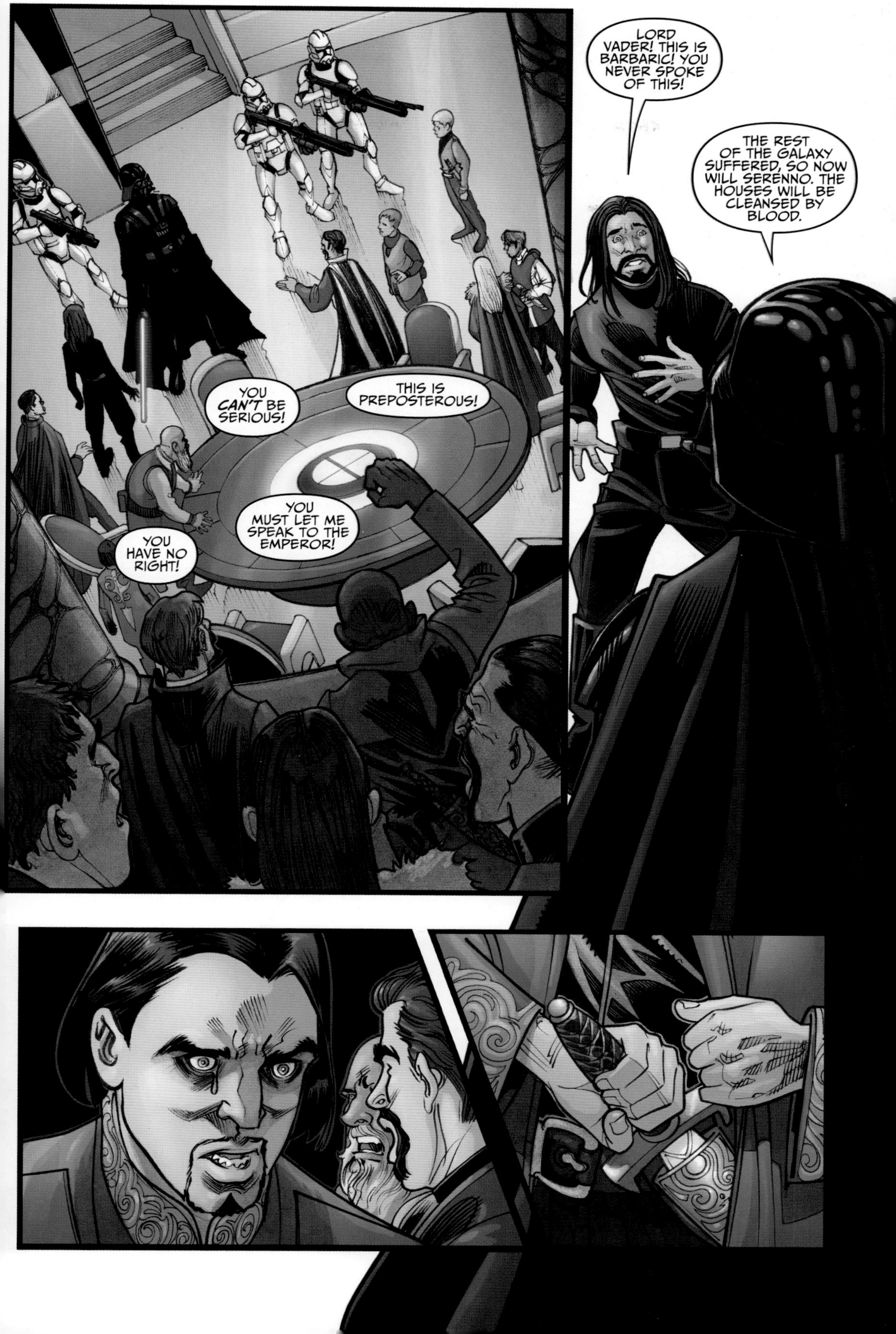
YOU CAN'T BE SERIOUS!
THIS IS PREPOSTEROUS!
YOU HAVE NO RIGHT!
YOU MUST LET ME SPEAK TO THE EMPEROR!
LORD VADER! THIS IS BARBARIC! YOU NEVER SPOKE OF THIS!
THE REST OF THE GALAXY SUFFERED, SO NOW WILL SERENNO. THE HOUSES WILL BE CLEANSED BY BLOOD.

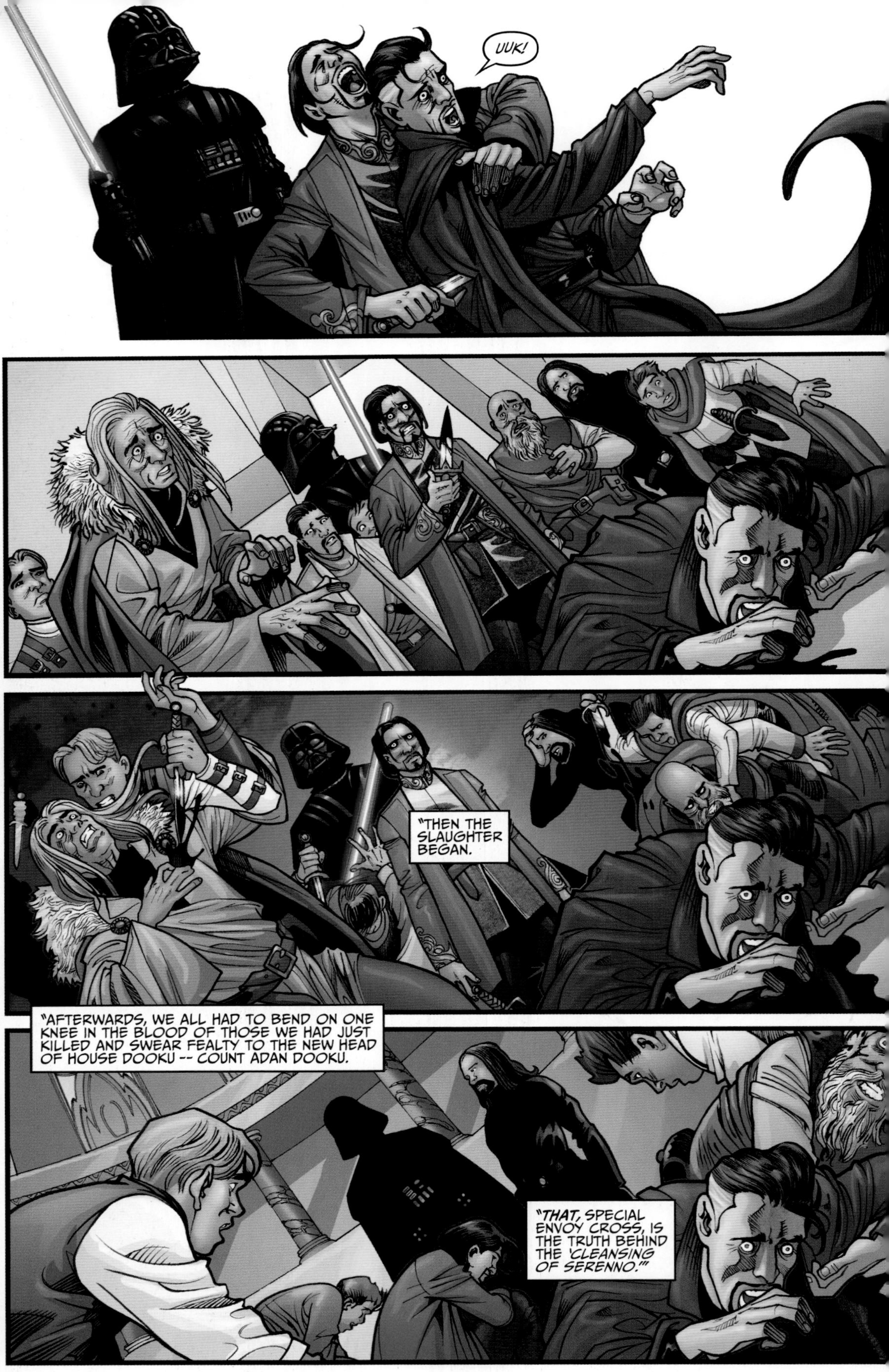
UUK!
"THEN THE SLAUGHTER BEGAN.
"AFTERWARDS, WE ALL HAD TO BEND ON ONE KNEE IN THE BLOOD OF THOSE WE HAD JUST KILLED AND SWEAR FEALTY TO THE NEW HEAD OF HOUSE DOOKU -- COUNT ADAN DOOKU.
"THAT, SPECIAL ENVOY CROSS, IS THE TRUTH BEHIND THE 'CLEANSING OF SERENNO.'"

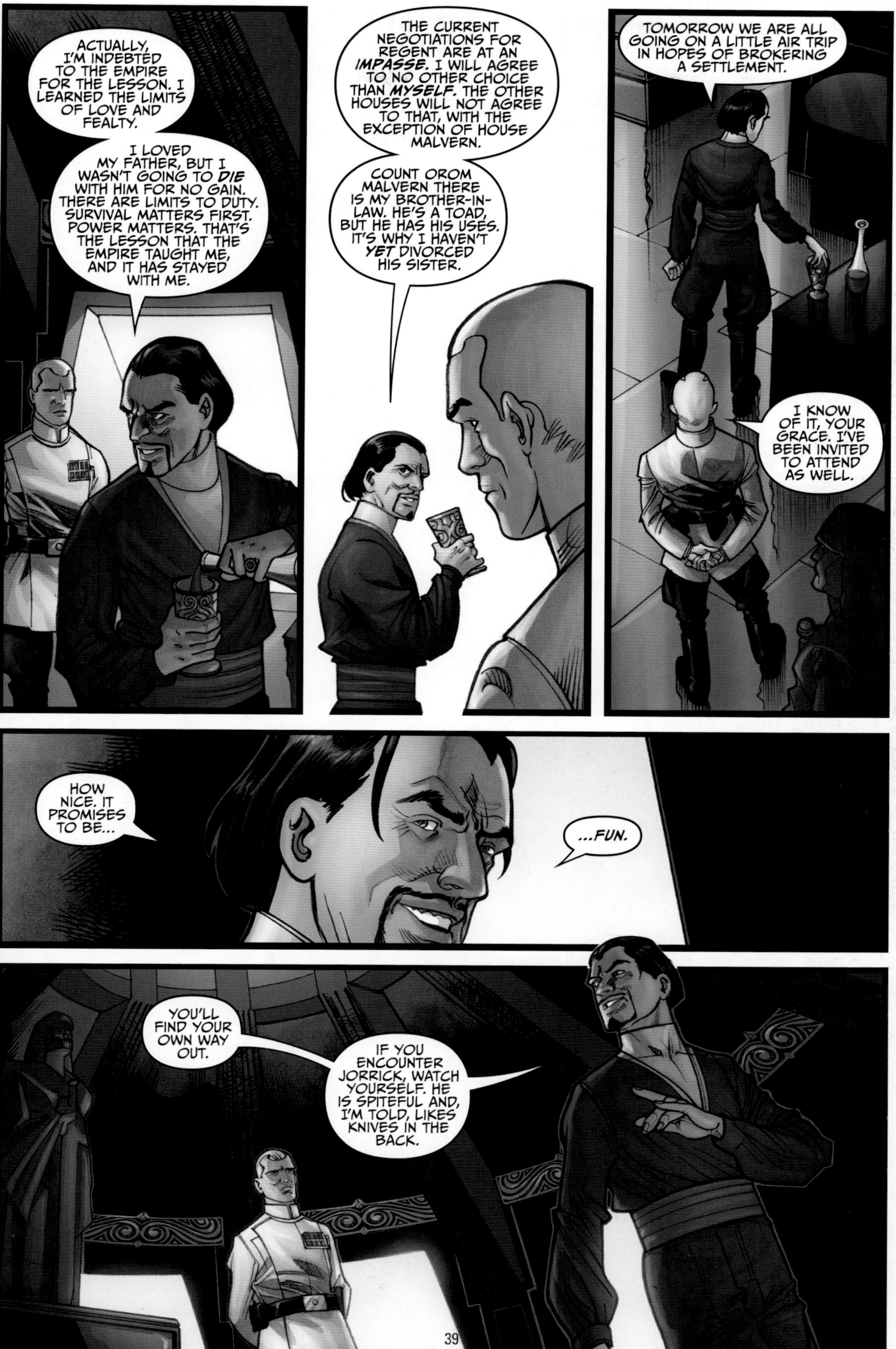
ACTUALLY, I'M INDEBTED TO THE EMPIRE FOR THE LESSON. I LEARNED THE LIMITS OF LOVE AND FEALTY.
I LOVED MY FATHER, BUT I WASN'T GOING TO *DIE* WITH HIM FOR NO GAIN. THERE ARE LIMITS TO DUTY. SURVIVAL MATTERS FIRST. POWER MATTERS. THAT'S THE LESSON THAT THE EMPIRE TAUGHT ME, AND IT HAS STAYED WITH ME.
THE CURRENT NEGOTIATIONS FOR REGENT ARE AT AN *IMPASSE.* I WILL AGREE TO NO OTHER CHOICE THAN *MYSELF.* THE OTHER HOUSES WILL NOT AGREE TO THAT, WITH THE EXCEPTION OF HOUSE MALVERN.
COUNT OROM MALVERN THERE IS MY BROTHER-IN-LAW. HE'S A TOAD, BUT HE HAS HIS USES. IT'S WHY I HAVEN'T *YET* DIVORCED HIS SISTER.
TOMORROW WE ARE ALL GOING ON A LITTLE AIR TRIP IN HOPES OF BROKERING A SETTLEMENT.
I KNOW OF IT, YOUR GRACE. I'VE BEEN INVITED TO ATTEND AS WELL.
HOW NICE. IT PROMISES TO BE...
...FUN.
YOU'LL FIND YOUR OWN WAY OUT.
IF YOU ENCOUNTER JORRICK, WATCH YOURSELF. HE IS SPITEFUL AND, I'M TOLD, LIKES KNIVES IN THE BACK.

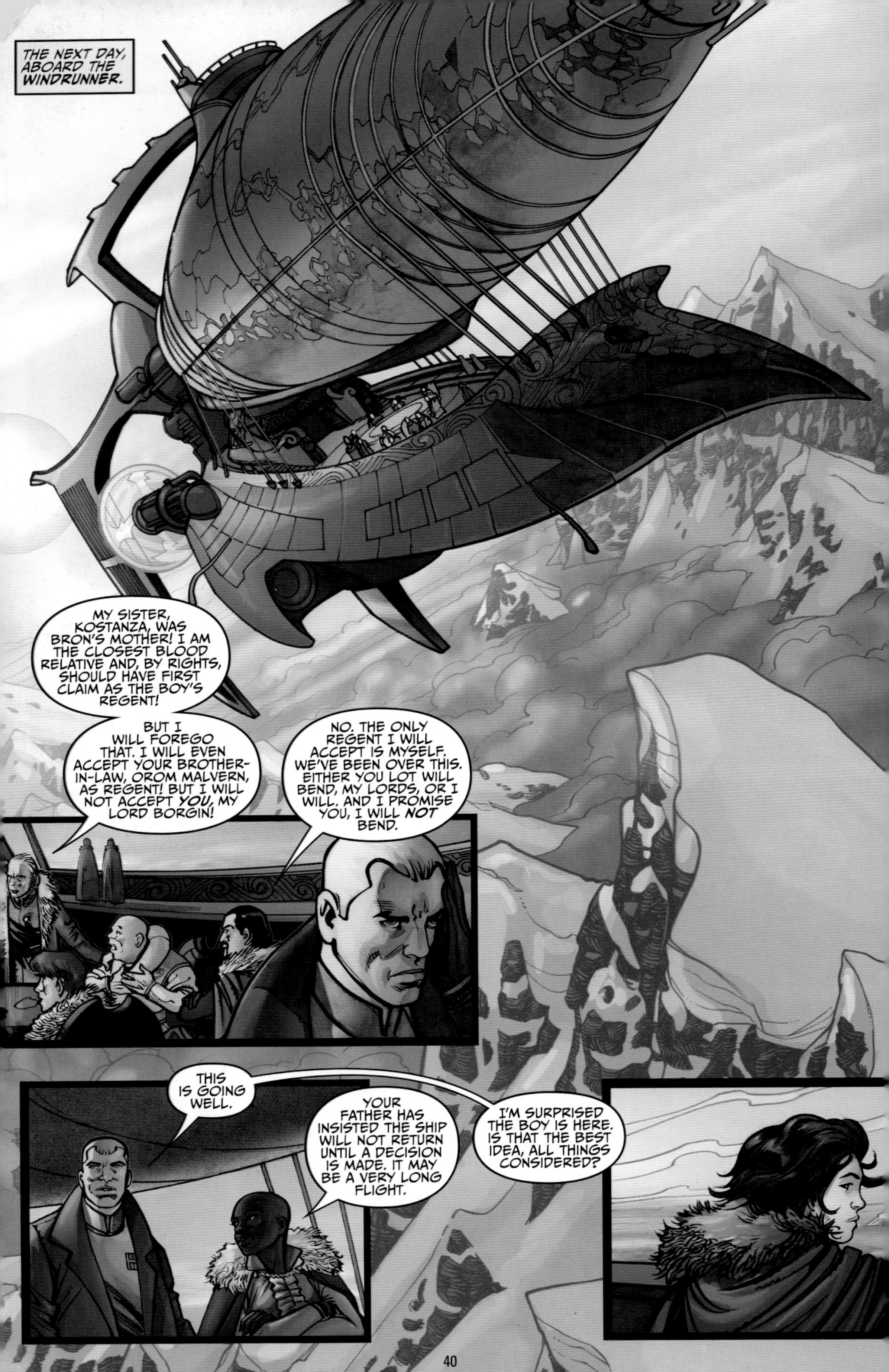
THE NEXT DAY, ABOARD THE WINDRUNNER.
MY SISTER, KOSTANZA, WAS BRON'S MOTHER! I AM THE CLOSEST BLOOD RELATIVE AND, BY RIGHTS, SHOULD HAVE FIRST CLAIM AS THE BOY'S REGENT!
BUT I WILL FOREGO THAT. I WILL EVEN ACCEPT YOUR BROTHER-IN-LAW, OROM MALVERN, AS REGENT! BUT I WILL NOT ACCEPT YOU, MY LORD BORGIN!
NO. THE ONLY REGENT I WILL ACCEPT IS MYSELF. WE'VE BEEN OVER THIS. EITHER YOU LOT WILL BEND, MY LORDS, OR I WILL. AND I PROMISE YOU, I WILL NOT BEND.
THIS IS GOING WELL.
YOUR FATHER HAS INSISTED THE SHIP WILL NOT RETURN UNTIL A DECISION IS MADE. IT MAY BE A VERY LONG FLIGHT.
I'M SURPRISED THE BOY IS HERE. IS THAT THE BEST IDEA, ALL THINGS CONSIDERED?

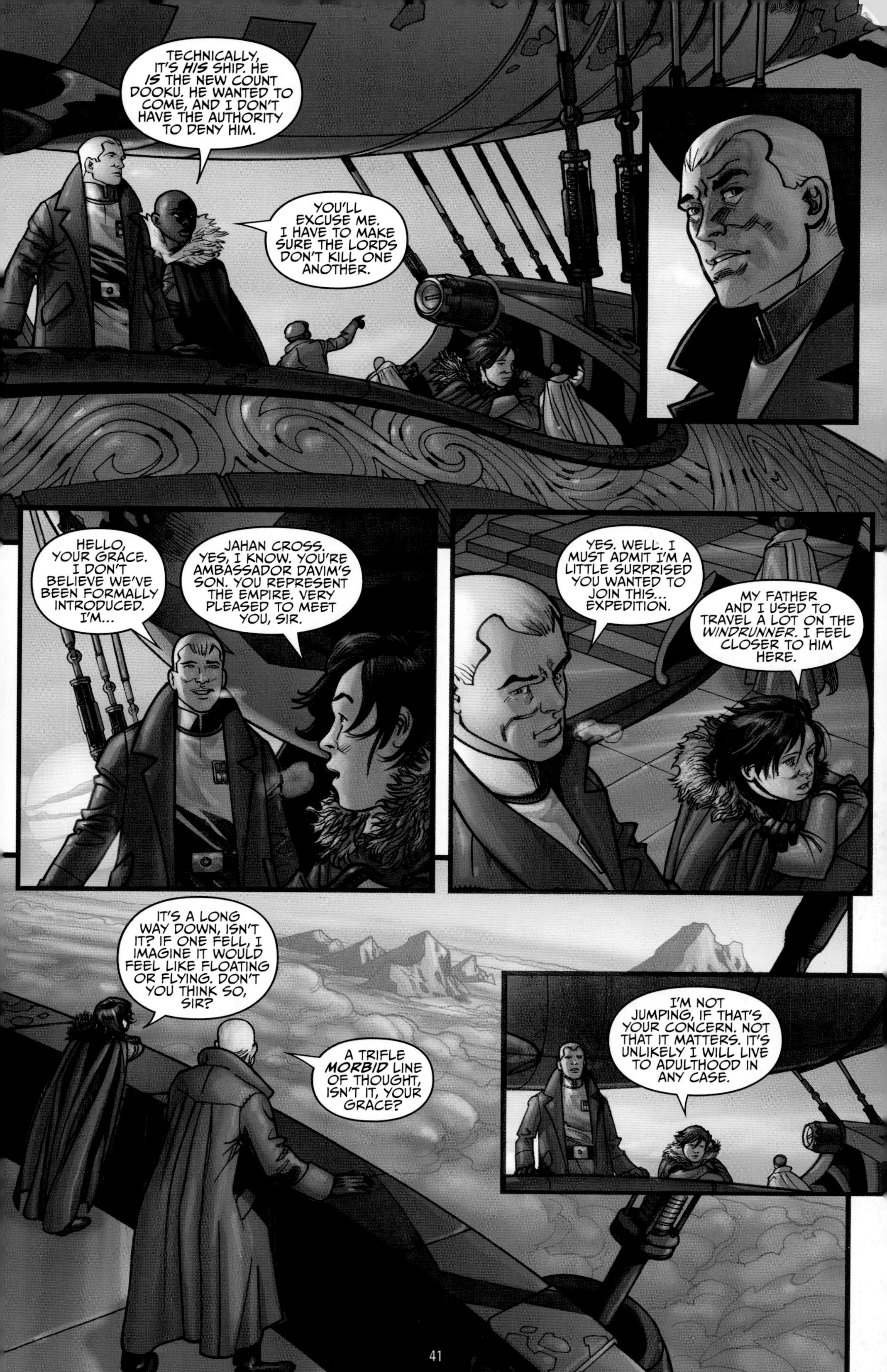
TECHNICALLY, IT'S HIS SHIP. HE IS THE NEW COUNT DOOKU. HE WANTED TO COME, AND I DON'T HAVE THE AUTHORITY TO DENY HIM.
YOU'LL EXCUSE ME. I HAVE TO MAKE SURE THE LORDS DON'T KILL ONE ANOTHER.
HELLO, YOUR GRACE. I DON'T BELIEVE WE'VE BEEN FORMALLY INTRODUCED. I'M...
JAHAN CROSS. YES, I KNOW. YOU'RE AMBASSADOR DAVIM'S SON. YOU REPRESENT THE EMPIRE. VERY PLEASED TO MEET YOU, SIR.
YES. WELL. I MUST ADMIT I'M A LITTLE SURPRISED YOU WANTED TO JOIN THIS... EXPEDITION.
MY FATHER AND I USED TO TRAVEL A LOT ON THE WINDRUNNER. I FEEL CLOSER TO HIM HERE.
IT'S A LONG WAY DOWN, ISN'T IT? IF ONE FELL, I IMAGINE IT WOULD FEEL LIKE FLOATING OR FLYING. DON'T YOU THINK SO, SIR?
A TRIFLE MORBID LINE OF THOUGHT, ISN'T IT, YOUR GRACE?
I'M NOT JUMPING, IF THAT'S YOUR CONCERN. NOT THAT IT MATTERS. IT'S UNLIKELY I WILL LIVE TO ADULTHOOD IN ANY CASE.

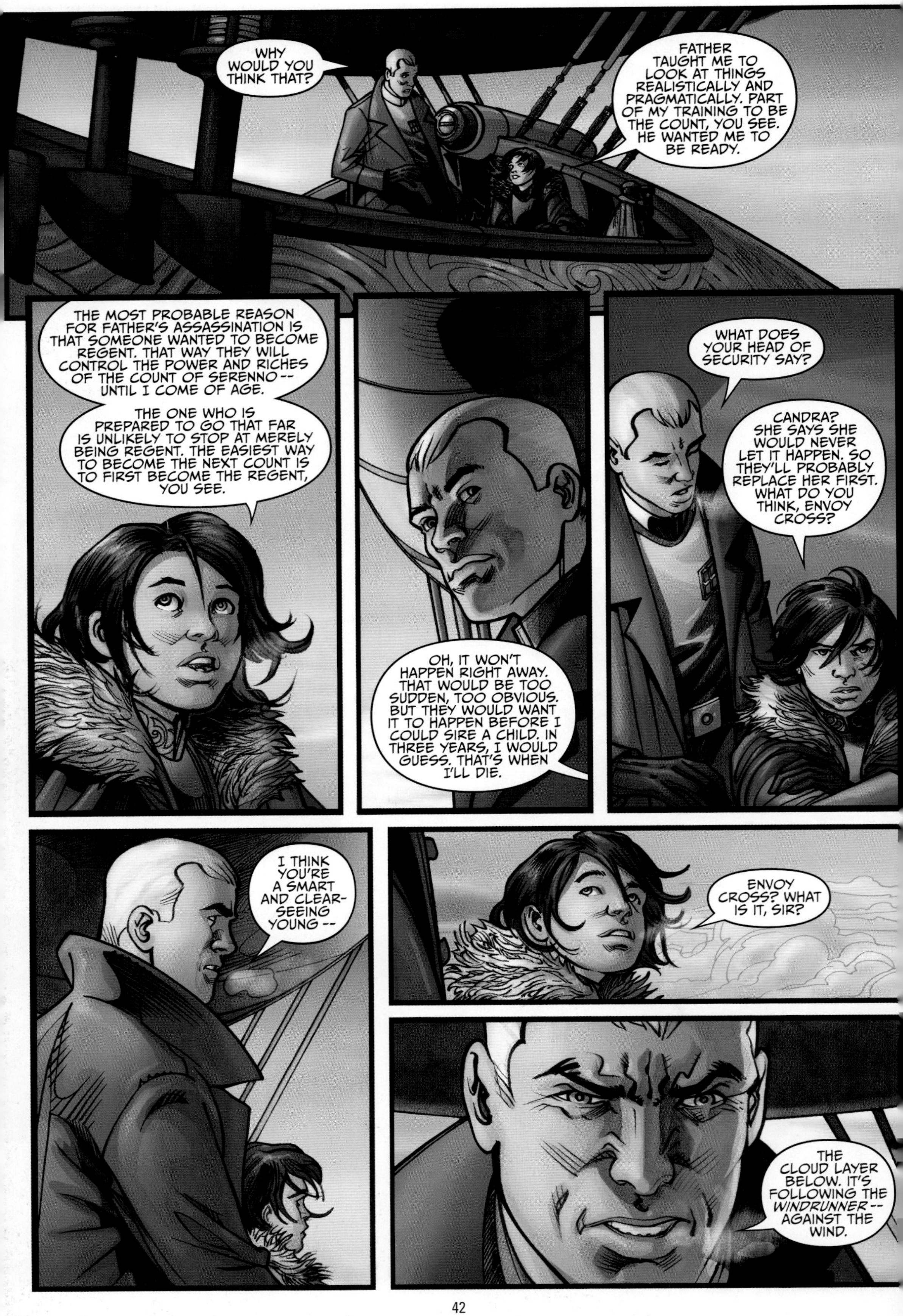
WHY WOULD YOU THINK THAT?
FATHER TAUGHT ME TO LOOK AT THINGS REALISTICALLY AND PRAGMATICALLY. PART OF MY TRAINING TO BE THE COUNT, YOU SEE. HE WANTED ME TO BE READY.
THE MOST PROBABLE REASON FOR FATHER'S ASSASSINATION IS THAT SOMEONE WANTED TO BECOME REGENT. THAT WAY THEY WILL CONTROL THE POWER AND RICHES OF THE COUNT OF SERENNO -- UNTIL I COME OF AGE.
THE ONE WHO IS PREPARED TO GO THAT FAR IS UNLIKELY TO STOP AT MERELY BEING REGENT. THE EASIEST WAY TO BECOME THE NEXT COUNT IS TO FIRST BECOME THE REGENT, YOU SEE.
OH, IT WON'T HAPPEN RIGHT AWAY. THAT WOULD BE TOO SUDDEN, TOO OBVIOUS. BUT THEY WOULD WANT IT TO HAPPEN BEFORE I COULD SIRE A CHILD. IN THREE YEARS, I WOULD GUESS. THAT'S WHEN I'LL DIE.
WHAT DOES YOUR HEAD OF SECURITY SAY?
CANDRA? SHE SAYS SHE WOULD NEVER LET IT HAPPEN. SO THEY'LL PROBABLY REPLACE HER FIRST. WHAT DO YOU THINK, ENVOY CROSS?
I THINK YOU'RE A SMART AND CLEAR-SEEING YOUNG --
ENVOY CROSS? WHAT IS IT, SIR?
THE CLOUD LAYER BELOW. IT'S FOLLOWING THE *WINDRUNNER* -- AGAINST THE WIND.

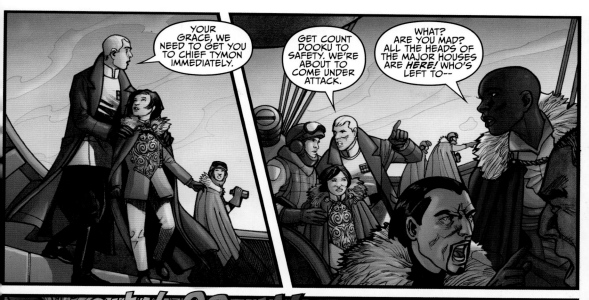

YOUR GRACE, WE NEED TO GET YOU TO CHIEF TYMON IMMEDIATELY.

GET COUNT DOOKU TO SAFETY. WE'RE ABOUT TO COME UNDER ATTACK.

WHAT? ARE YOU MAD? ALL THE HEADS OF THE MAJOR HOUSES ARE *HERE!* WHO'S LEFT TO--

SHWOOOOM!

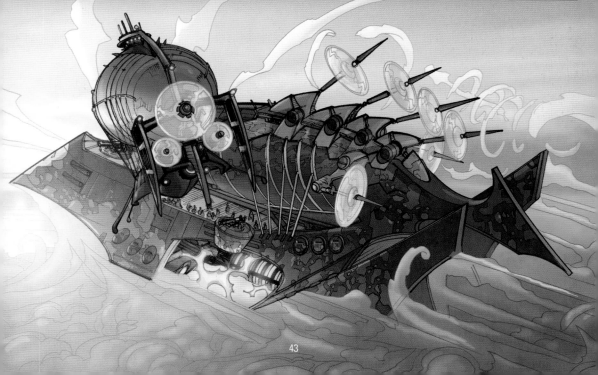

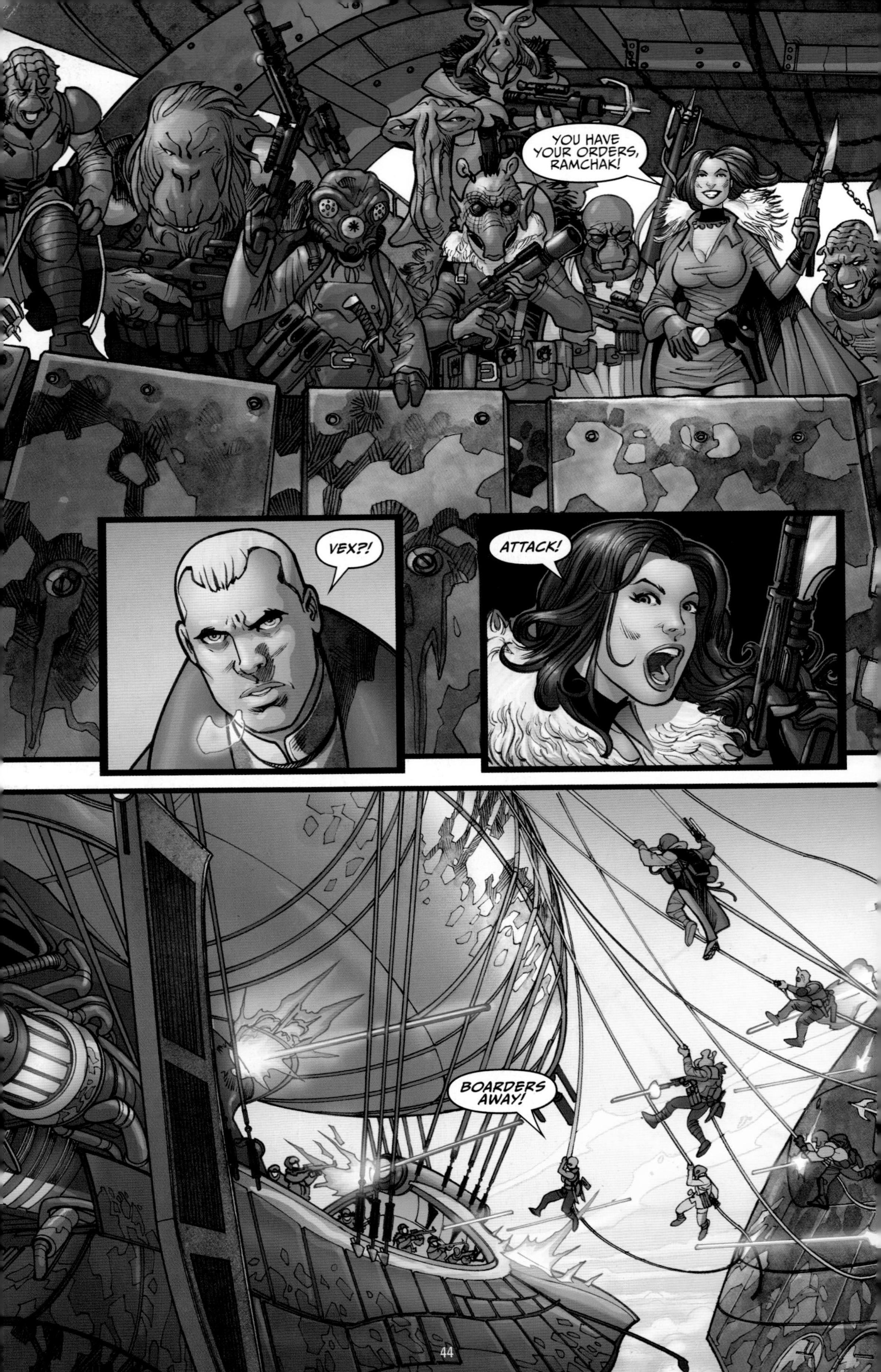
YOU HAVE YOUR ORDERS, RAMCHAK!
VEX?!
ATTACK!
BOARDERS AWAY!

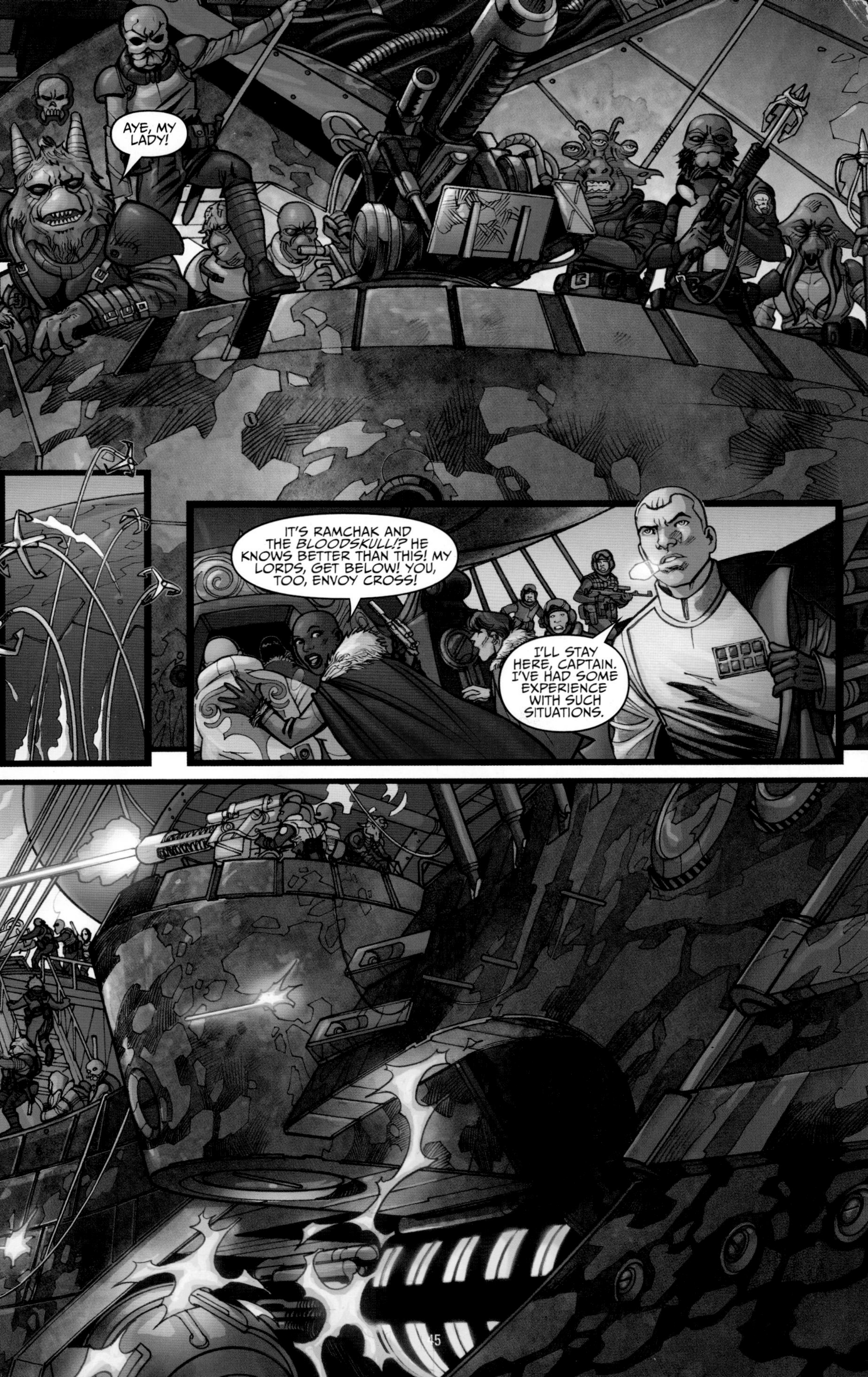
AYE, MY LADY!
IT'S RAMCHAK AND THE BLOODSKULL!? HE KNOWS BETTER THAN THIS! MY LORDS, GET BELOW! YOU, TOO, ENVOY CROSS!
I'LL STAY HERE, CAPTAIN. I'VE HAD SOME EXPERIENCE WITH SUCH SITUATIONS.

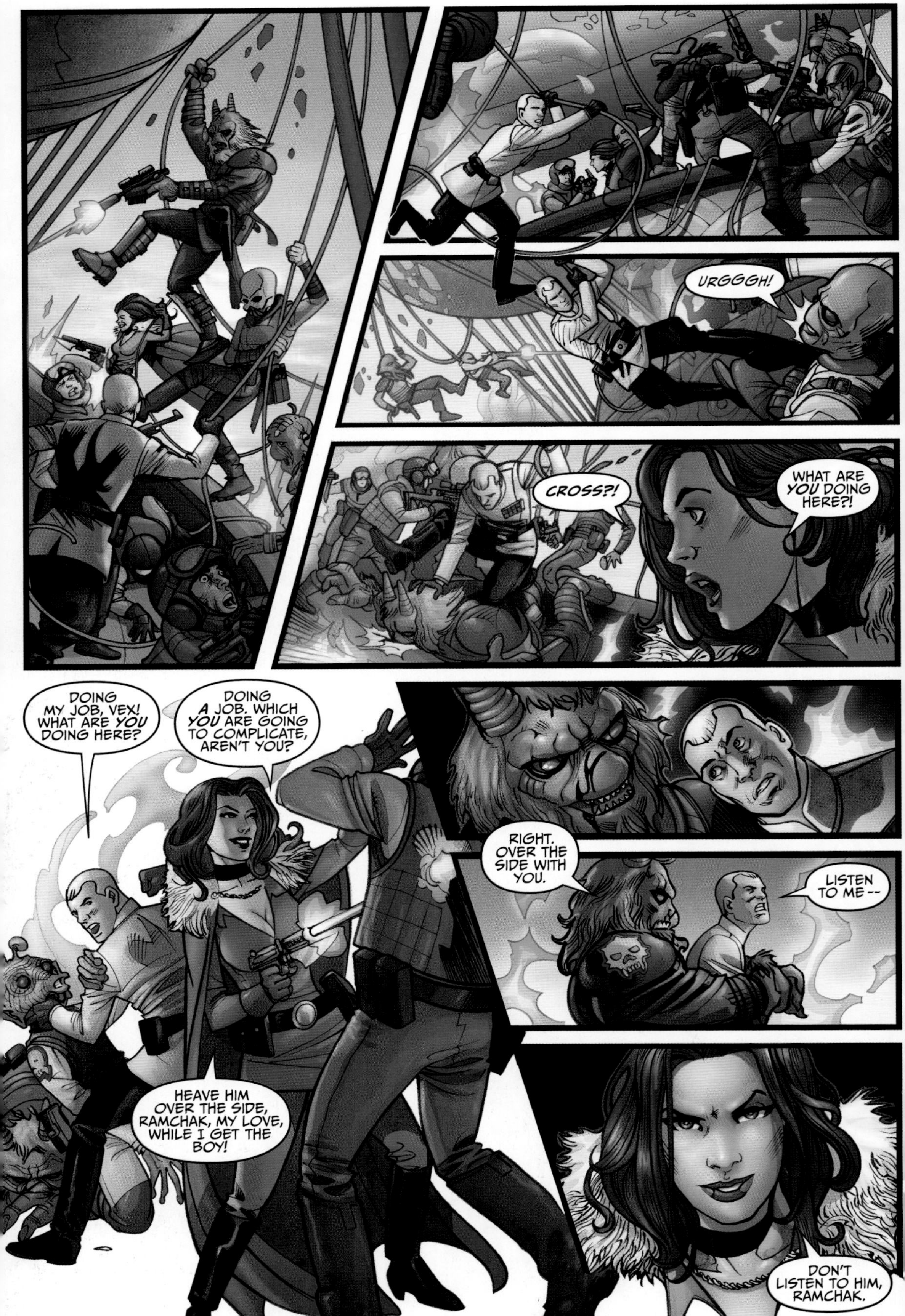
URGGGH!
CROSS?!
WHAT ARE YOU DOING HERE?!
DOING MY JOB, VEX! WHAT ARE YOU DOING HERE?
DOING A JOB. WHICH YOU ARE GOING TO COMPLICATE, AREN'T YOU?
HEAVE HIM OVER THE SIDE, RAMCHAK, MY LOVE, WHILE I GET THE BOY!
RIGHT. OVER THE SIDE WITH YOU.
LISTEN TO ME --
DON'T LISTEN TO HIM, RAMCHAK.

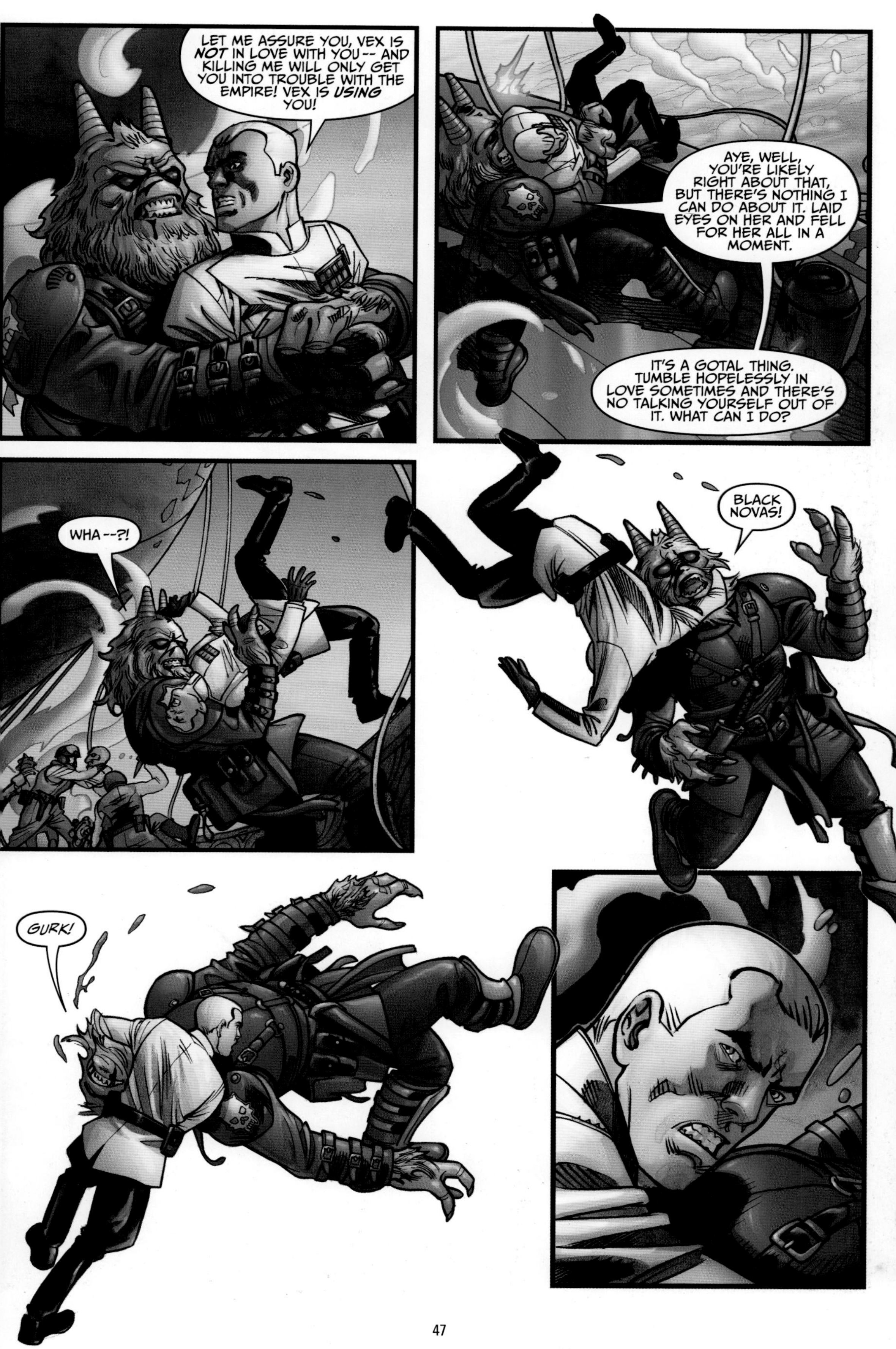
LET ME ASSURE YOU, VEX IS *NOT* IN LOVE WITH YOU-- AND KILLING ME WILL ONLY GET YOU INTO TROUBLE WITH THE EMPIRE! VEX IS *USING* YOU!
AYE, WELL, YOU'RE LIKELY RIGHT ABOUT THAT, BUT THERE'S NOTHING I CAN DO ABOUT IT. LAID EYES ON HER AND FELL FOR HER ALL IN A MOMENT.
IT'S A GOTAL THING. TUMBLE HOPELESSLY IN LOVE SOMETIMES AND THERE'S NO TALKING YOURSELF OUT OF IT. WHAT CAN I DO?
WHA--?!
BLACK NOVAS!
GURK!

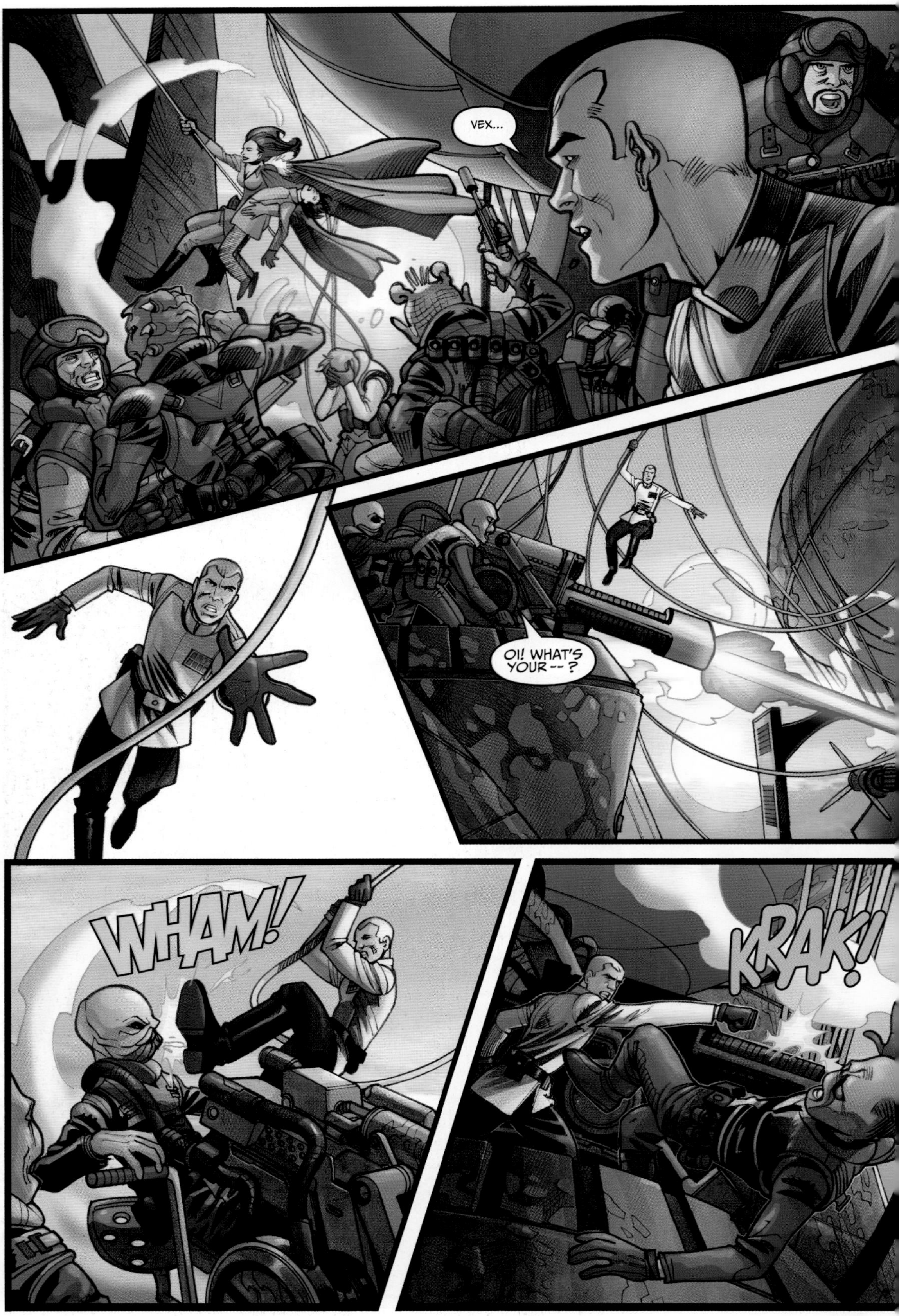
VEX...
OI! WHAT'S YOUR -- ?
WHAM!
KRAK!

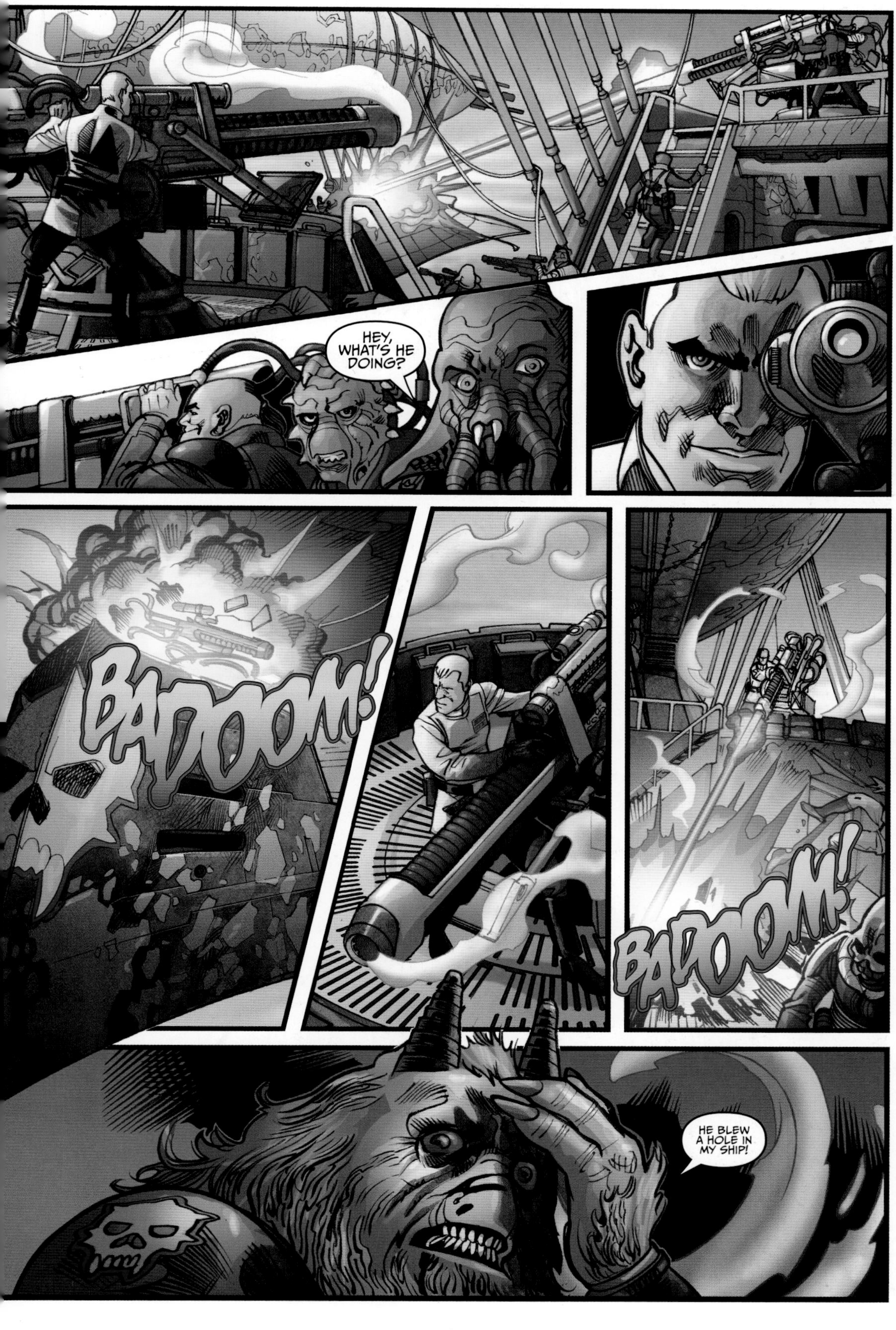
HEY, WHAT'S HE DOING?
BADOOM!
BADOOM!
HE BLEW A HOLE IN MY SHIP!

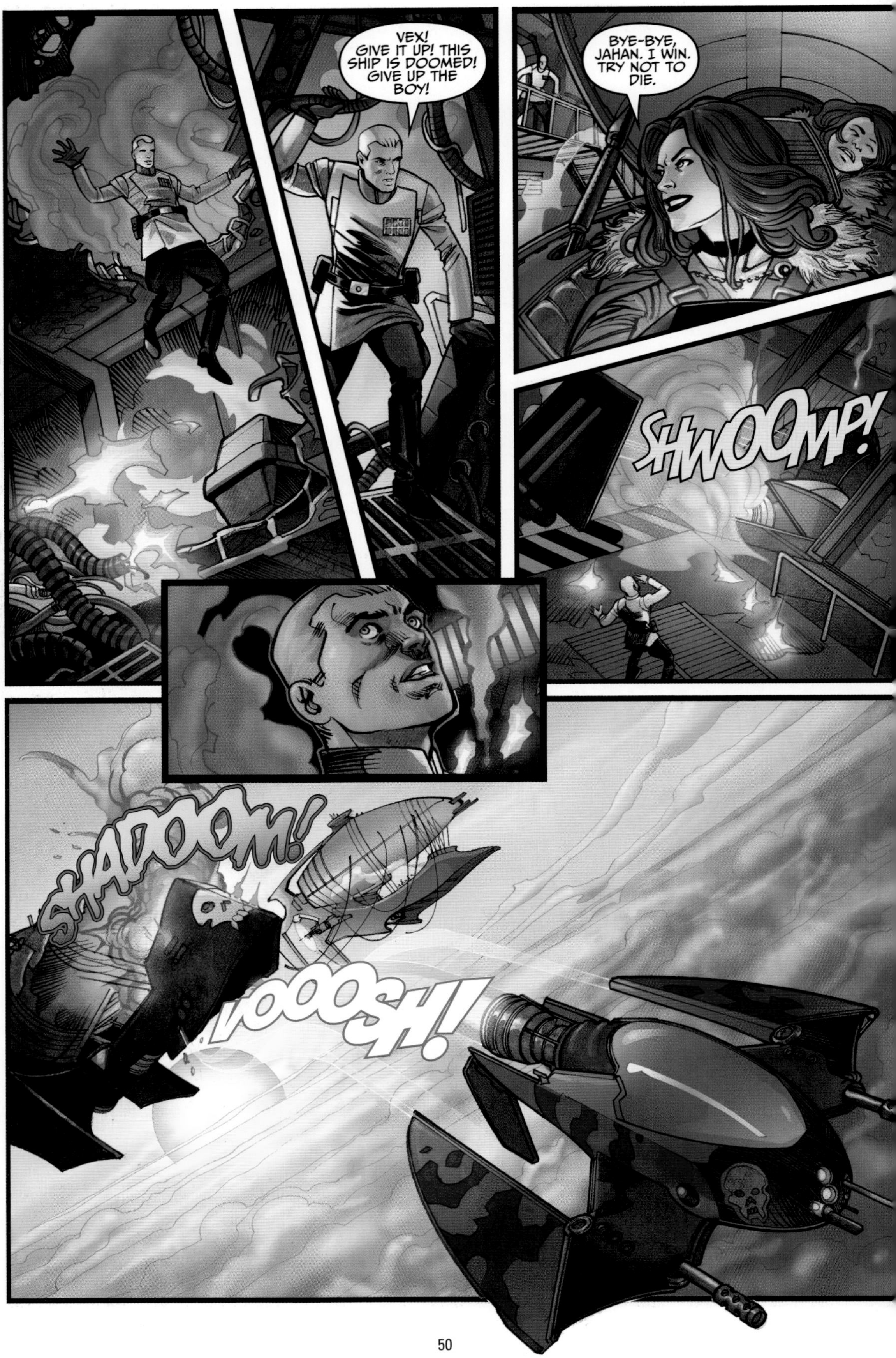
VEX! GIVE IT UP! THIS SHIP IS DOOMED! GIVE UP THE BOY!
BYE-BYE, JAHAN. I WIN. TRY NOT TO DIE.
SHWOOMP!
SHADOOM!
VOOOSH!

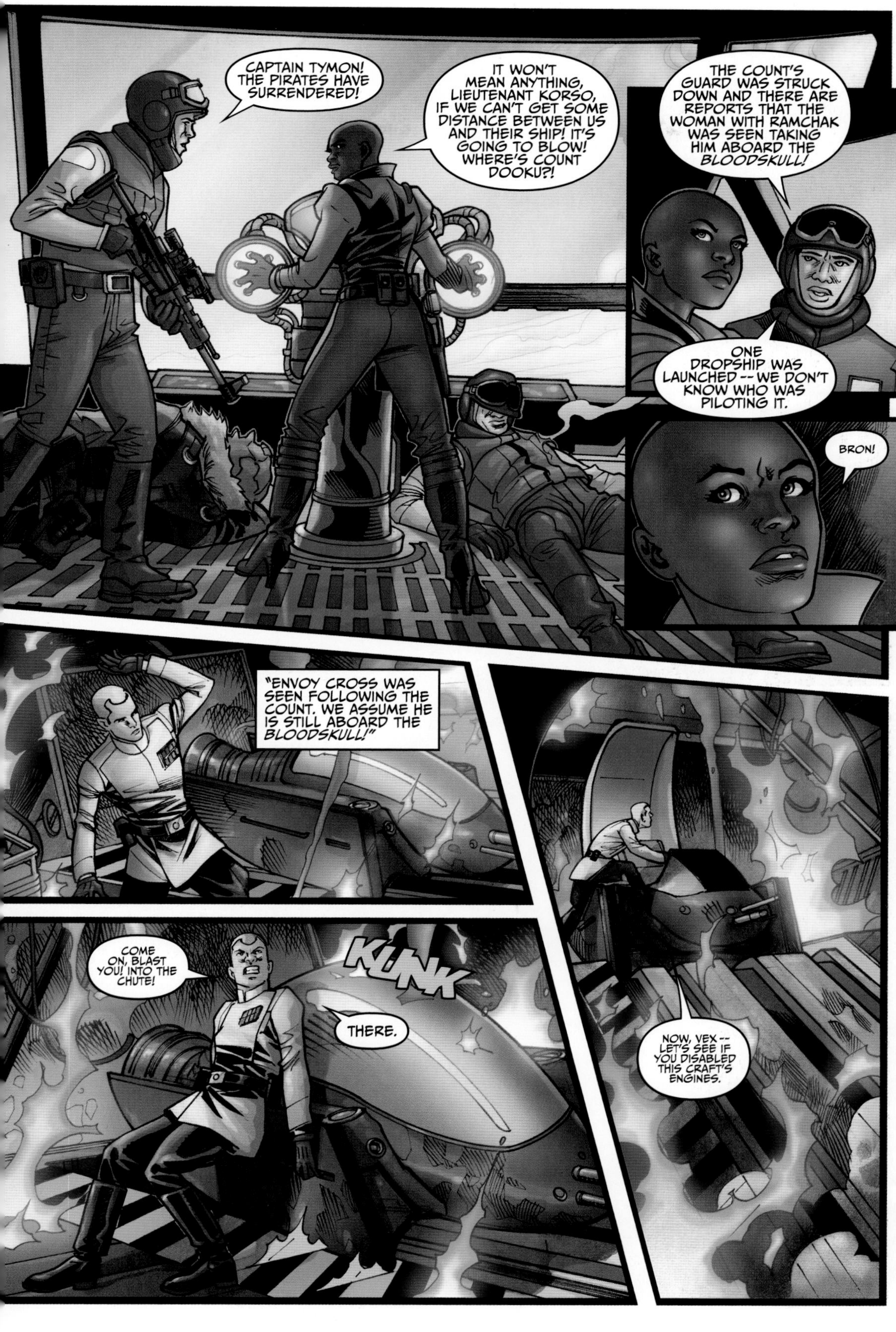
CAPTAIN TYMON! THE PIRATES HAVE SURRENDERED!
IT WON'T MEAN ANYTHING, LIEUTENANT KORSO, IF WE CAN'T GET SOME DISTANCE BETWEEN US AND THEIR SHIP! IT'S GOING TO BLOW! WHERE'S COUNT DOOKU?!
THE COUNT'S GUARD WAS STRUCK DOWN AND THERE ARE REPORTS THAT THE WOMAN WITH RAMCHAK WAS SEEN TAKING HIM ABOARD THE *BLOODSKULL!*
ONE DROPSHIP WAS LAUNCHED -- WE DON'T KNOW WHO WAS PILOTING IT.
BRON!
"ENVOY CROSS WAS SEEN FOLLOWING THE COUNT. WE ASSUME HE IS STILL ABOARD THE *BLOODSKULL!*"
COME ON, BLAST YOU! INTO THE CHUTE!
KUNK
THERE.
NOW, VEX -- LET'S SEE IF YOU DISABLED THIS CRAFT'S ENGINES.

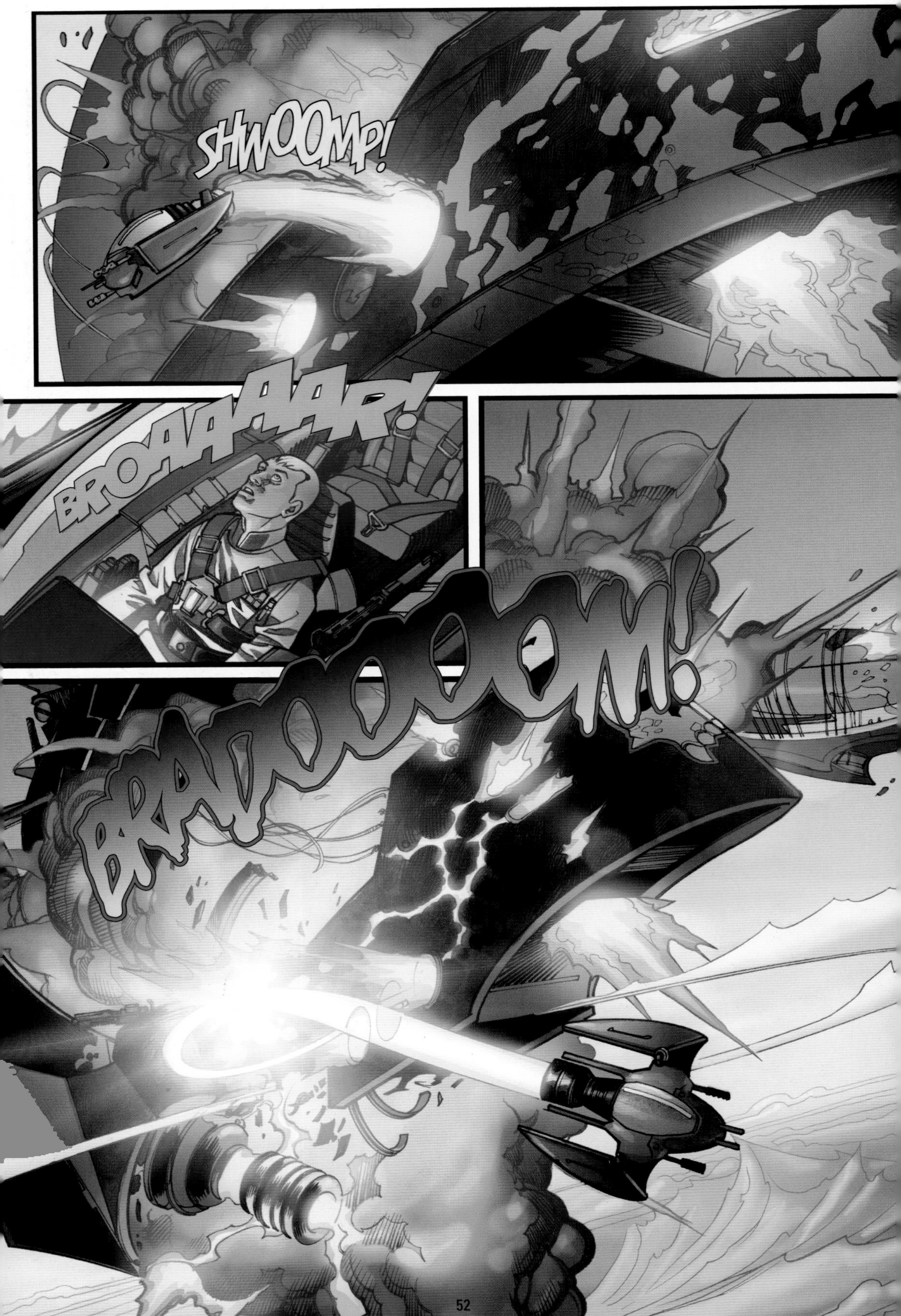
SHWOOMP!
BROAAAAAR!
BRADOOOOOM!

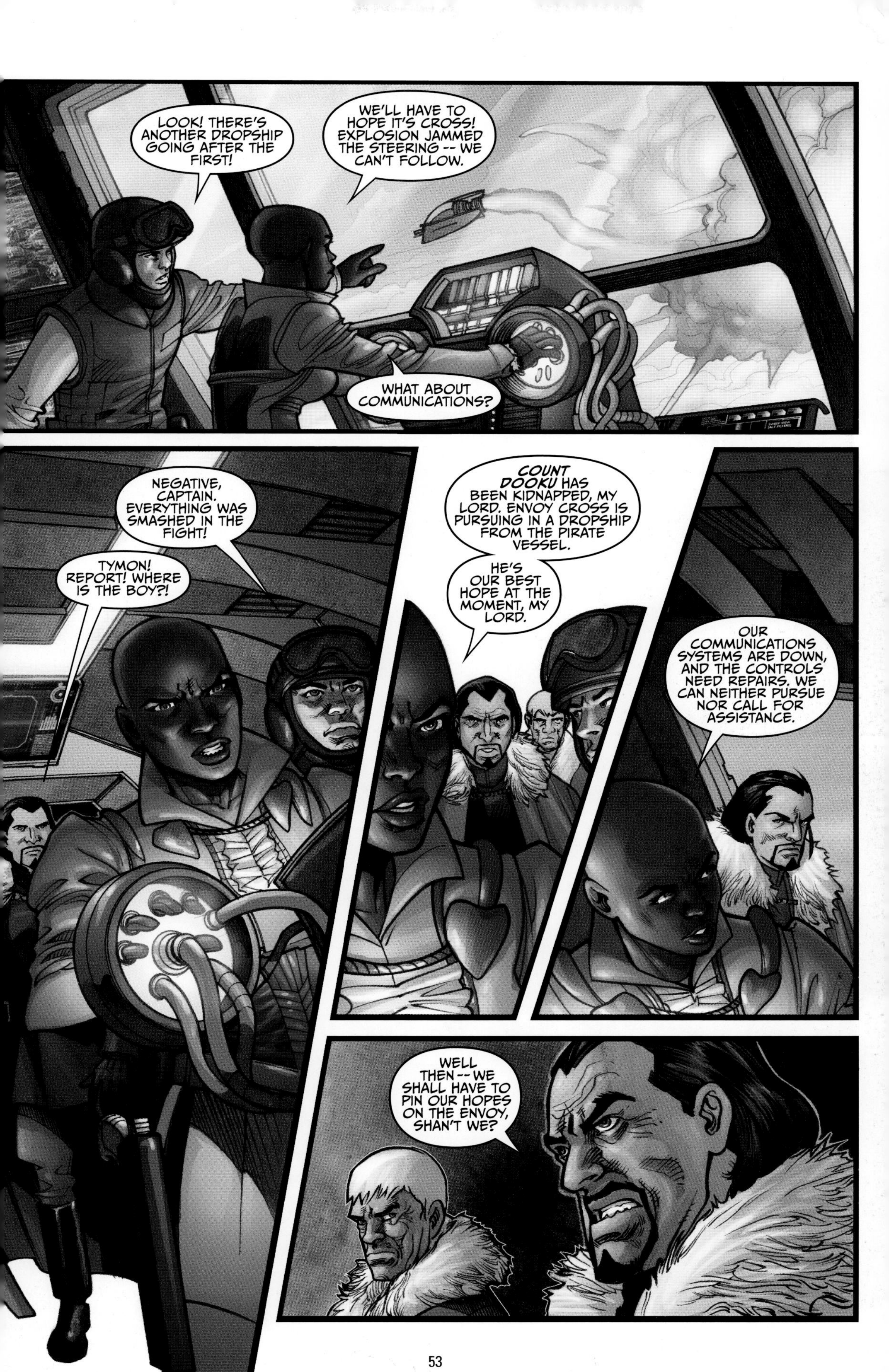
LOOK! THERE'S ANOTHER DROPSHIP GOING AFTER THE FIRST!
WE'LL HAVE TO HOPE IT'S CROSS! EXPLOSION JAMMED THE STEERING -- WE CAN'T FOLLOW.
WHAT ABOUT COMMUNICATIONS?
NEGATIVE, CAPTAIN. EVERYTHING WAS SMASHED IN THE FIGHT!
TYMON! REPORT! WHERE IS THE BOY?!
COUNT DOOKU HAS BEEN KIDNAPPED, MY LORD. ENVOY CROSS IS PURSUING IN A DROPSHIP FROM THE PIRATE VESSEL.
HE'S OUR BEST HOPE AT THE MOMENT, MY LORD.
OUR COMMUNICATIONS SYSTEMS ARE DOWN, AND THE CONTROLS NEED REPAIRS. WE CAN NEITHER PURSUE NOR CALL FOR ASSISTANCE.
WELL THEN -- WE SHALL HAVE TO PIN OUR HOPES ON THE ENVOY, SHAN'T WE?

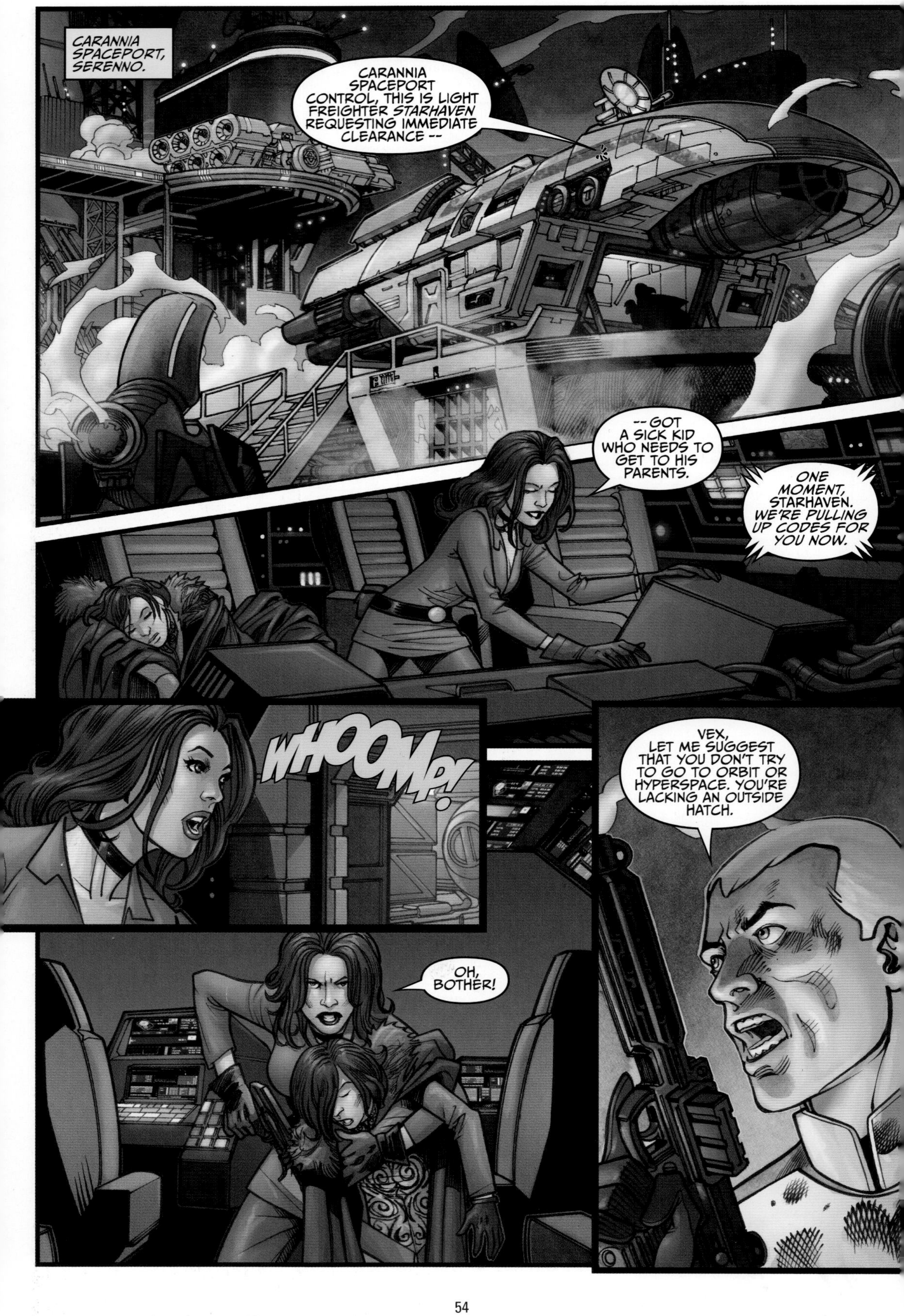
CARANNIA SPACEPORT, SERENNO.
CARANNIA SPACEPORT CONTROL, THIS IS LIGHT FREIGHTER STARHAVEN REQUESTING IMMEDIATE CLEARANCE --
-- GOT A SICK KID WHO NEEDS TO GET TO HIS PARENTS.
ONE MOMENT, STARHAVEN. WE'RE PULLING UP CODES FOR YOU NOW.
WHOOMP!
VEX, LET ME SUGGEST THAT YOU DON'T TRY TO GO TO ORBIT OR HYPERSPACE. YOU'RE LACKING AN OUTSIDE HATCH.
OH, BOTHER!

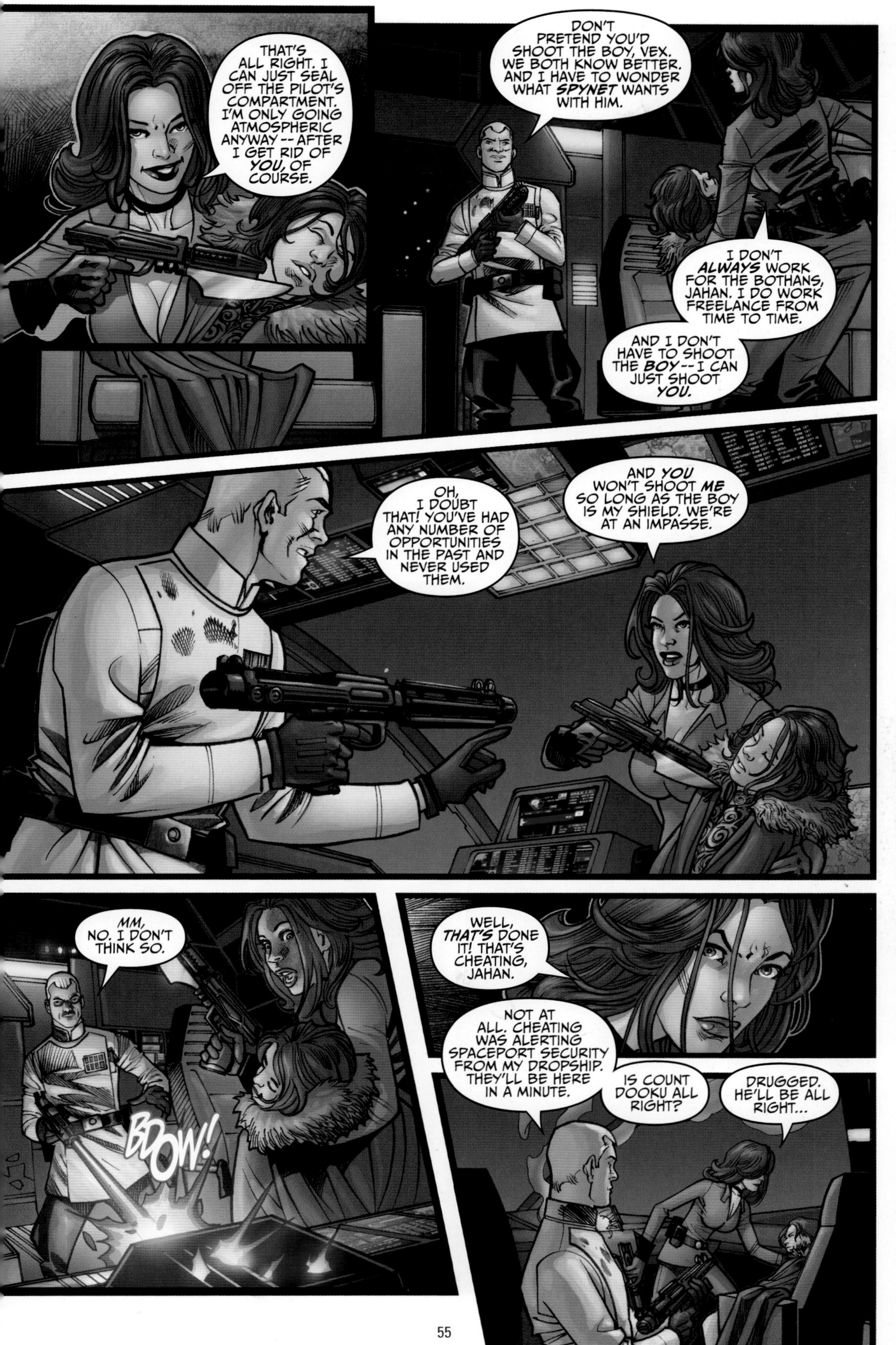
THAT'S ALL RIGHT. I CAN JUST SEAL OFF THE PILOT'S COMPARTMENT. I'M ONLY GOING ATMOSPHERIC ANYWAY -- AFTER I GET RID OF YOU, OF COURSE.
DON'T PRETEND YOU'D SHOOT THE BOY, VEX. WE BOTH KNOW BETTER. AND I HAVE TO WONDER WHAT SPYNET WANTS WITH HIM.
I DON'T ALWAYS WORK FOR THE BOTHANS, JAHAN. I DO WORK FREELANCE FROM TIME TO TIME.
AND I DON'T HAVE TO SHOOT THE BOY -- I CAN JUST SHOOT YOU.
OH, I DOUBT THAT! YOU'VE HAD ANY NUMBER OF OPPORTUNITIES IN THE PAST AND NEVER USED THEM.
AND YOU WON'T SHOOT ME SO LONG AS THE BOY IS MY SHIELD. WE'RE AT AN IMPASSE.
MM, NO. I DON'T THINK SO.
BDOW!
WELL, THAT'S DONE IT! THAT'S CHEATING, JAHAN.
NOT AT ALL. CHEATING WAS ALERTING SPACEPORT SECURITY FROM MY DROPSHIP. THEY'LL BE HERE IN A MINUTE.
IS COUNT DOOKU ALL RIGHT?
DRUGGED. HE'LL BE ALL RIGHT...

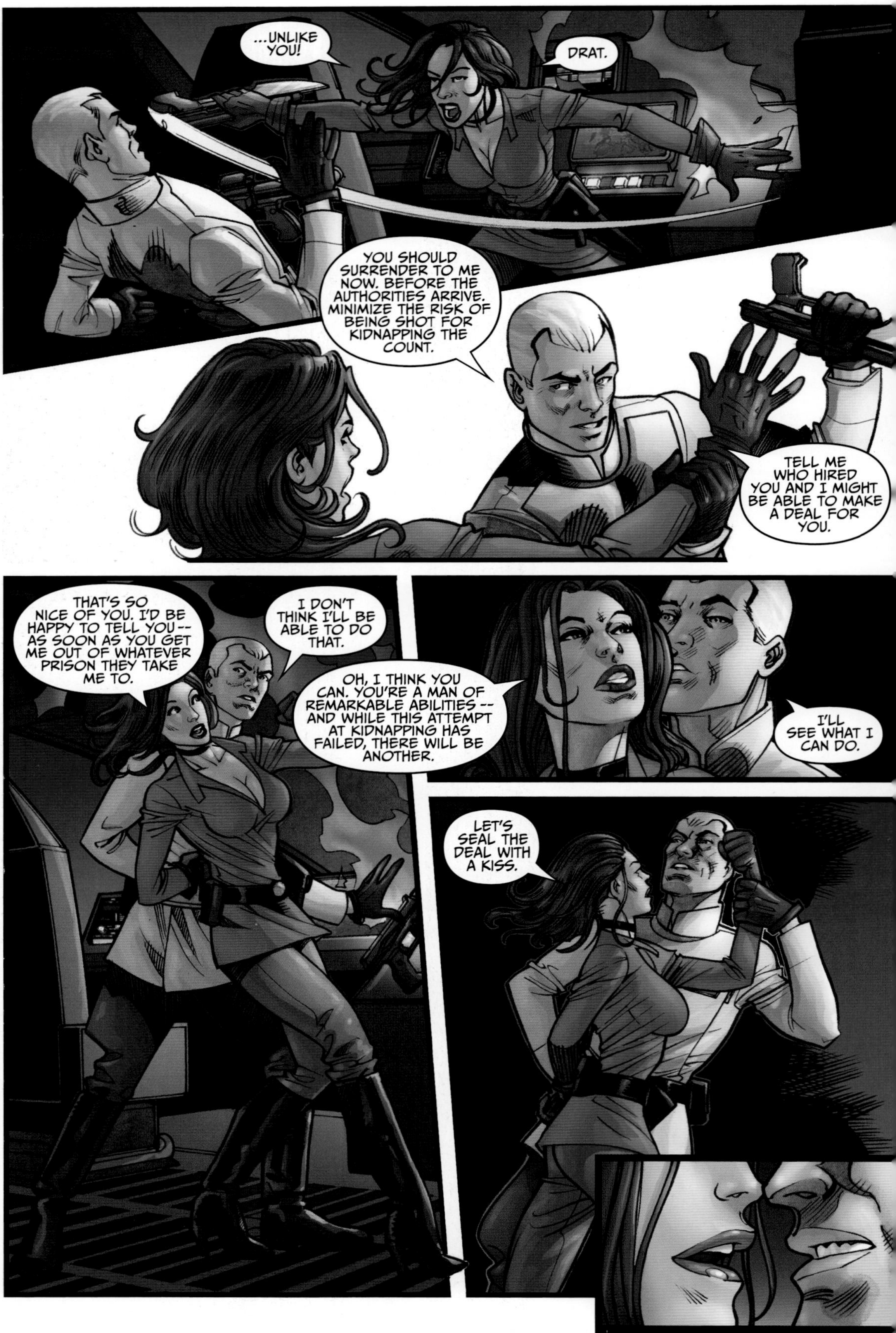
...UNLIKE YOU!
DRAT.
YOU SHOULD SURRENDER TO ME NOW. BEFORE THE AUTHORITIES ARRIVE. MINIMIZE THE RISK OF BEING SHOT FOR KIDNAPPING THE COUNT.
TELL ME WHO HIRED YOU AND I MIGHT BE ABLE TO MAKE A DEAL FOR YOU.
THAT'S SO NICE OF YOU. I'D BE HAPPY TO TELL YOU-- AS SOON AS YOU GET ME OUT OF WHATEVER PRISON THEY TAKE ME TO.
I DON'T THINK I'LL BE ABLE TO DO THAT.
OH, I THINK YOU CAN. YOU'RE A MAN OF REMARKABLE ABILITIES -- AND WHILE THIS ATTEMPT AT KIDNAPPING HAS FAILED, THERE WILL BE ANOTHER.
I'LL SEE WHAT I CAN DO.
LET'S SEAL THE DEAL WITH A KISS.

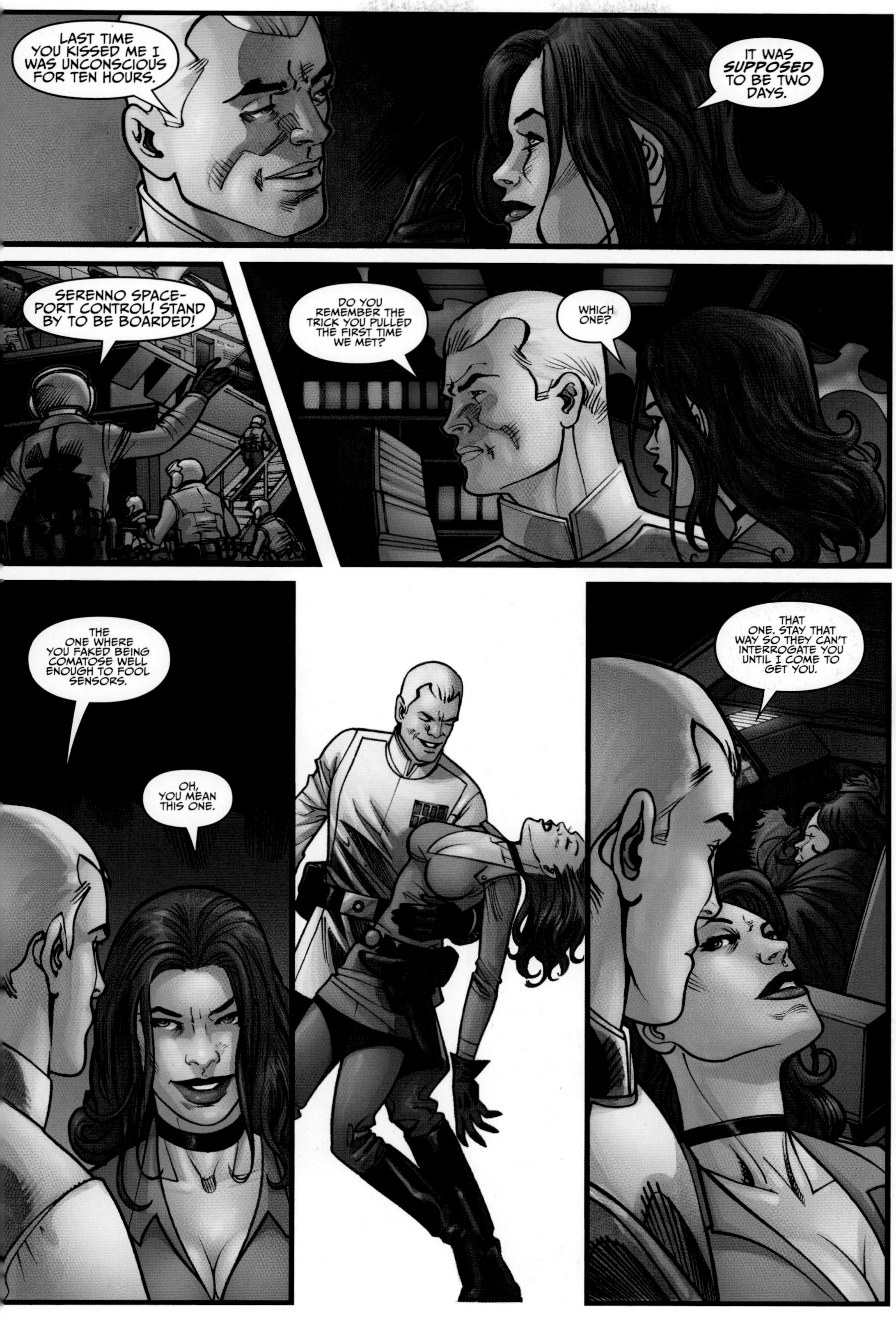
LAST TIME YOU KISSED ME I WAS UNCONSCIOUS FOR TEN HOURS.
IT WAS *SUPPOSED* TO BE TWO DAYS.
SERENNO SPACE-PORT CONTROL! STAND BY TO BE BOARDED!
DO YOU REMEMBER THE TRICK YOU PULLED THE FIRST TIME WE MET?
WHICH ONE?
THE ONE WHERE YOU FAKED BEING COMATOSE WELL ENOUGH TO FOOL SENSORS.
OH, YOU MEAN THIS ONE.
THAT ONE. STAY THAT WAY SO THEY CAN'T INTERROGATE YOU UNTIL I COME TO GET YOU.

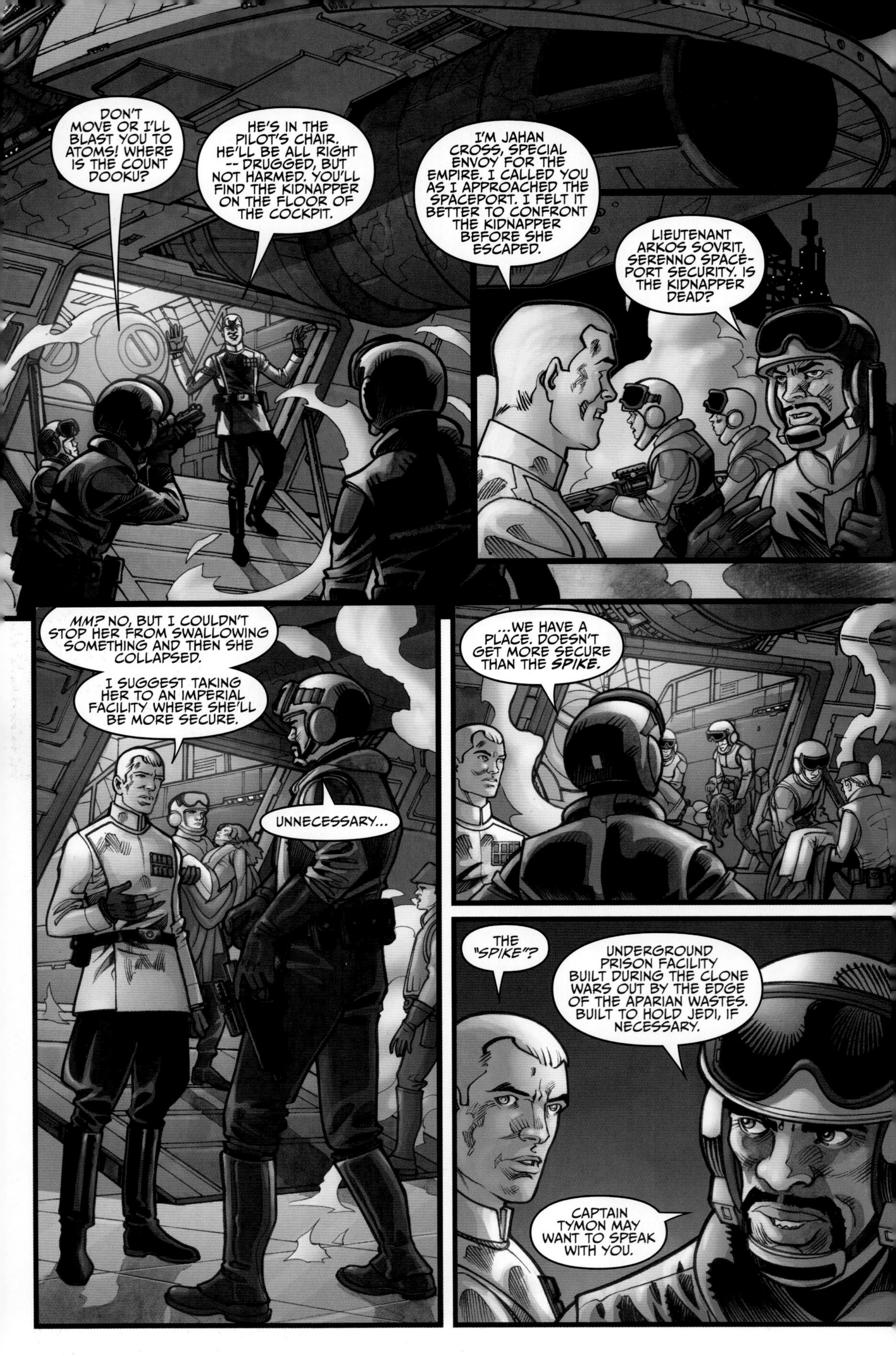
DON'T MOVE OR I'LL BLAST YOU TO ATOMS! WHERE IS THE COUNT DOOKU?
HE'S IN THE PILOT'S CHAIR. HE'LL BE ALL RIGHT -- DRUGGED, BUT NOT HARMED. YOU'LL FIND THE KIDNAPPER ON THE FLOOR OF THE COCKPIT.
I'M JAHAN CROSS, SPECIAL ENVOY FOR THE EMPIRE. I CALLED YOU AS I APPROACHED THE SPACEPORT. I FELT IT BETTER TO CONFRONT THE KIDNAPPER BEFORE SHE ESCAPED.
LIEUTENANT ARKOS SOVRIT, SERENNO SPACE-PORT SECURITY. IS THE KIDNAPPER DEAD?
MM? NO, BUT I COULDN'T STOP HER FROM SWALLOWING SOMETHING AND THEN SHE COLLAPSED.
I SUGGEST TAKING HER TO AN IMPERIAL FACILITY WHERE SHE'LL BE MORE SECURE.
UNNECESSARY...
...WE HAVE A PLACE. DOESN'T GET MORE SECURE THAN THE SPIKE.
THE "SPIKE"?
UNDERGROUND PRISON FACILITY BUILT DURING THE CLONE WARS OUT BY THE EDGE OF THE APARIAN WASTES. BUILT TO HOLD JEDI, IF NECESSARY.
CAPTAIN TYMON MAY WANT TO SPEAK WITH YOU.

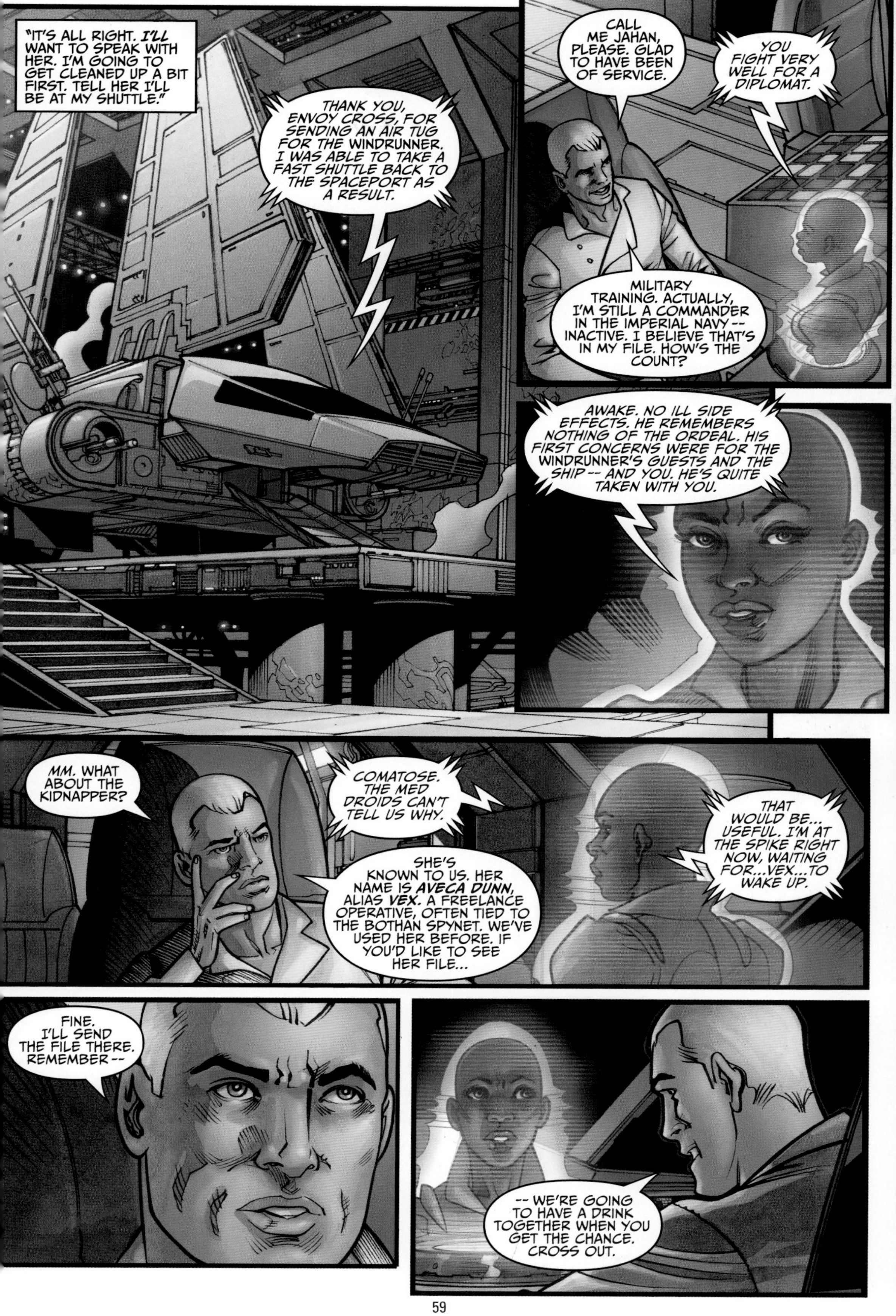
"IT'S ALL RIGHT. I'LL WANT TO SPEAK WITH HER. I'M GOING TO GET CLEANED UP A BIT FIRST. TELL HER I'LL BE AT MY SHUTTLE."
THANK YOU, ENVOY CROSS, FOR SENDING AN AIR TUG FOR THE WINDRUNNER. I WAS ABLE TO TAKE A FAST SHUTTLE BACK TO THE SPACEPORT AS A RESULT.
CALL ME JAHAN, PLEASE. GLAD TO HAVE BEEN OF SERVICE.
YOU FIGHT VERY WELL FOR A DIPLOMAT.
MILITARY TRAINING. ACTUALLY, I'M STILL A COMMANDER IN THE IMPERIAL NAVY -- INACTIVE. I BELIEVE THAT'S IN MY FILE. HOW'S THE COUNT?
AWAKE. NO ILL SIDE EFFECTS. HE REMEMBERS NOTHING OF THE ORDEAL. HIS FIRST CONCERNS WERE FOR THE WINDRUNNER'S GUESTS AND THE SHIP -- AND YOU. HE'S QUITE TAKEN WITH YOU.
MM. WHAT ABOUT THE KIDNAPPER?
COMATOSE. THE MED DROIDS CAN'T TELL US WHY.
SHE'S KNOWN TO US. HER NAME IS AVECA DUNN, ALIAS VEX. A FREELANCE OPERATIVE, OFTEN TIED TO THE BOTHAN SPYNET. WE'VE USED HER BEFORE. IF YOU'D LIKE TO SEE HER FILE...
THAT WOULD BE... USEFUL. I'M AT THE SPIKE RIGHT NOW, WAITING FOR...VEX...TO WAKE UP.
FINE. I'LL SEND THE FILE THERE. REMEMBER --
-- WE'RE GOING TO HAVE A DRINK TOGETHER WHEN YOU GET THE CHANCE. CROSS OUT.

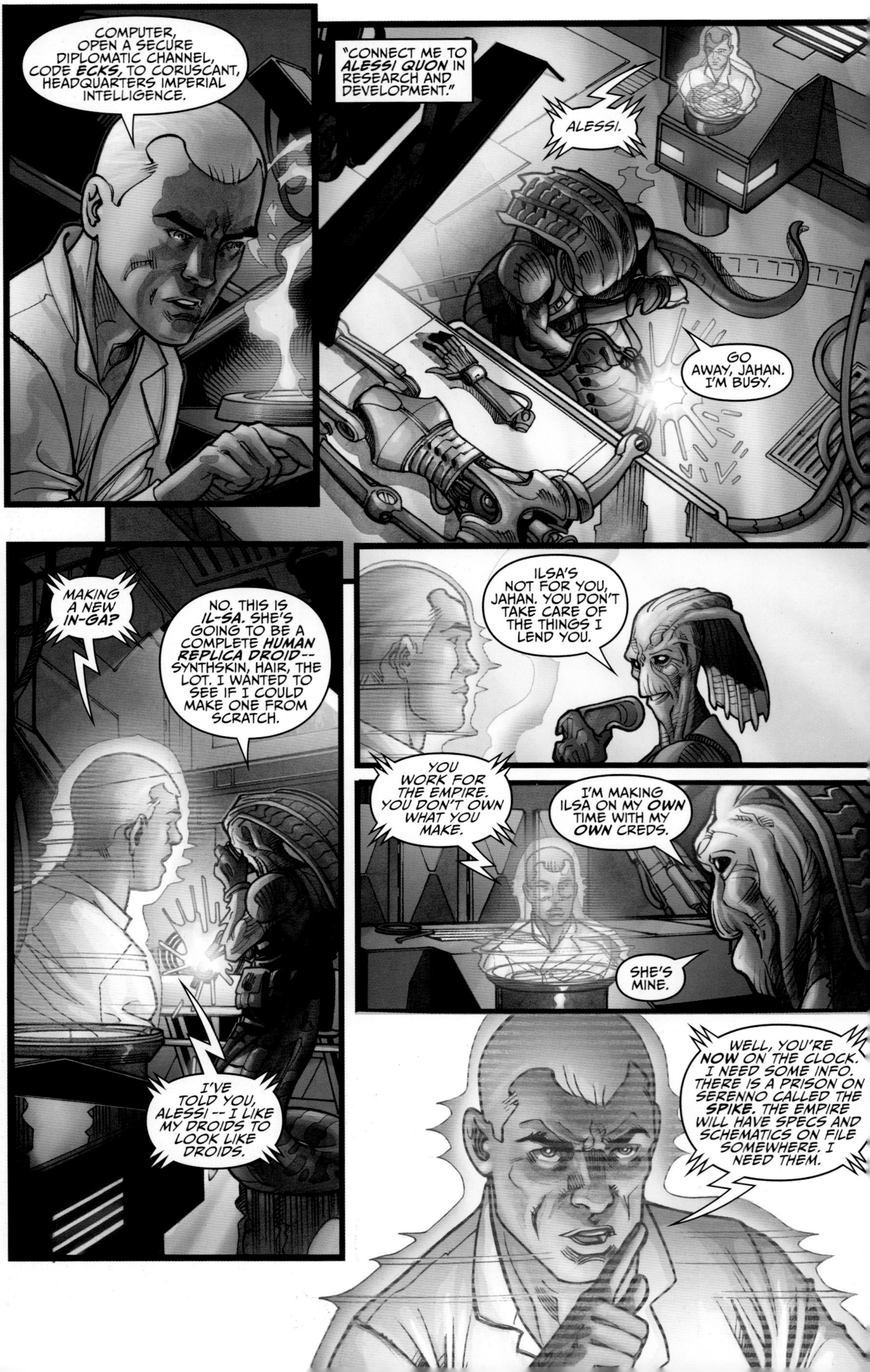
COMPUTER, OPEN A SECURE DIPLOMATIC CHANNEL, CODE ECKS, TO CORUSCANT, HEADQUARTERS IMPERIAL INTELLIGENCE.
"CONNECT ME TO ALESSI QUON IN RESEARCH AND DEVELOPMENT."
ALESSI.
GO AWAY, JAHAN. I'M BUSY.
MAKING A NEW IN-GA?
NO. THIS IS IL-SA. SHE'S GOING TO BE A COMPLETE HUMAN REPLICA DROID-- SYNTHSKIN, HAIR, THE LOT. I WANTED TO SEE IF I COULD MAKE ONE FROM SCRATCH.
I'VE TOLD YOU, ALESSI -- I LIKE MY DROIDS TO LOOK LIKE DROIDS.
ILSA'S NOT FOR YOU, JAHAN. YOU DON'T TAKE CARE OF THE THINGS I LEND YOU.
YOU WORK FOR THE EMPIRE. YOU DON'T OWN WHAT YOU MAKE.
I'M MAKING ILSA ON MY OWN TIME WITH MY OWN CREDS.
SHE'S MINE.
WELL, YOU'RE NOW ON THE CLOCK. I NEED SOME INFO. THERE IS A PRISON ON SERENNO CALLED THE SPIKE. THE EMPIRE WILL HAVE SPECS AND SCHEMATICS ON FILE SOMEWHERE. I NEED THEM.

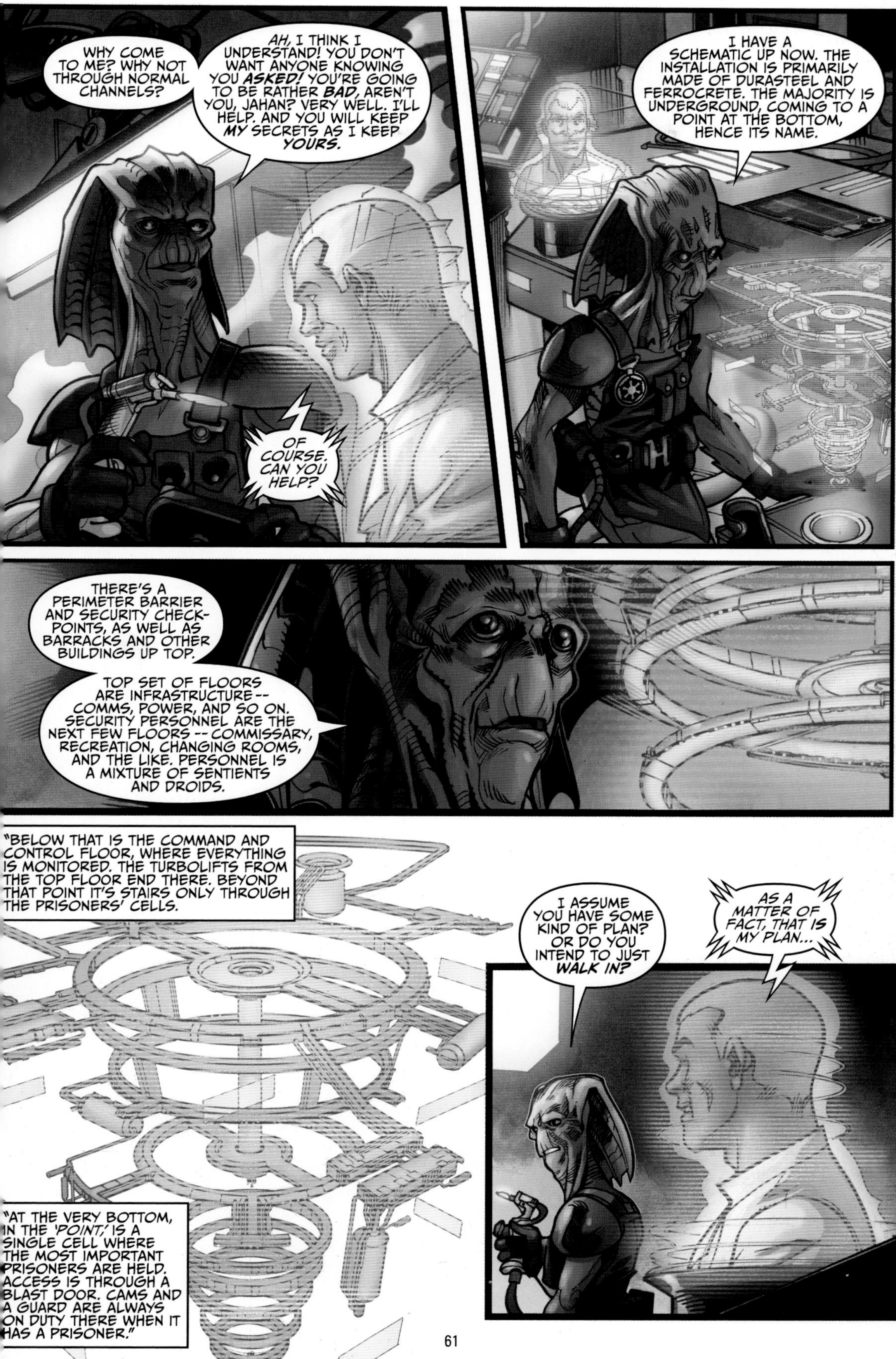

WHY COME TO ME? WHY NOT THROUGH NORMAL CHANNELS?
AH, I THINK I UNDERSTAND! YOU DON'T WANT ANYONE KNOWING YOU ASKED! YOU'RE GOING TO BE RATHER BAD, AREN'T YOU, JAHAN? VERY WELL. I'LL HELP. AND YOU WILL KEEP MY SECRETS AS I KEEP YOURS.
OF COURSE. CAN YOU HELP?
I HAVE A SCHEMATIC UP NOW. THE INSTALLATION IS PRIMARILY MADE OF DURASTEEL AND FERROCRETE. THE MAJORITY IS UNDERGROUND, COMING TO A POINT AT THE BOTTOM, HENCE ITS NAME.
THERE'S A PERIMETER BARRIER AND SECURITY CHECK-POINTS, AS WELL AS BARRACKS AND OTHER BUILDINGS UP TOP.
TOP SET OF FLOORS ARE INFRASTRUCTURE-- COMMS, POWER, AND SO ON. SECURITY PERSONNEL ARE THE NEXT FEW FLOORS -- COMMISSARY, RECREATION, CHANGING ROOMS, AND THE LIKE. PERSONNEL IS A MIXTURE OF SENTIENTS AND DROIDS.
"BELOW THAT IS THE COMMAND AND CONTROL FLOOR, WHERE EVERYTHING IS MONITORED. THE TURBOLIFTS FROM THE TOP FLOOR END THERE. BEYOND THAT POINT IT'S STAIRS ONLY THROUGH THE PRISONERS' CELLS.
"AT THE VERY BOTTOM, IN THE 'POINT,' IS A SINGLE CELL WHERE THE MOST IMPORTANT PRISONERS ARE HELD. ACCESS IS THROUGH A BLAST DOOR. CAMS AND A GUARD ARE ALWAYS ON DUTY THERE WHEN IT HAS A PRISONER."
I ASSUME YOU HAVE SOME KIND OF PLAN? OR DO YOU INTEND TO JUST WALK IN?
AS A MATTER OF FACT, THAT IS MY PLAN...

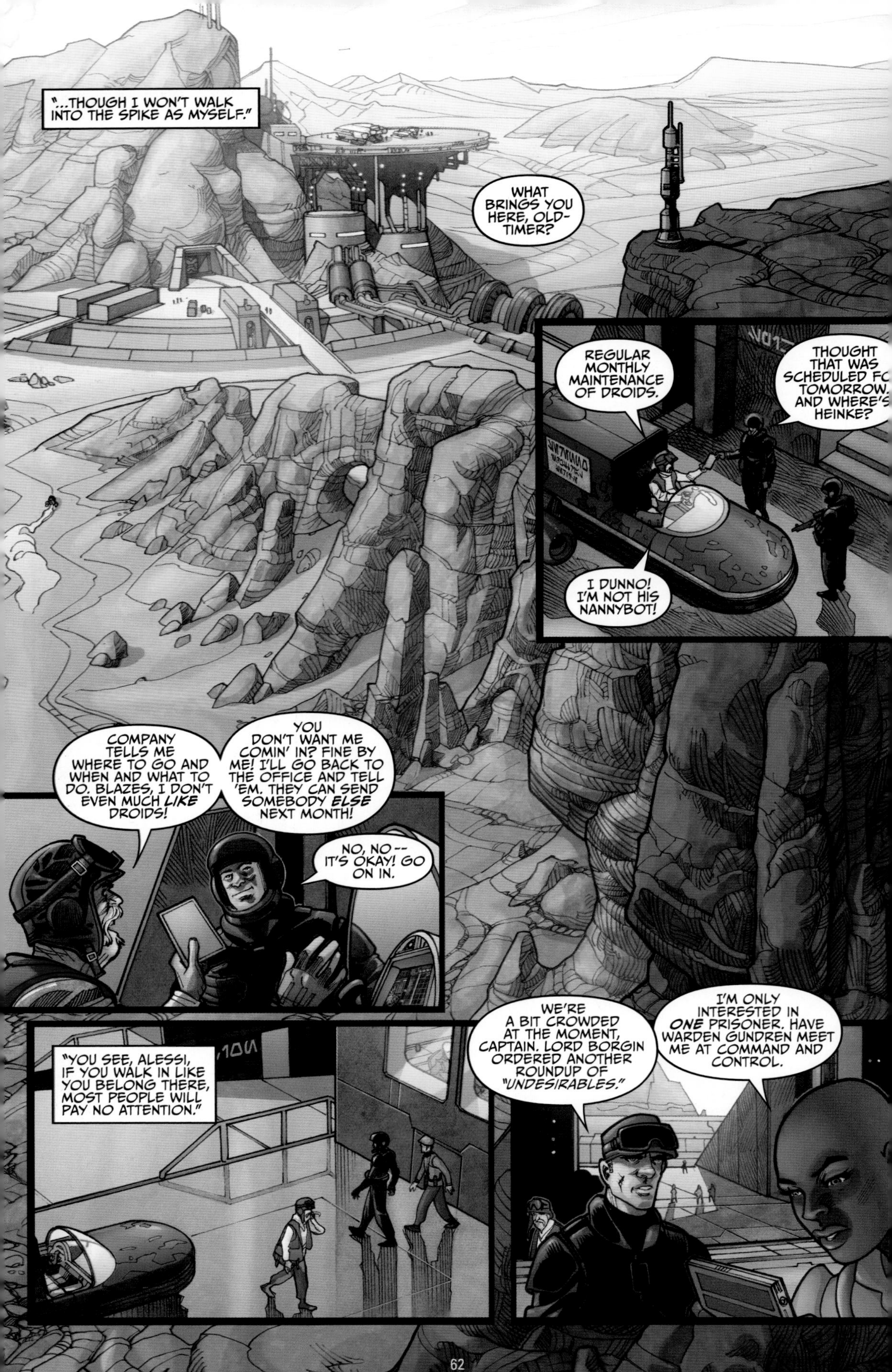
"...THOUGH I WON'T WALK INTO THE SPIKE AS MYSELF."
WHAT BRINGS YOU HERE, OLD-TIMER?
REGULAR MONTHLY MAINTENANCE OF DROIDS.
THOUGHT THAT WAS SCHEDULED FO TOMORROW. AND WHERE'S HEINKE?
I DUNNO! I'M NOT HIS NANNYBOT!
COMPANY TELLS ME WHERE TO GO AND WHEN AND WHAT TO DO. BLAZES, I DON'T EVEN MUCH LIKE DROIDS!
YOU DON'T WANT ME COMIN' IN? FINE BY ME! I'LL GO BACK TO THE OFFICE AND TELL 'EM. THEY CAN SEND SOMEBODY ELSE NEXT MONTH!
NO, NO-- IT'S OKAY! GO ON IN.
"YOU SEE, ALESSI, IF YOU WALK IN LIKE YOU BELONG THERE, MOST PEOPLE WILL PAY NO ATTENTION."
WE'RE A BIT CROWDED AT THE MOMENT, CAPTAIN. LORD BORGIN ORDERED ANOTHER ROUNDUP OF "UNDESIRABLES."
I'M ONLY INTERESTED IN ONE PRISONER. HAVE WARDEN GUNDREN MEET ME AT COMMAND AND CONTROL.

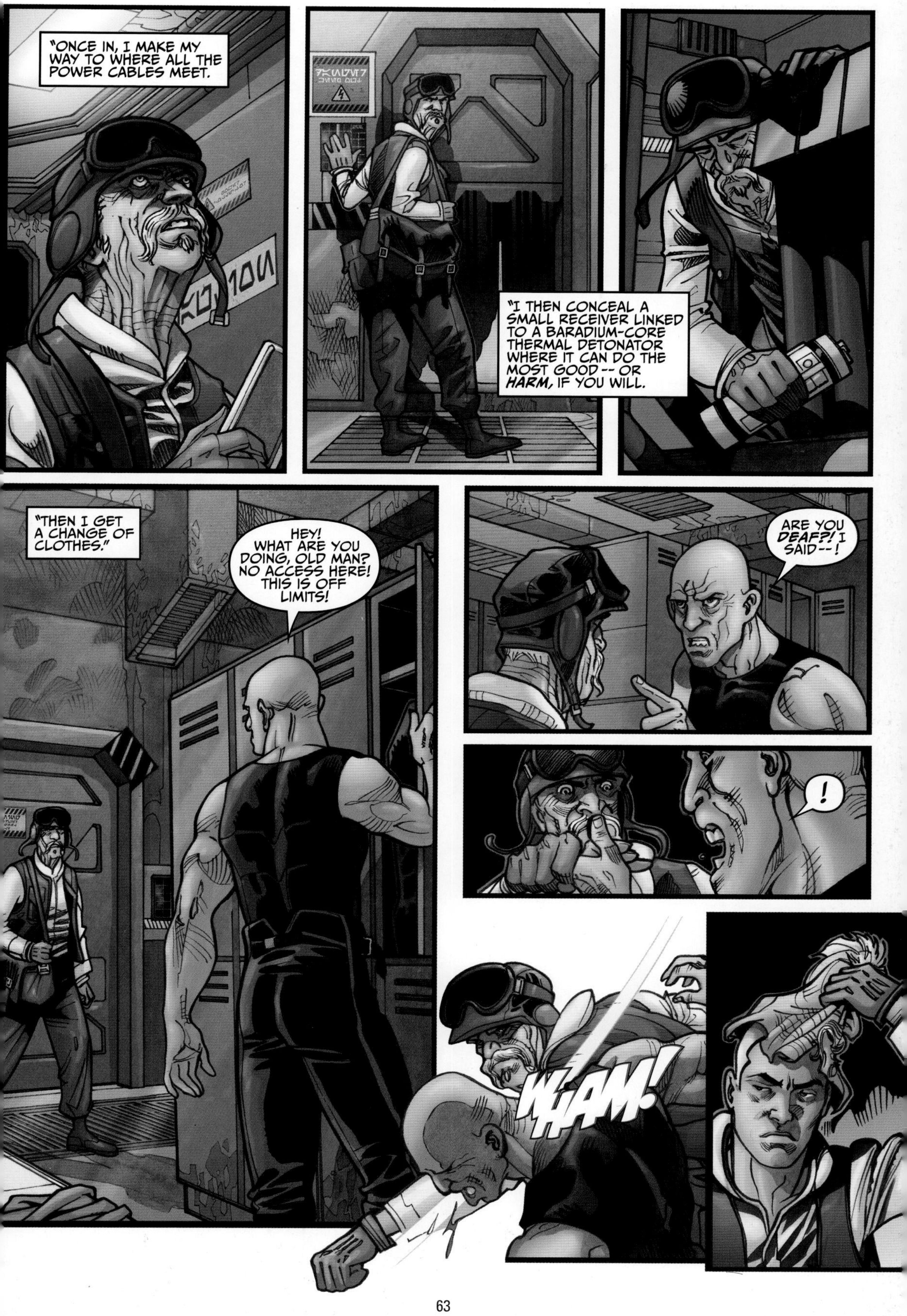
"ONCE IN, I MAKE MY WAY TO WHERE ALL THE POWER CABLES MEET.
"I THEN CONCEAL A SMALL RECEIVER LINKED TO A BARADIUM-CORE THERMAL DETONATOR WHERE IT CAN DO THE MOST GOOD -- OR HARM, IF YOU WILL.
"THEN I GET A CHANGE OF CLOTHES."
HEY! WHAT ARE YOU DOING, OLD MAN? NO ACCESS HERE! THIS IS OFF LIMITS!
ARE YOU DEAF?! I SAID--!
!
WHAM!

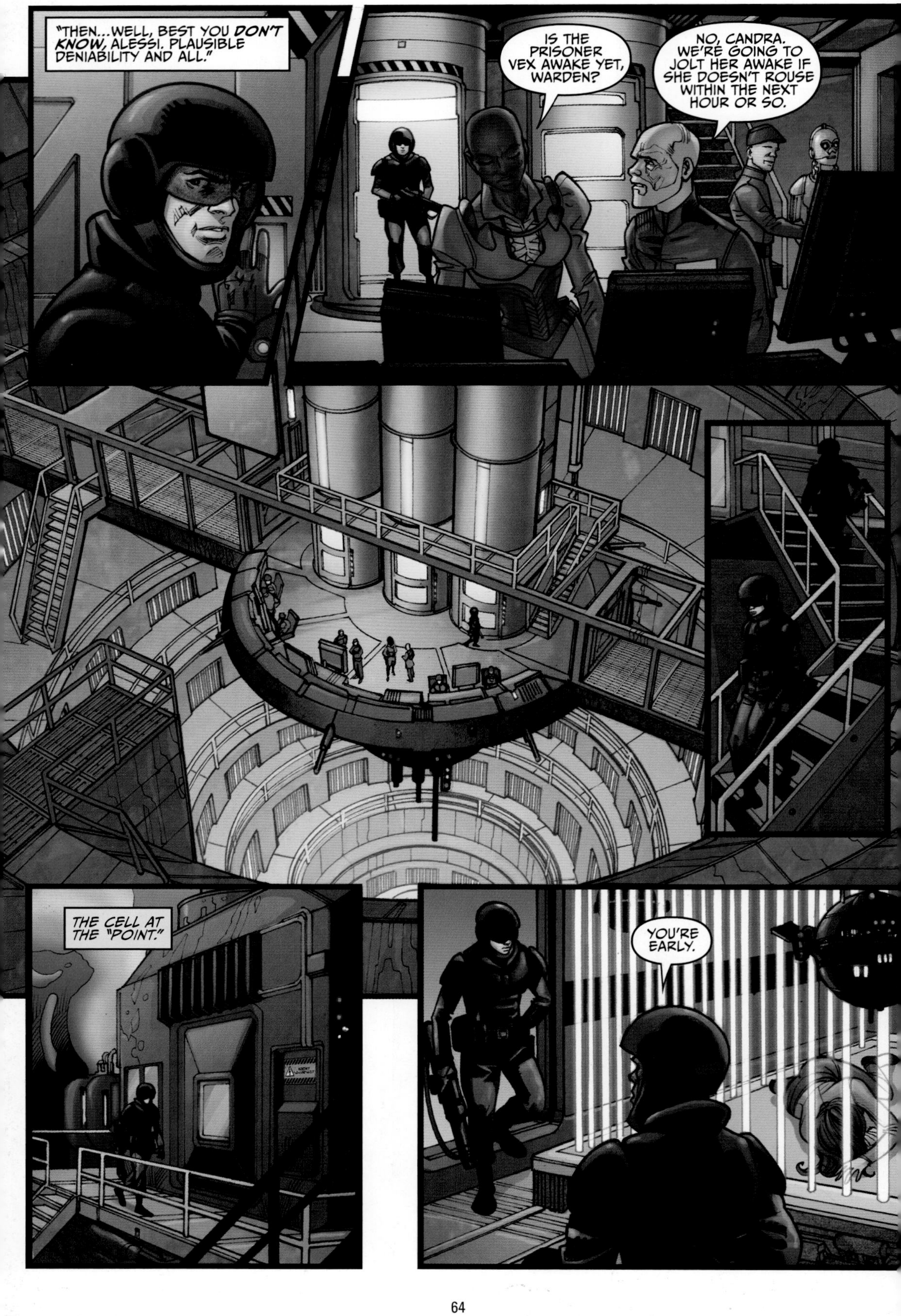
"THEN...WELL, BEST YOU DON'T KNOW, ALESSI. PLAUSIBLE DENIABILITY AND ALL."
IS THE PRISONER VEX AWAKE YET, WARDEN?
NO, CANDRA. WE'RE GOING TO JOLT HER AWAKE IF SHE DOESN'T ROUSE WITHIN THE NEXT HOUR OR SO.
THE CELL AT THE "POINT."
YOU'RE EARLY.

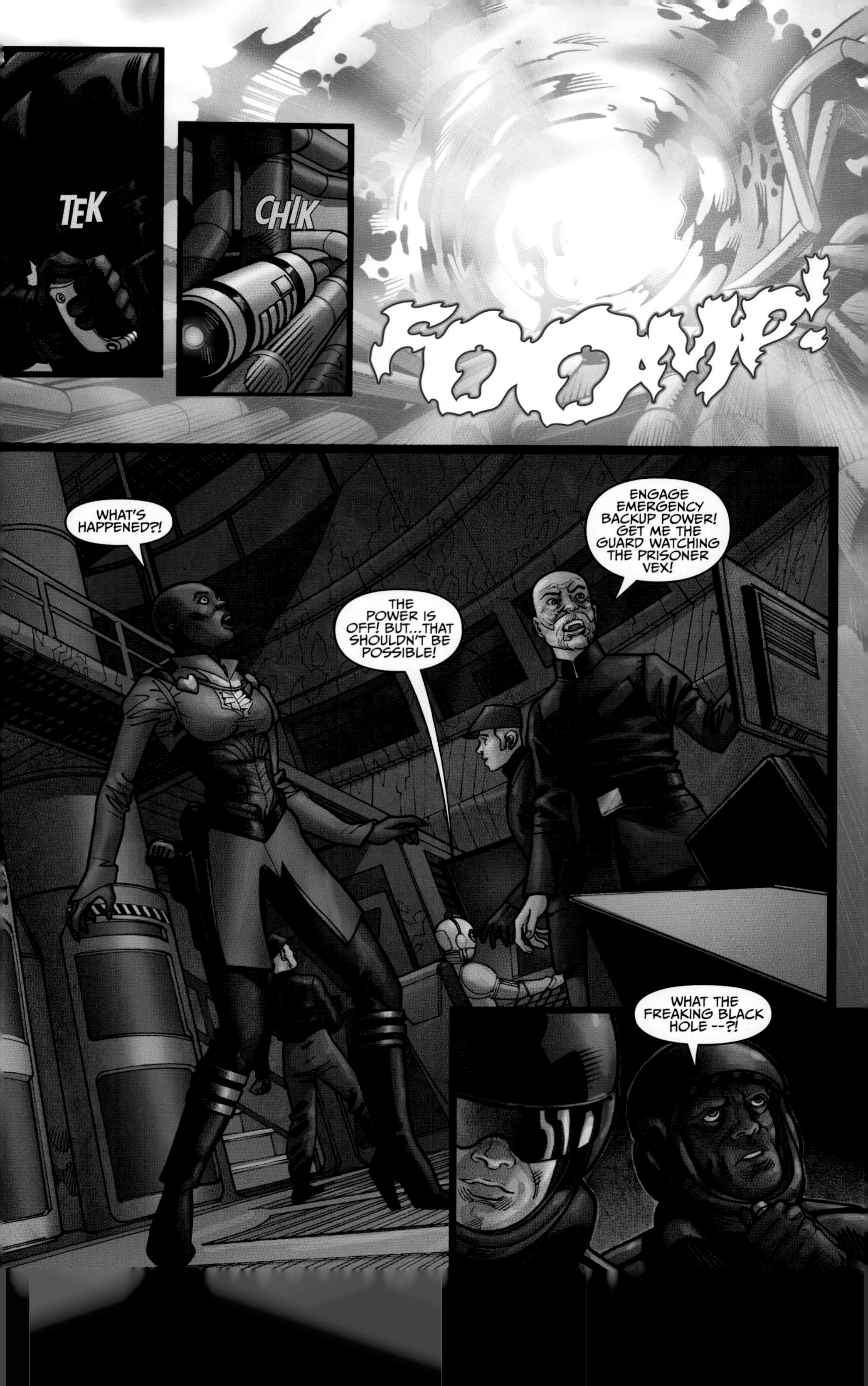
TEK
CHIK
FOOMP!
WHAT'S HAPPENED?!
THE POWER IS OFF! BUT...THAT SHOULDN'T BE POSSIBLE!
ENGAGE EMERGENCY BACKUP POWER! GET ME THE GUARD WATCHING THE PRISONER VEX!
WHAT THE FREAKING BLACK HOLE --?!

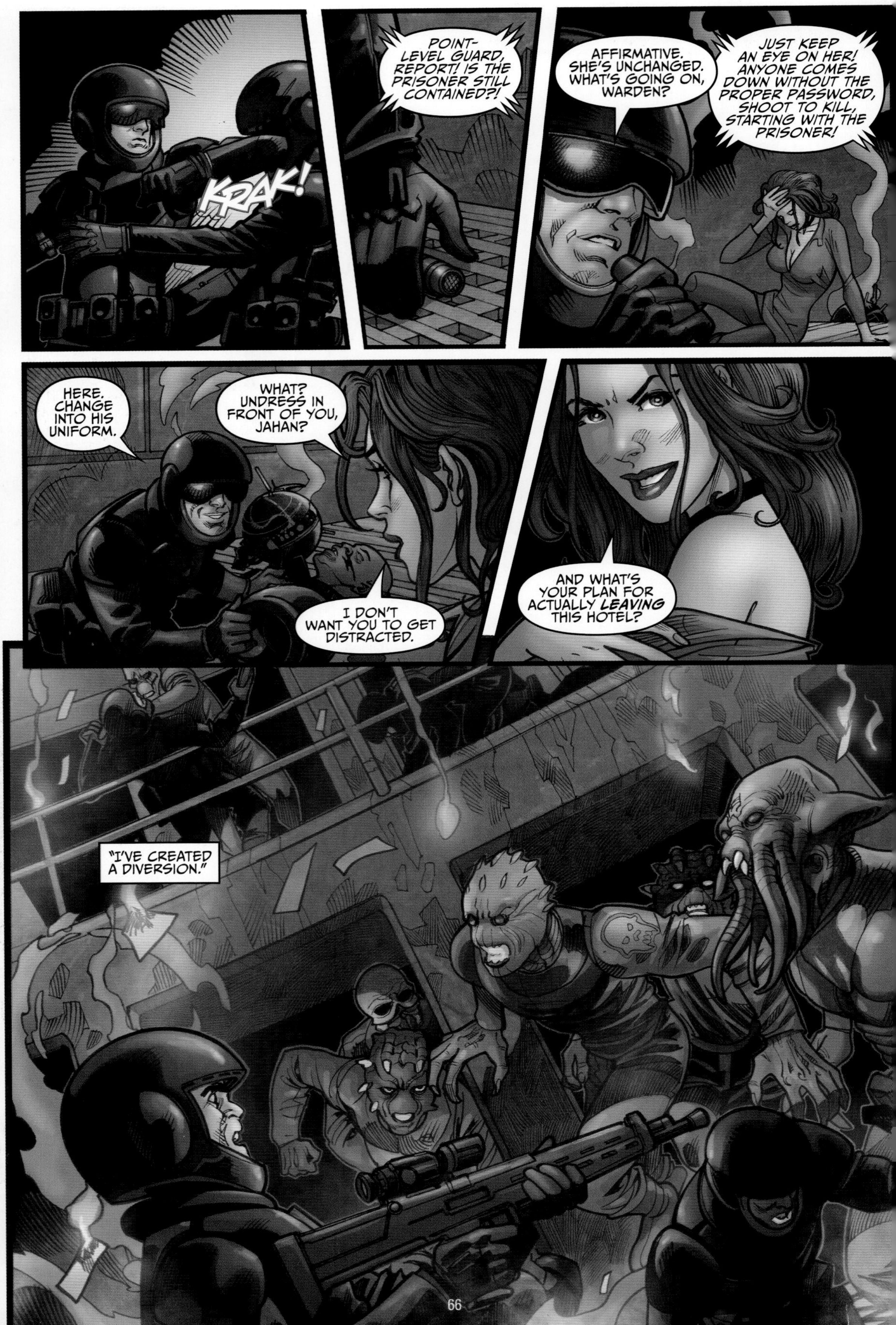
KRAK!
POINT-LEVEL GUARD, REPORT! IS THE PRISONER STILL CONTAINED?!
AFFIRMATIVE. SHE'S UNCHANGED. WHAT'S GOING ON, WARDEN?
JUST KEEP AN EYE ON HER! ANYONE COMES DOWN WITHOUT THE PROPER PASSWORD, SHOOT TO KILL, STARTING WITH THE PRISONER!
HERE. CHANGE INTO HIS UNIFORM.
WHAT? UNDRESS IN FRONT OF YOU, JAHAN?
I DON'T WANT YOU TO GET DISTRACTED.
AND WHAT'S YOUR PLAN FOR ACTUALLY *LEAVING* THIS HOTEL?
"I'VE CREATED A DIVERSION."

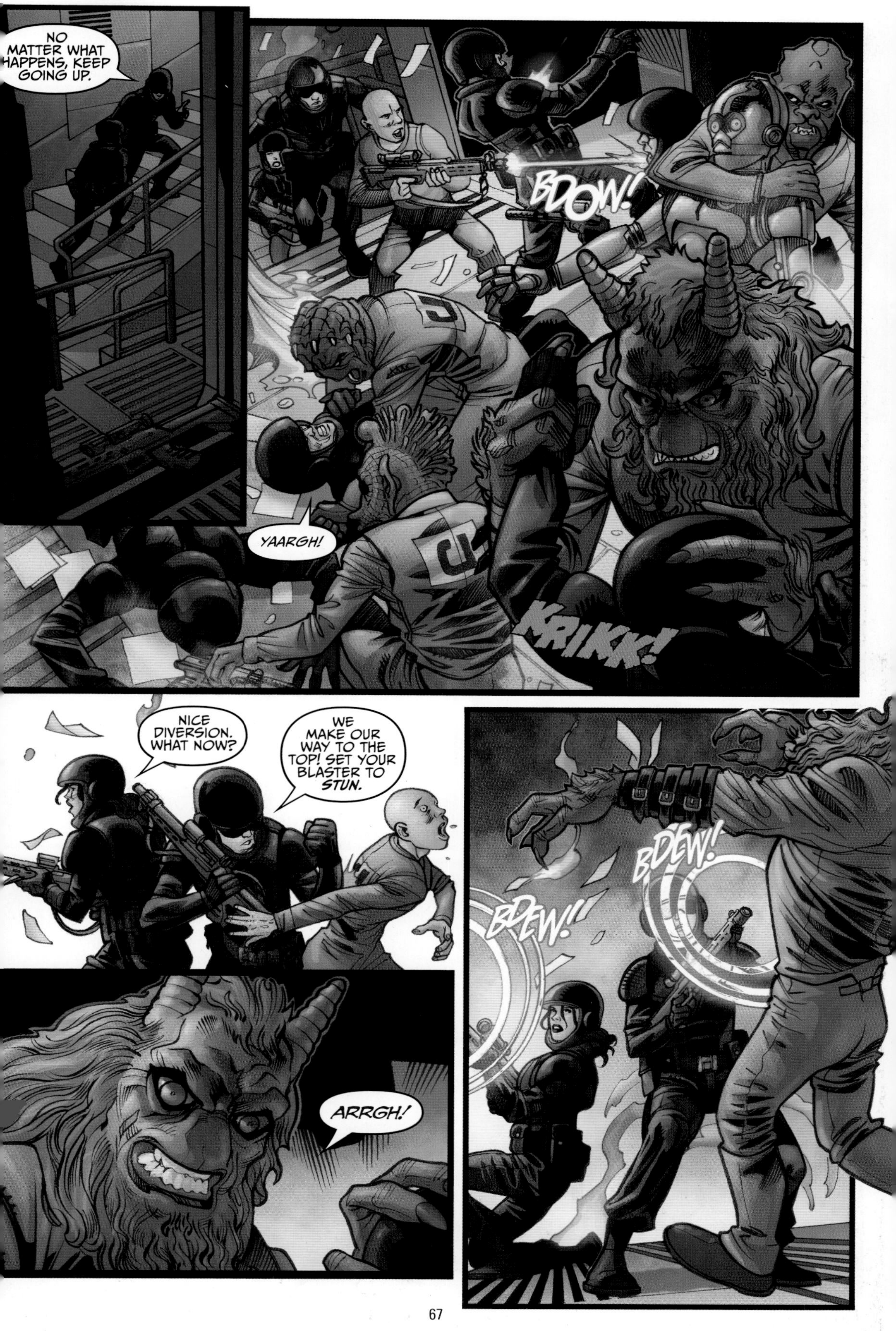
NO MATTER WHAT HAPPENS, KEEP GOING UP.
BDOW!
YAARGH!
KRIKK!
NICE DIVERSION. WHAT NOW?
WE MAKE OUR WAY TO THE TOP! SET YOUR BLASTER TO STUN.
ARRGH!
BDEW!
BDEW!

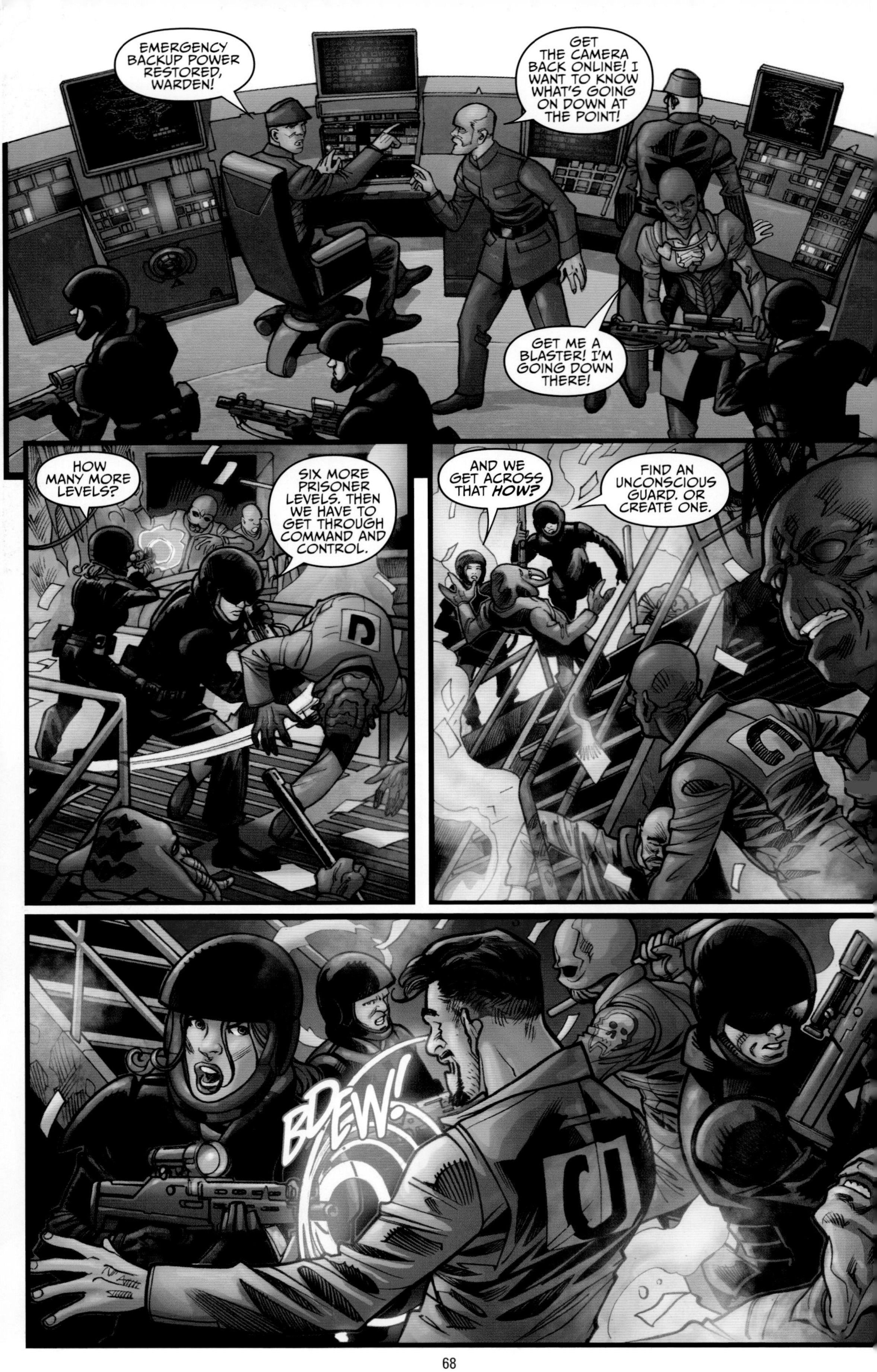
EMERGENCY BACKUP POWER RESTORED, WARDEN!
GET THE CAMERA BACK ONLINE! I WANT TO KNOW WHAT'S GOING ON DOWN AT THE POINT!
GET ME A BLASTER! I'M GOING DOWN THERE!
HOW MANY MORE LEVELS?
SIX MORE PRISONER LEVELS. THEN WE HAVE TO GET THROUGH COMMAND AND CONTROL.
AND WE GET ACROSS THAT HOW?
FIND AN UNCONSCIOUS GUARD. OR CREATE ONE.
BDEW!

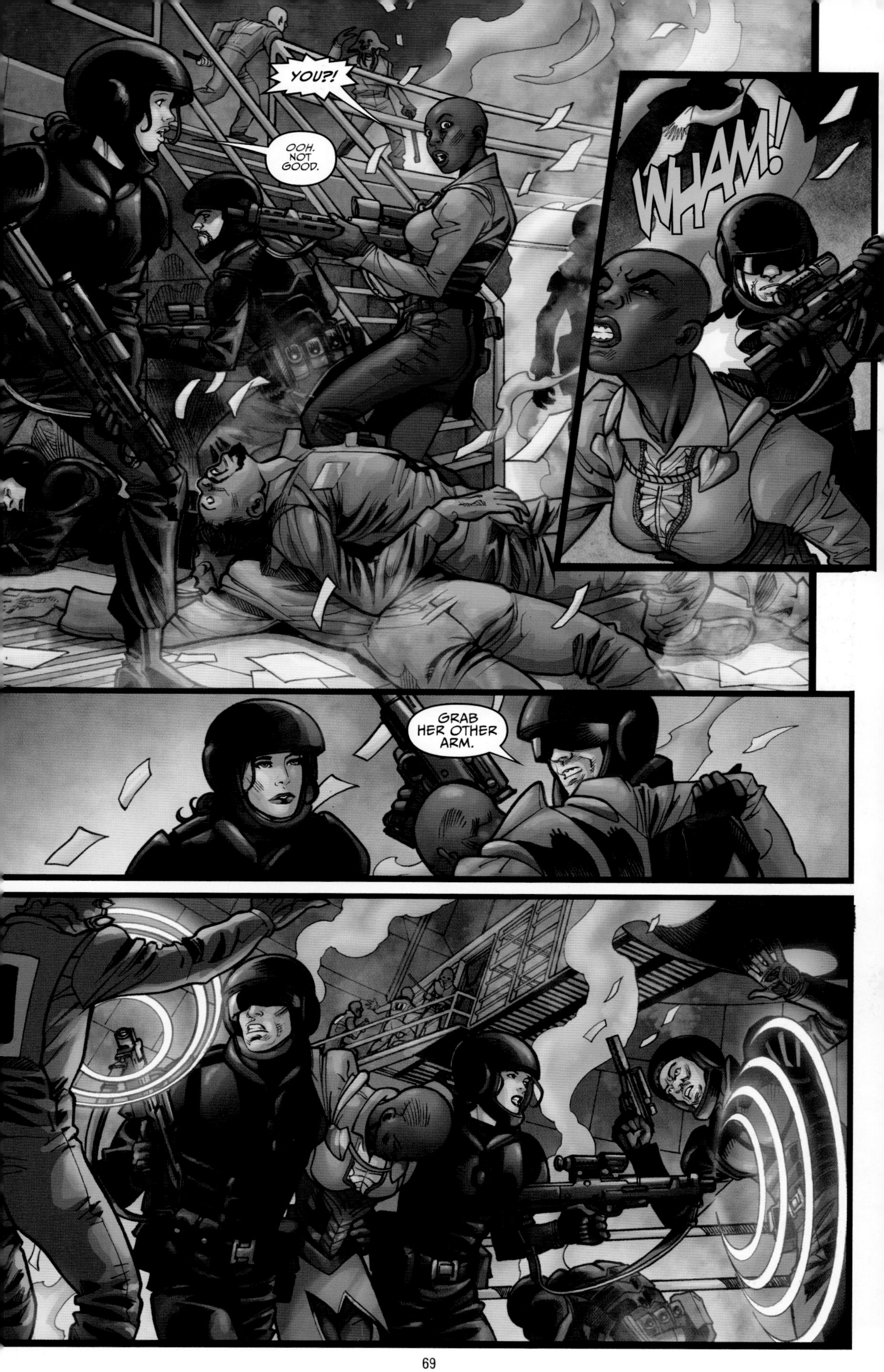
YOU?!
OOH. NOT GOOD.
WHAM!!
GRAB HER OTHER ARM.

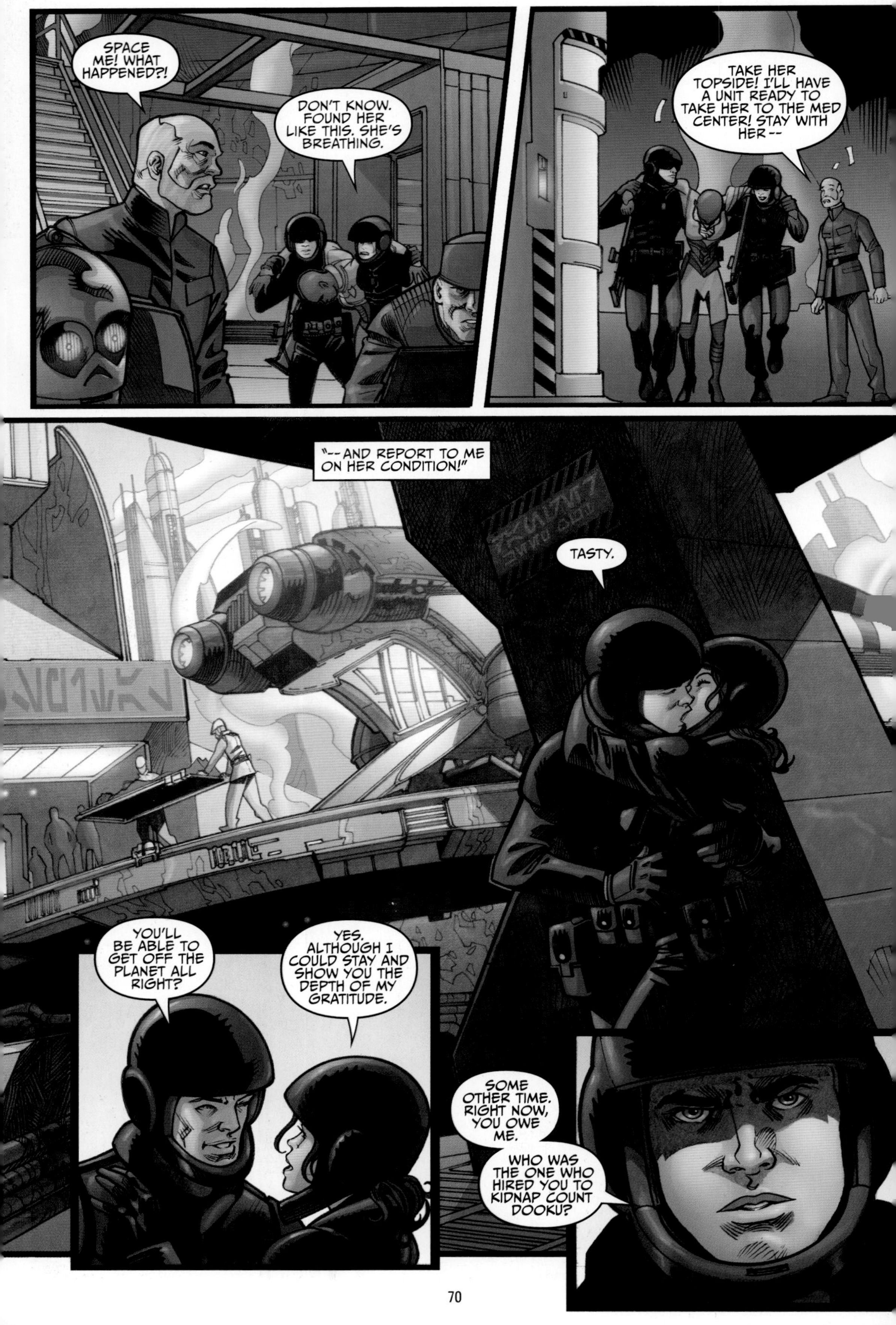
SPACE ME! WHAT HAPPENED?!
DON'T KNOW. FOUND HER LIKE THIS. SHE'S BREATHING.
TAKE HER TOPSIDE! I'LL HAVE A UNIT READY TO TAKE HER TO THE MED CENTER! STAY WITH HER --
"-- AND REPORT TO ME ON HER CONDITION!"
TASTY.
YOU'LL BE ABLE TO GET OFF THE PLANET ALL RIGHT?
YES. ALTHOUGH I COULD STAY AND SHOW YOU THE DEPTH OF MY GRATITUDE.
SOME OTHER TIME. RIGHT NOW, YOU OWE ME.
WHO WAS THE ONE WHO HIRED YOU TO KIDNAP COUNT DOOKU?

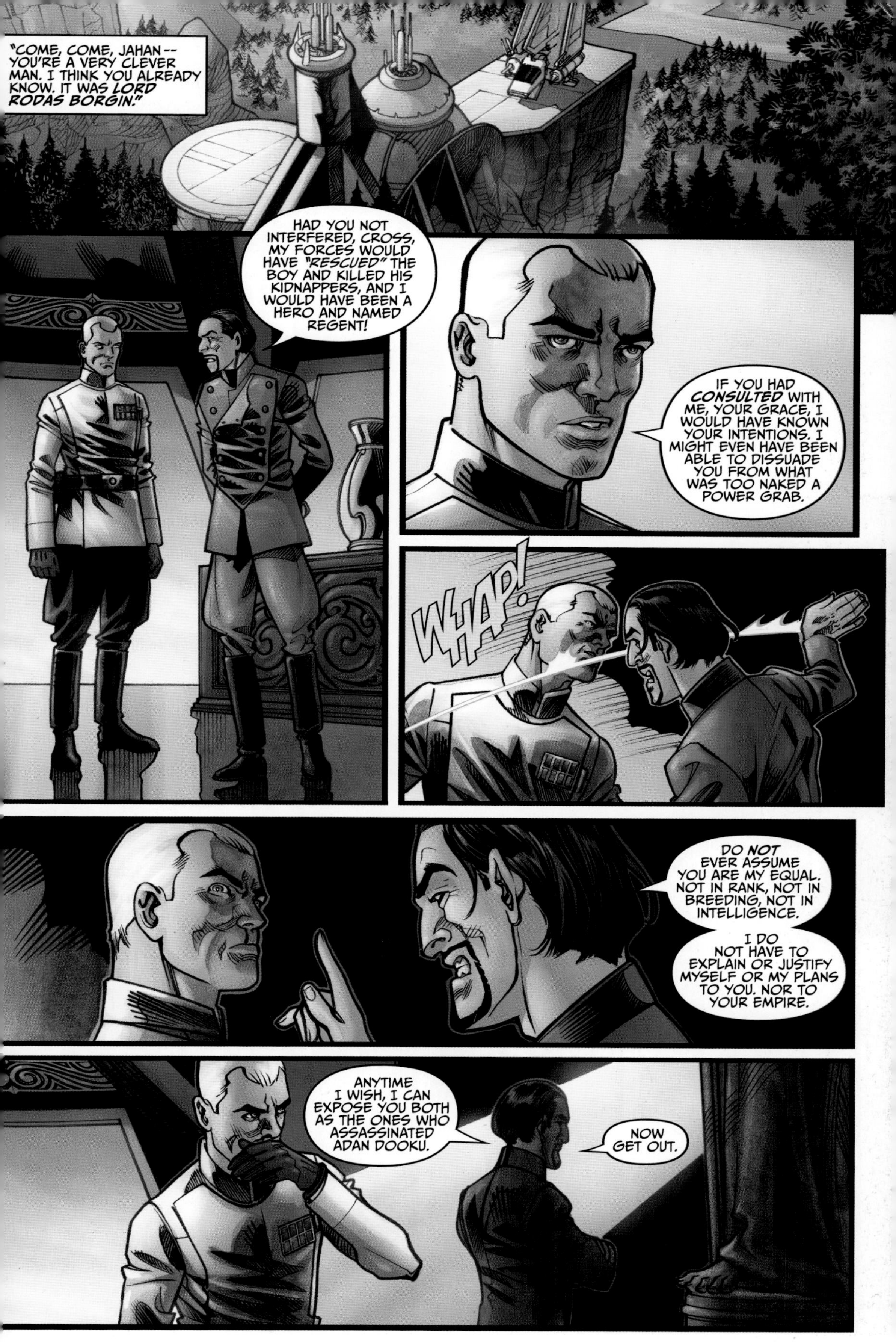
"COME, COME, JAHAN -- YOU'RE A VERY CLEVER MAN. I THINK YOU ALREADY KNOW. IT WAS LORD RODAS BORGIN."
HAD YOU NOT INTERFERED, CROSS, MY FORCES WOULD HAVE "RESCUED" THE BOY AND KILLED HIS KIDNAPPERS, AND I WOULD HAVE BEEN A HERO AND NAMED REGENT!
IF YOU HAD CONSULTED WITH ME, YOUR GRACE, I WOULD HAVE KNOWN YOUR INTENTIONS. I MIGHT EVEN HAVE BEEN ABLE TO DISSUADE YOU FROM WHAT WAS TOO NAKED A POWER GRAB.
WHAP!
DO NOT EVER ASSUME YOU ARE MY EQUAL. NOT IN RANK, NOT IN BREEDING, NOT IN INTELLIGENCE.
I DO NOT HAVE TO EXPLAIN OR JUSTIFY MYSELF OR MY PLANS TO YOU. NOR TO YOUR EMPIRE.
ANYTIME I WISH, I CAN EXPOSE YOU BOTH AS THE ONES WHO ASSASSINATED ADAN DOOKU.
NOW GET OUT.

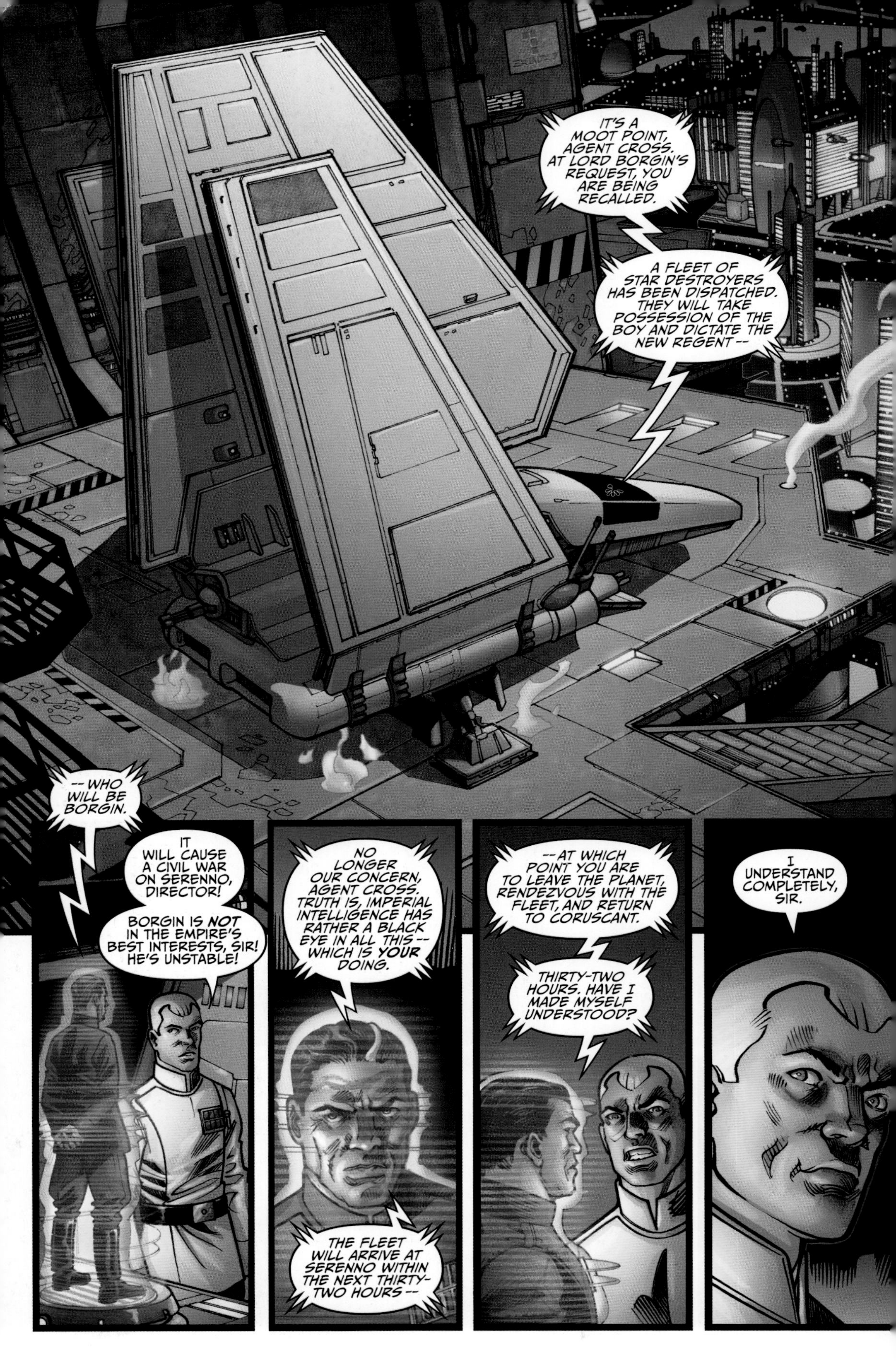
IT'S A MOOT POINT, AGENT CROSS. AT LORD BORGIN'S REQUEST, YOU ARE BEING RECALLED.
A FLEET OF STAR DESTROYERS HAS BEEN DISPATCHED. THEY WILL TAKE POSSESSION OF THE BOY AND DICTATE THE NEW REGENT --
-- WHO WILL BE BORGIN.
IT WILL CAUSE A CIVIL WAR ON SERENNO, DIRECTOR!
BORGIN IS **NOT** IN THE EMPIRE'S BEST INTERESTS, SIR! HE'S UNSTABLE!
NO LONGER OUR CONCERN, AGENT CROSS. TRUTH IS, IMPERIAL INTELLIGENCE HAS RATHER A BLACK EYE IN ALL THIS -- WHICH IS **YOUR** DOING.
THE FLEET WILL ARRIVE AT SERENNO WITHIN THE NEXT THIRTY-TWO HOURS --
-- AT WHICH POINT YOU ARE TO LEAVE THE PLANET, RENDEZVOUS WITH THE FLEET, AND RETURN TO CORUSCANT.
THIRTY-TWO HOURS. HAVE I MADE MYSELF UNDERSTOOD?
I UNDERSTAND COMPLETELY, SIR.

THAT EVENING. A CANTINA, NEAR THE SERENNO SPACEPORT.

THERE YOU ARE, CHIEF TYMON. YOU'VE BEEN HARD TO TRACK DOWN.

YOU'VE HEARD?

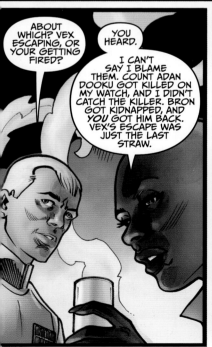

ABOUT WHICH? VEX ESCAPING, OR YOUR GETTING FIRED?

YOU HEARD.

I CAN'T SAY I BLAME THEM. COUNT ADAN DOOKU GOT KILLED ON MY WATCH, AND I DIDN'T CATCH THE KILLER. BRON GOT KIDNAPPED, AND *YOU* GOT HIM BACK. VEX'S ESCAPE WAS JUST THE LAST STRAW.

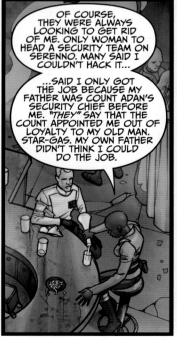

OF COURSE, THEY WERE ALWAYS LOOKING TO GET RID OF ME. ONLY WOMAN TO HEAD A SECURITY TEAM ON SERENNO. MANY SAID I COULDN'T HACK IT...

...SAID I ONLY GOT THE JOB BECAUSE MY FATHER WAS COUNT ADAN'S SECURITY CHIEF BEFORE ME. *"THEY"* SAY THAT THE COUNT APPOINTED ME OUT OF LOYALTY TO MY OLD MAN. STAR-GAS. MY OWN FATHER DIDN'T THINK I COULD DO THE JOB.

COUNT ADAN CHAMPIONED ME. I WORKED TWICE AS HARD TO MAKE GOOD HIS FAITH IN ME. LOOKS LIKE HE WAS WRONG AND *"THEY"* WERE RIGHT.

MY BEST WAS A LONG WAYS FROM GOOD ENOUGH.

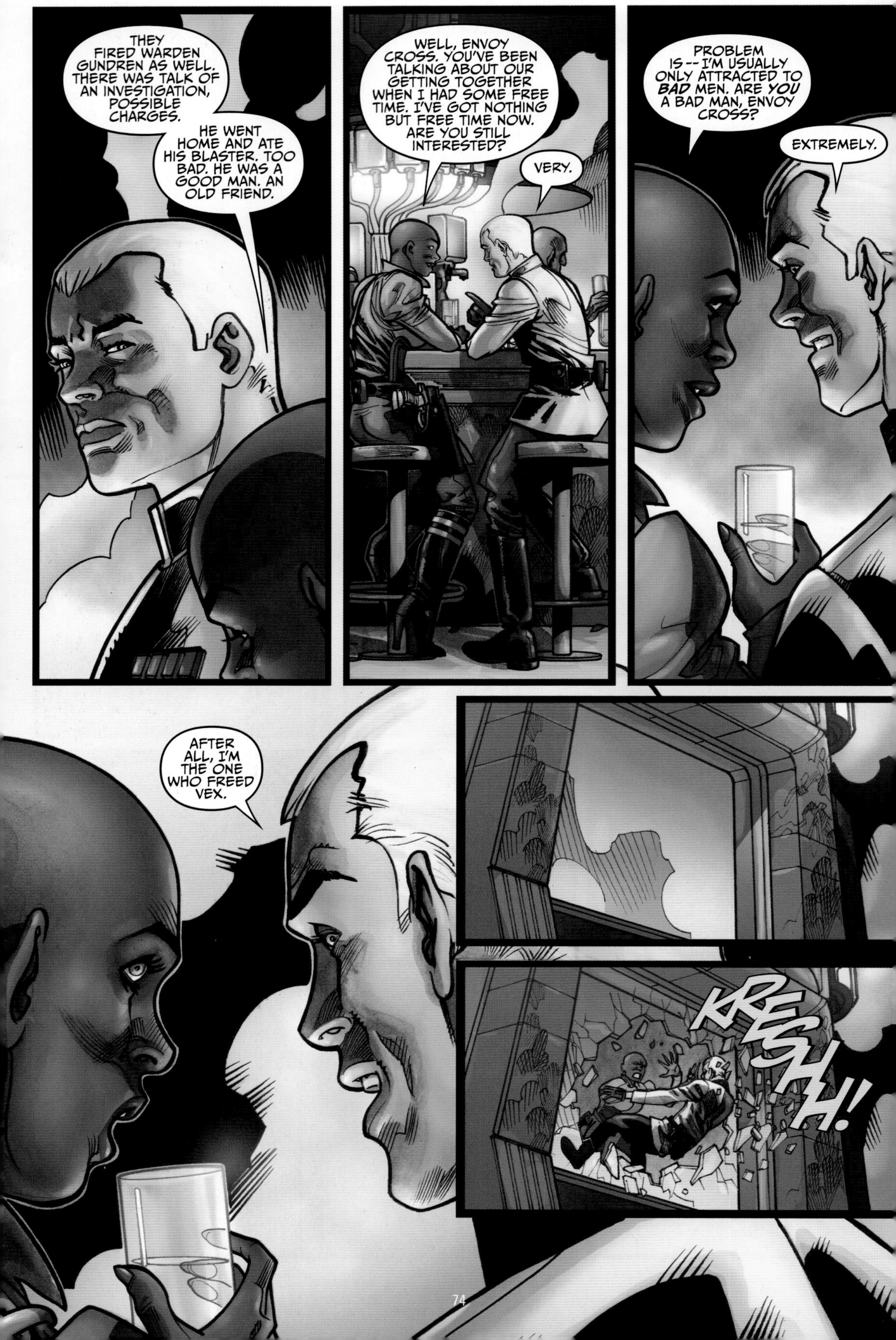
THEY FIRED WARDEN GUNDREN AS WELL. THERE WAS TALK OF AN INVESTIGATION, POSSIBLE CHARGES.
HE WENT HOME AND ATE HIS BLASTER. TOO BAD. HE WAS A GOOD MAN. AN OLD FRIEND.
WELL, ENVOY CROSS. YOU'VE BEEN TALKING ABOUT OUR GETTING TOGETHER WHEN I HAD SOME FREE TIME. I'VE GOT NOTHING BUT FREE TIME NOW. ARE YOU STILL INTERESTED?
VERY.
PROBLEM IS -- I'M USUALLY ONLY ATTRACTED TO *BAD* MEN. ARE *YOU* A BAD MAN, ENVOY CROSS?
EXTREMELY.
AFTER ALL, I'M THE ONE WHO FREED VEX.
KRESHH!

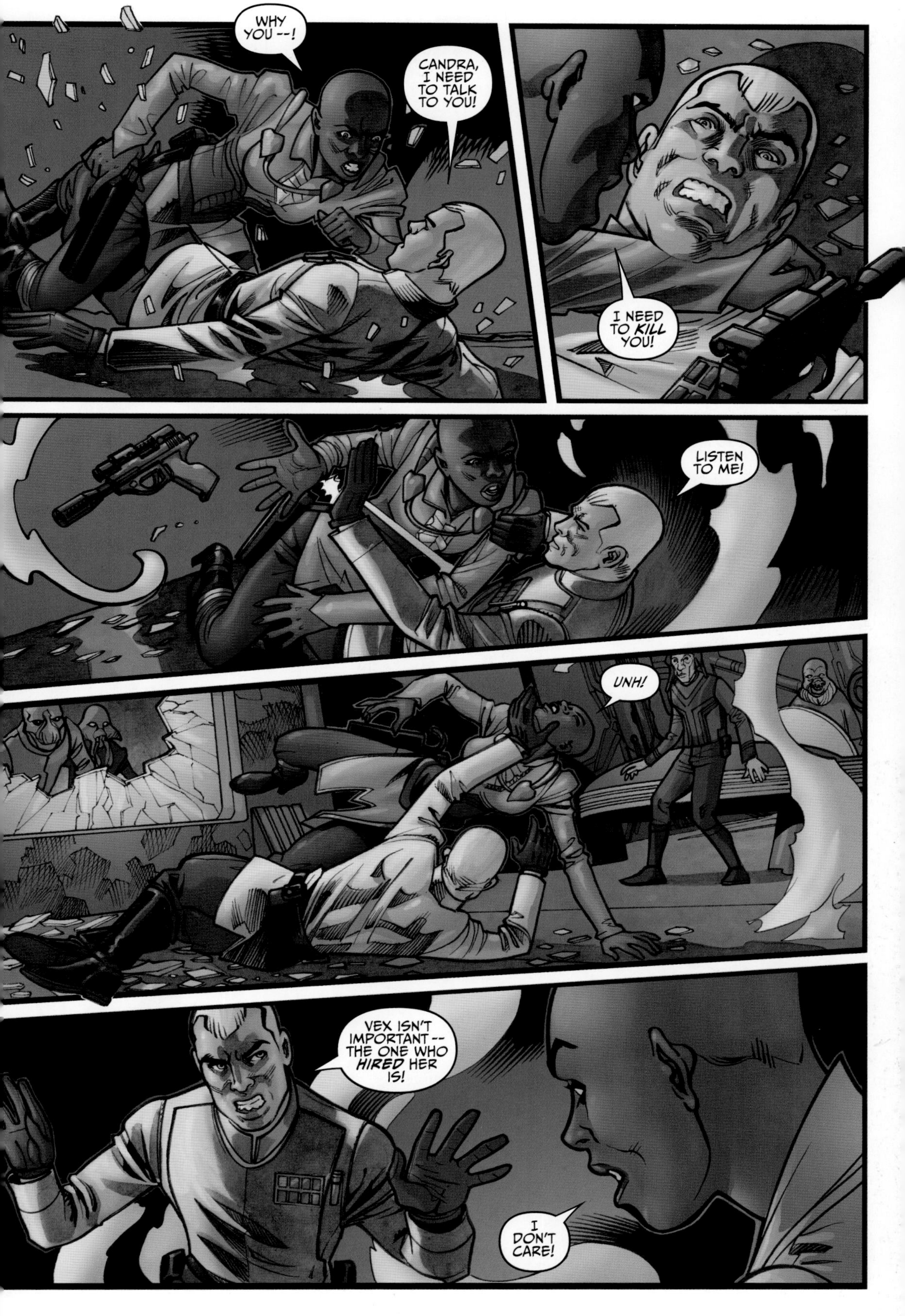
WHY YOU --!
CANDRA, I NEED TO TALK TO YOU!
I NEED TO KILL YOU!
LISTEN TO ME!
UNH!
VEX ISN'T IMPORTANT -- THE ONE WHO HIRED HER IS!
I DON'T CARE!

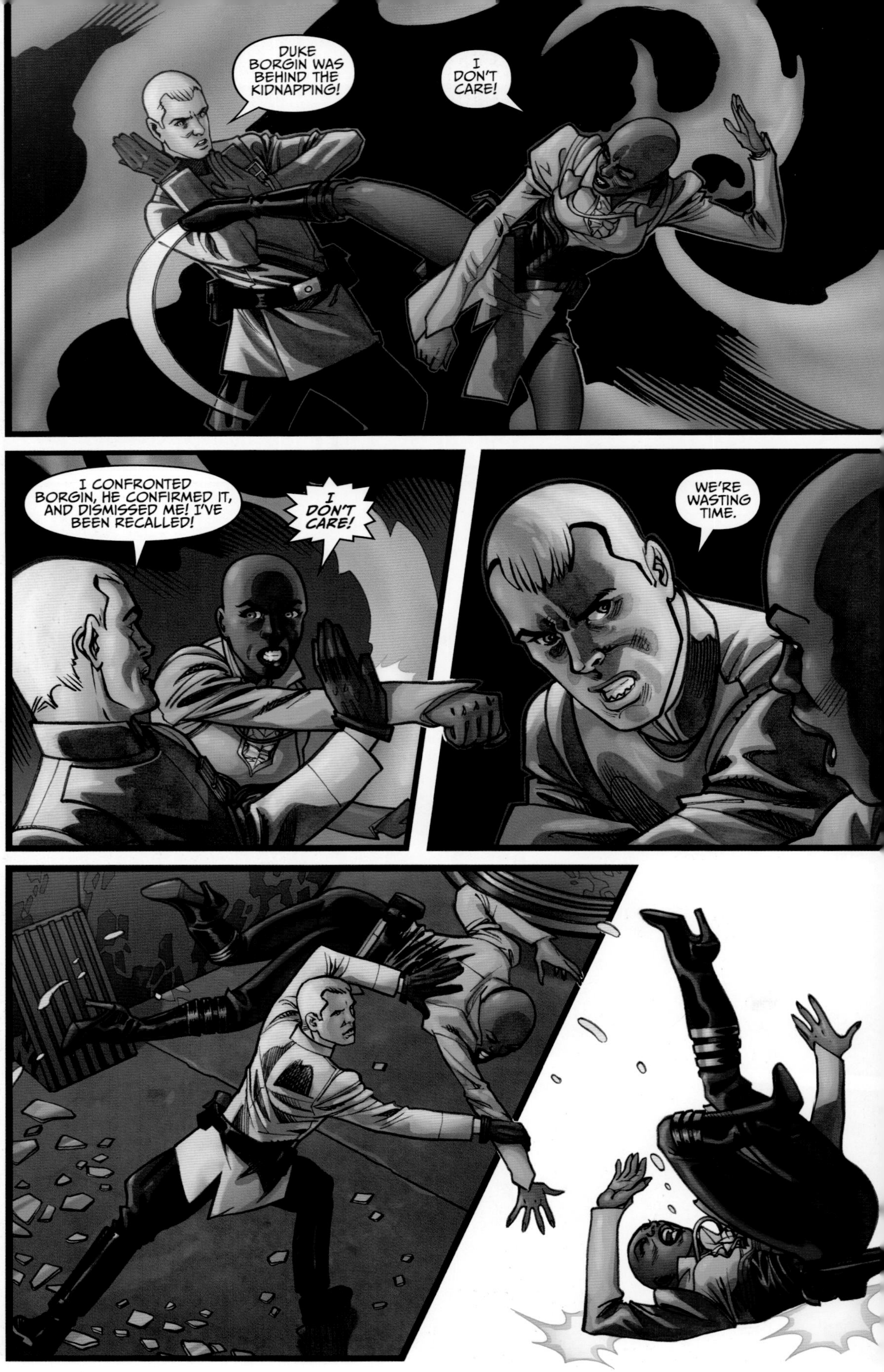
DUKE BORGIN WAS BEHIND THE KIDNAPPING!
I DON'T CARE!
I CONFRONTED BORGIN, HE CONFIRMED IT, AND DISMISSED ME! I'VE BEEN RECALLED!
I DON'T CARE!
WE'RE WASTING TIME.

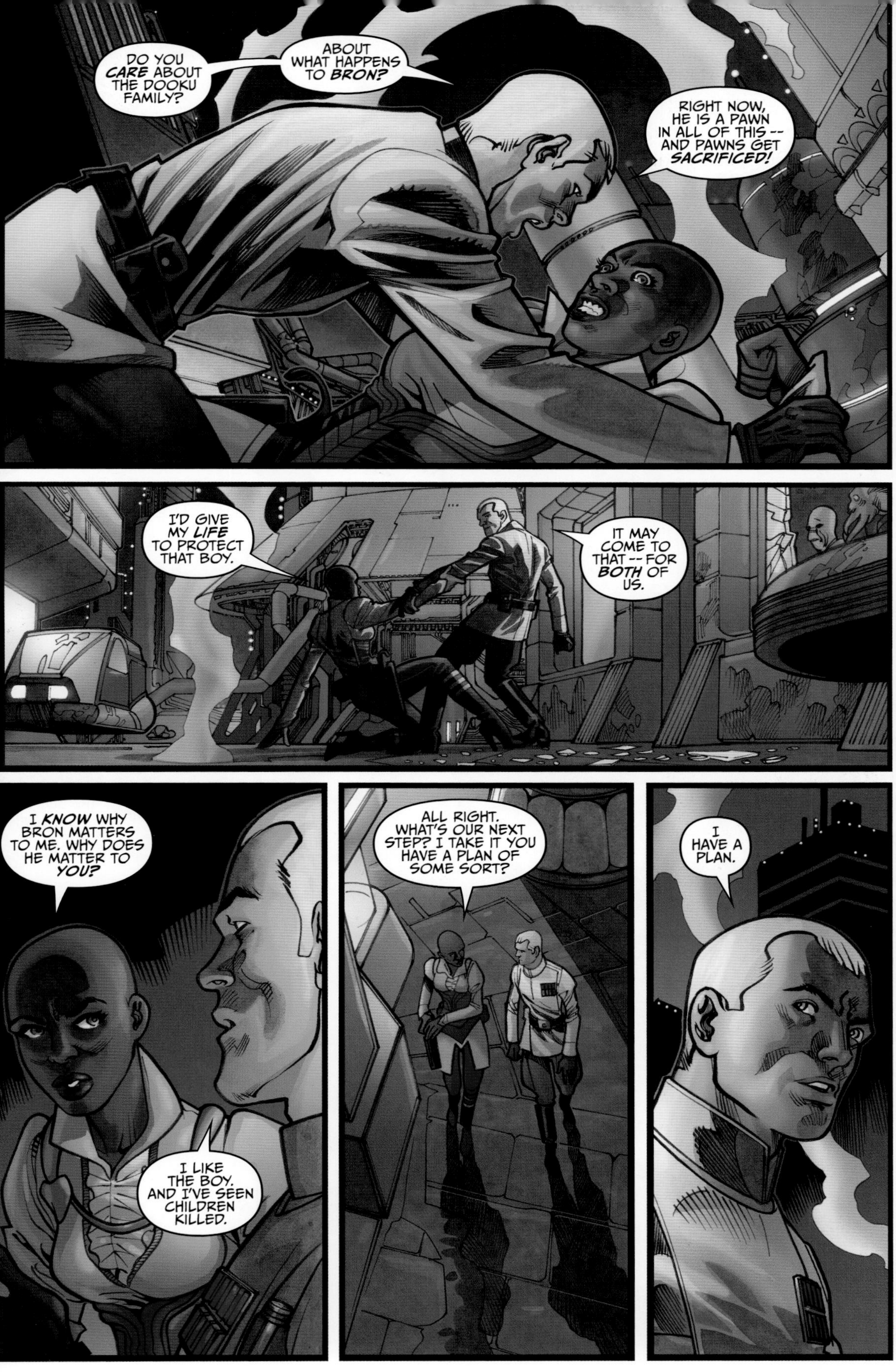
DO YOU CARE ABOUT THE DOOKU FAMILY?
ABOUT WHAT HAPPENS TO BRON?
RIGHT NOW, HE IS A PAWN IN ALL OF THIS -- AND PAWNS GET SACRIFICED!
I'D GIVE MY LIFE TO PROTECT THAT BOY.
IT MAY COME TO THAT -- FOR BOTH OF US.
I KNOW WHY BRON MATTERS TO ME. WHY DOES HE MATTER TO YOU?
I LIKE THE BOY. AND I'VE SEEN CHILDREN KILLED.
ALL RIGHT. WHAT'S OUR NEXT STEP? I TAKE IT YOU HAVE A PLAN OF SOME SORT?
I HAVE A PLAN.

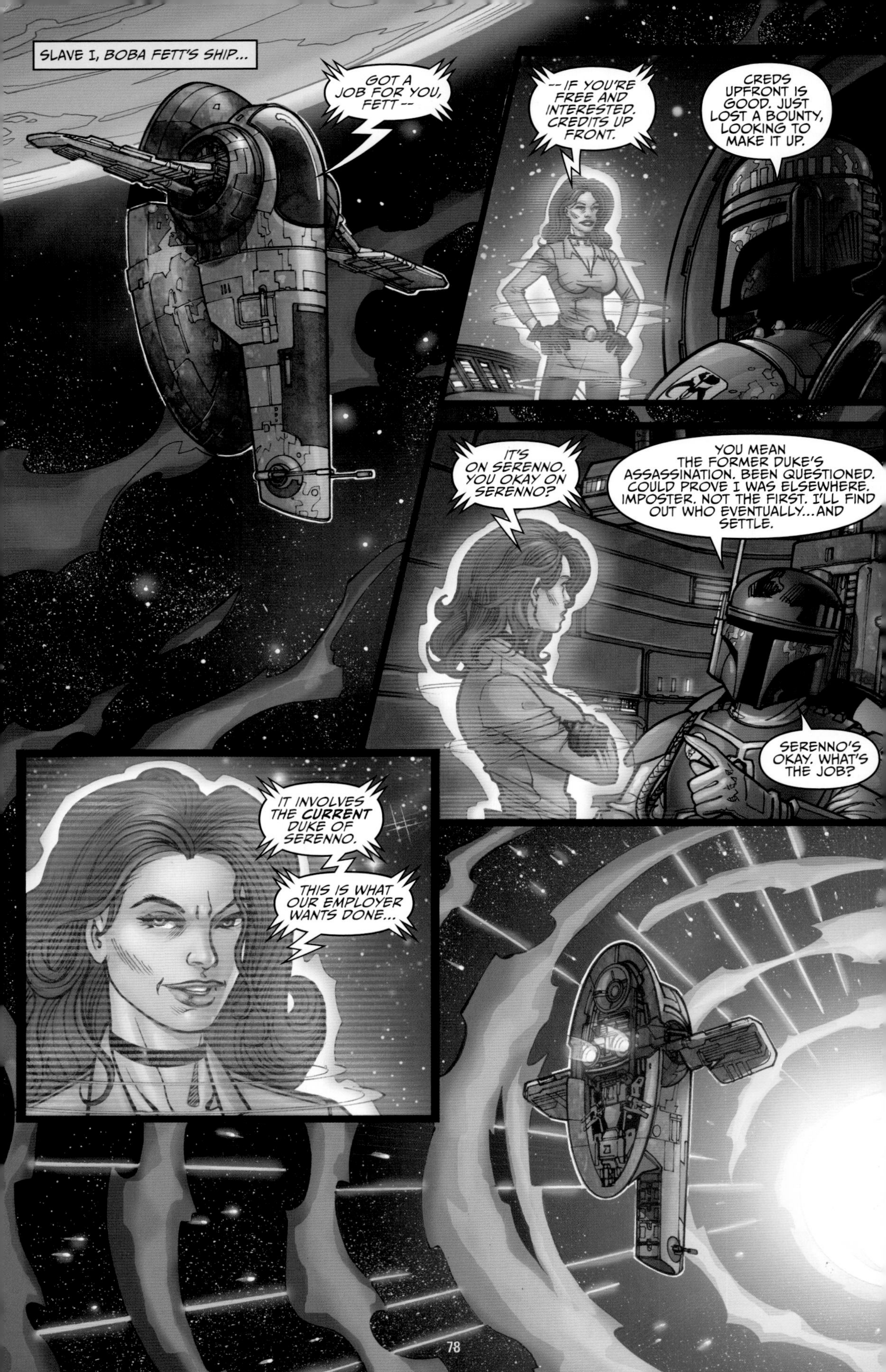
SLAVE I, BOBA FETT'S SHIP...
GOT A JOB FOR YOU, FETT --
-- IF YOU'RE FREE AND INTERESTED. CREDITS UP FRONT.
CREDS UPFRONT IS GOOD. JUST LOST A BOUNTY, LOOKING TO MAKE IT UP.
IT'S ON SERENNO. YOU OKAY ON SERENNO?
YOU MEAN THE FORMER DUKE'S ASSASSINATION. BEEN QUESTIONED. COULD PROVE I WAS ELSEWHERE. IMPOSTER. NOT THE FIRST. I'LL FIND OUT WHO EVENTUALLY...AND SETTLE.
SERENNO'S OKAY. WHAT'S THE JOB?
IT INVOLVES THE **CURRENT** DUKE OF SERENNO.
THIS IS WHAT OUR EMPLOYER WANTS DONE...

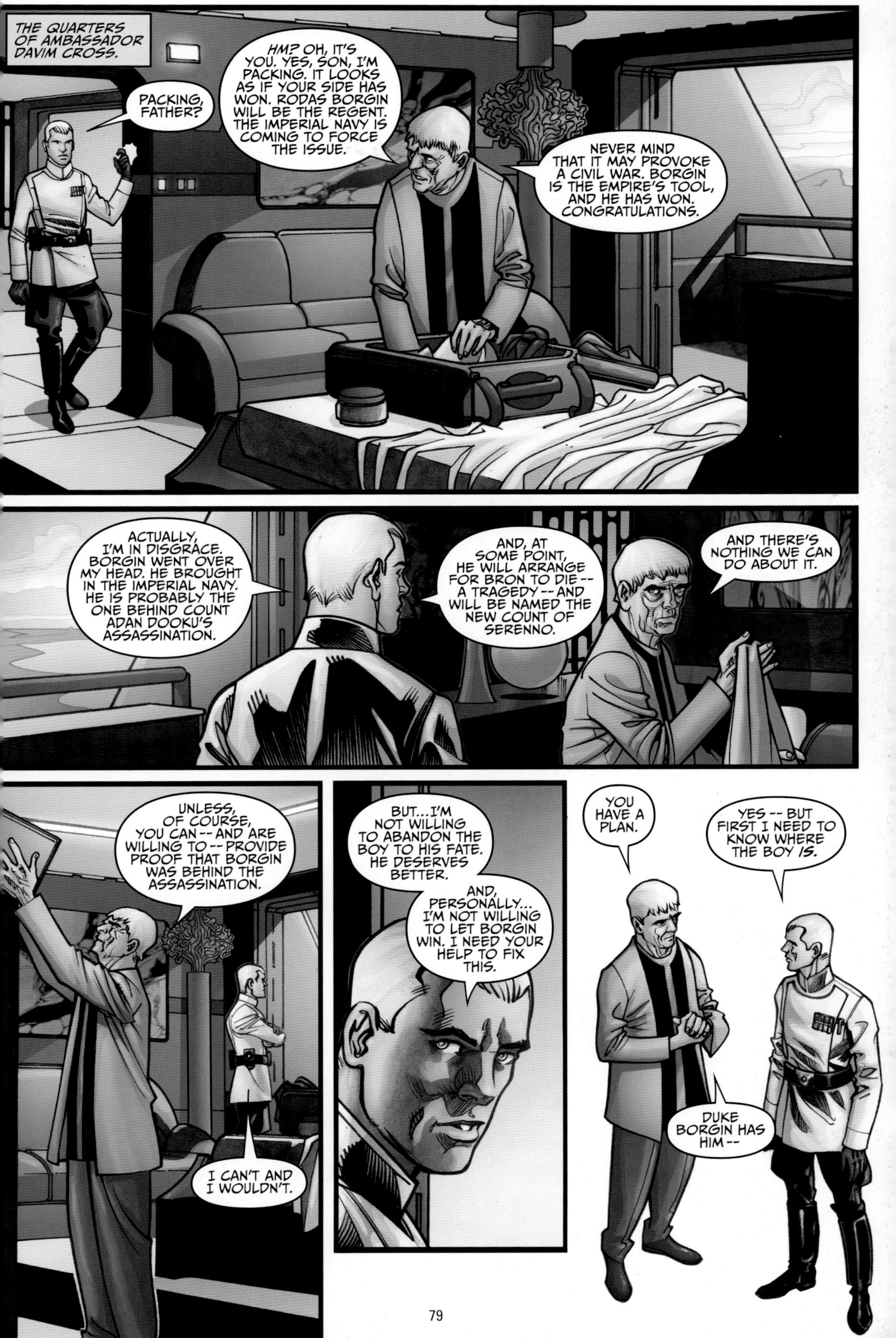
THE QUARTERS OF AMBASSADOR DAVIM CROSS.
PACKING, FATHER?
HM? OH, IT'S YOU. YES, SON, I'M PACKING. IT LOOKS AS IF YOUR SIDE HAS WON. RODAS BORGIN WILL BE THE REGENT. THE IMPERIAL NAVY IS COMING TO FORCE THE ISSUE.
NEVER MIND THAT IT MAY PROVOKE A CIVIL WAR. BORGIN IS THE EMPIRE'S TOOL, AND HE HAS WON. CONGRATULATIONS.
ACTUALLY, I'M IN DISGRACE. BORGIN WENT OVER MY HEAD. HE BROUGHT IN THE IMPERIAL NAVY. HE IS PROBABLY THE ONE BEHIND COUNT ADAN DOOKU'S ASSASSINATION.
AND, AT SOME POINT, HE WILL ARRANGE FOR BRON TO DIE -- A TRAGEDY -- AND WILL BE NAMED THE NEW COUNT OF SERENNO.
AND THERE'S NOTHING WE CAN DO ABOUT IT.
UNLESS, OF COURSE, YOU CAN -- AND ARE WILLING TO -- PROVIDE PROOF THAT BORGIN WAS BEHIND THE ASSASSINATION.
I CAN'T AND I WOULDN'T.
BUT... I'M NOT WILLING TO ABANDON THE BOY TO HIS FATE. HE DESERVES BETTER.
AND, PERSONALLY... I'M NOT WILLING TO LET BORGIN WIN. I NEED YOUR HELP TO FIX THIS.
YOU HAVE A PLAN.
YES -- BUT FIRST I NEED TO KNOW WHERE THE BOY *IS.*
DUKE BORGIN HAS HIM --

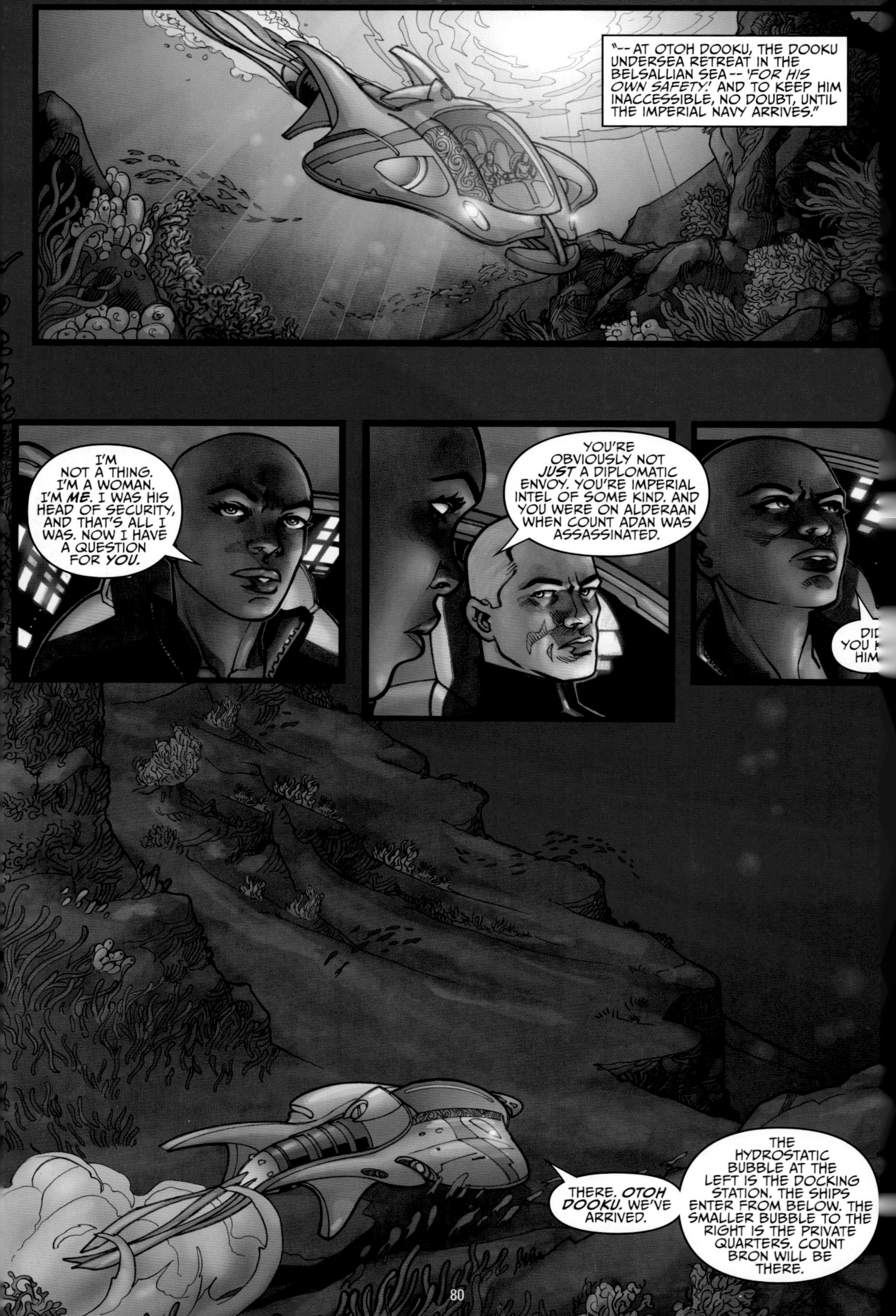
"-- AT OTOH DOOKU, THE DOOKU UNDERSEA RETREAT IN THE BELSALLIAN SEA -- 'FOR HIS OWN SAFETY!' AND TO KEEP HIM INACCESSIBLE, NO DOUBT, UNTIL THE IMPERIAL NAVY ARRIVES."
I'M NOT A THING. I'M A WOMAN. I'M ME. I WAS HIS HEAD OF SECURITY, AND THAT'S ALL I WAS. NOW I HAVE A QUESTION FOR YOU.
YOU'RE OBVIOUSLY NOT JUST A DIPLOMATIC ENVOY. YOU'RE IMPERIAL INTEL OF SOME KIND. AND YOU WERE ON ALDERAAN WHEN COUNT ADAN WAS ASSASSINATED.
THERE. OTOH DOOKU. WE'VE ARRIVED.
THE HYDROSTATIC BUBBLE AT THE LEFT IS THE DOCKING STATION. THE SHIPS ENTER FROM BELOW. THE SMALLER BUBBLE TO THE RIGHT IS THE PRIVATE QUARTERS. COUNT BRON WILL BE THERE.

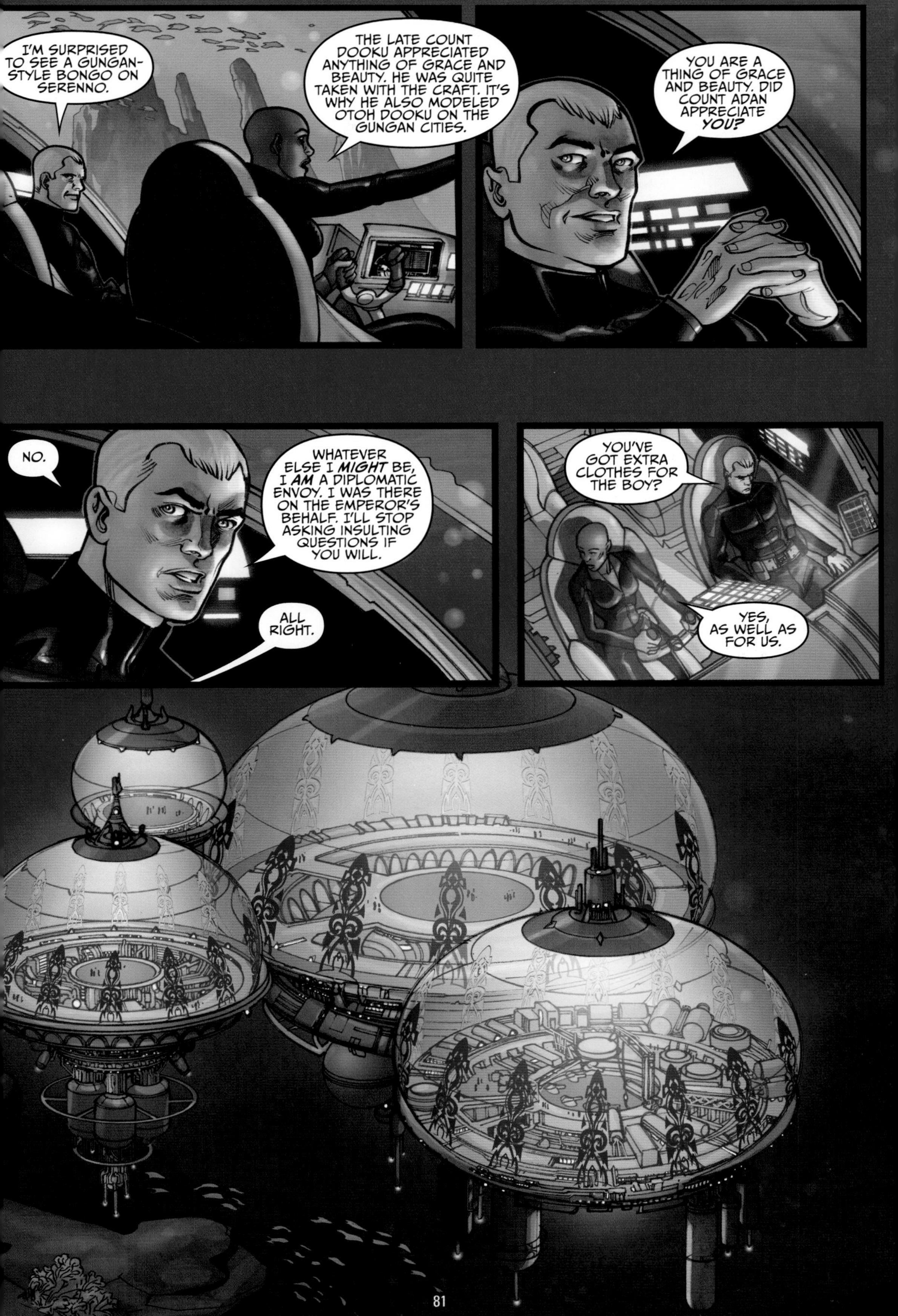
I'M SURPRISED TO SEE A GUNGAN-STYLE BONGO ON SERENNO.
THE LATE COUNT DOOKU APPRECIATED ANYTHING OF GRACE AND BEAUTY. HE WAS QUITE TAKEN WITH THE CRAFT. IT'S WHY HE ALSO MODELED OTOH DOOKU ON THE GUNGAN CITIES.
YOU ARE A THING OF GRACE AND BEAUTY. DID COUNT ADAN APPRECIATE *YOU?*
NO.
WHATEVER ELSE I *MIGHT* BE, I *AM* A DIPLOMATIC ENVOY. I WAS THERE ON THE EMPEROR'S BEHALF. I'LL STOP ASKING INSULTING QUESTIONS IF YOU WILL.
ALL RIGHT.
YOU'VE GOT EXTRA CLOTHES FOR THE BOY?
YES, AS WELL AS FOR US.

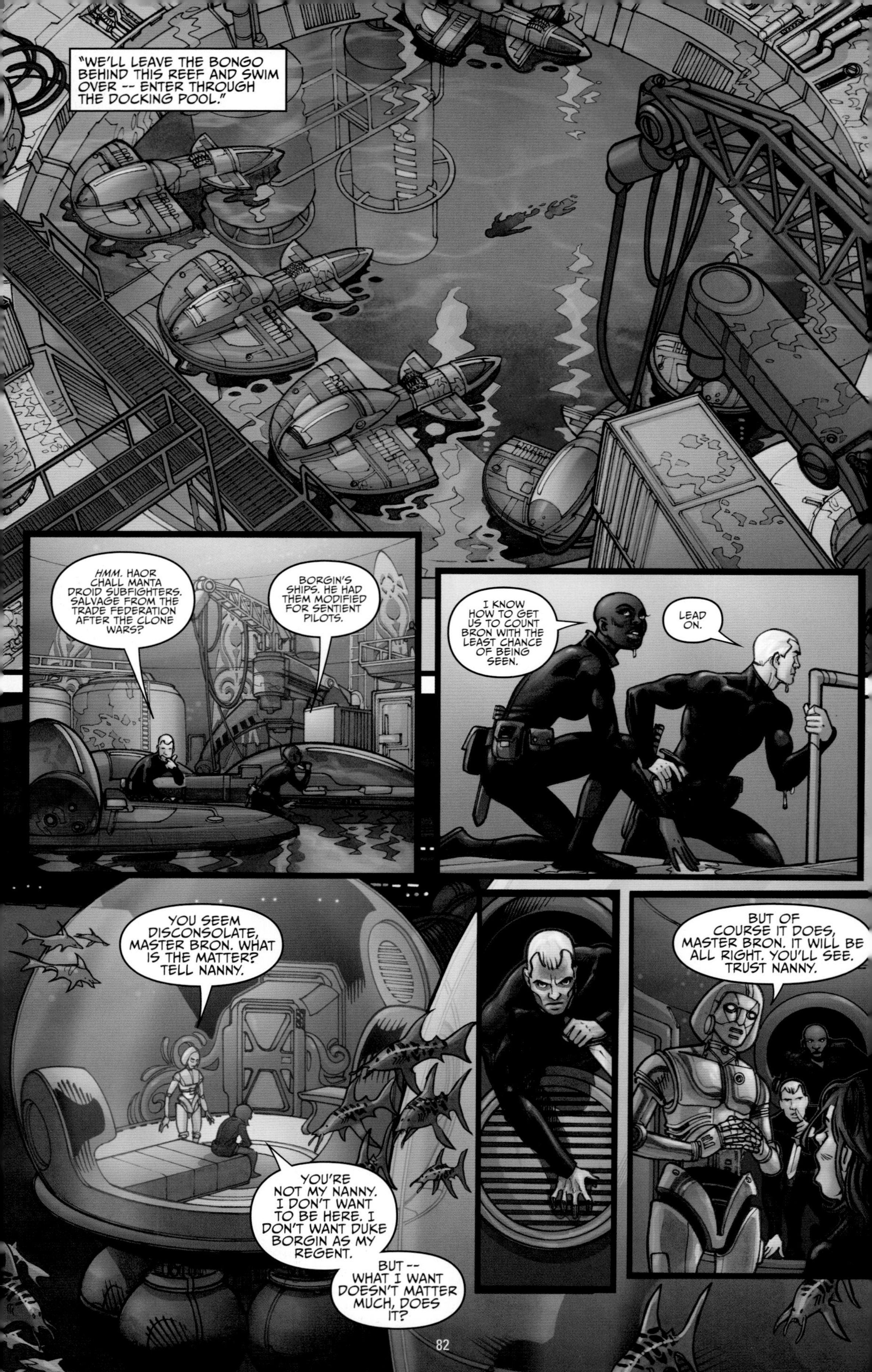
"WE'LL LEAVE THE BONGO BEHIND THIS REEF AND SWIM OVER -- ENTER THROUGH THE DOCKING POOL."
HMM. HAOR CHALL MANTA DROID SUBFIGHTERS. SALVAGE FROM THE TRADE FEDERATION AFTER THE CLONE WARS?
BORGIN'S SHIPS. HE HAD THEM MODIFIED FOR SENTIENT PILOTS.
I KNOW HOW TO GET US TO COUNT BRON WITH THE LEAST CHANCE OF BEING SEEN.
LEAD ON.
YOU SEEM DISCONSOLATE, MASTER BRON. WHAT IS THE MATTER? TELL NANNY.
YOU'RE NOT MY NANNY. I DON'T WANT TO BE HERE. I DON'T WANT DUKE BORGIN AS MY REGENT.
BUT -- WHAT I WANT DOESN'T MATTER MUCH, DOES IT?
BUT OF COURSE IT DOES, MASTER BRON. IT WILL BE ALL RIGHT. YOU'LL SEE. TRUST NANNY.

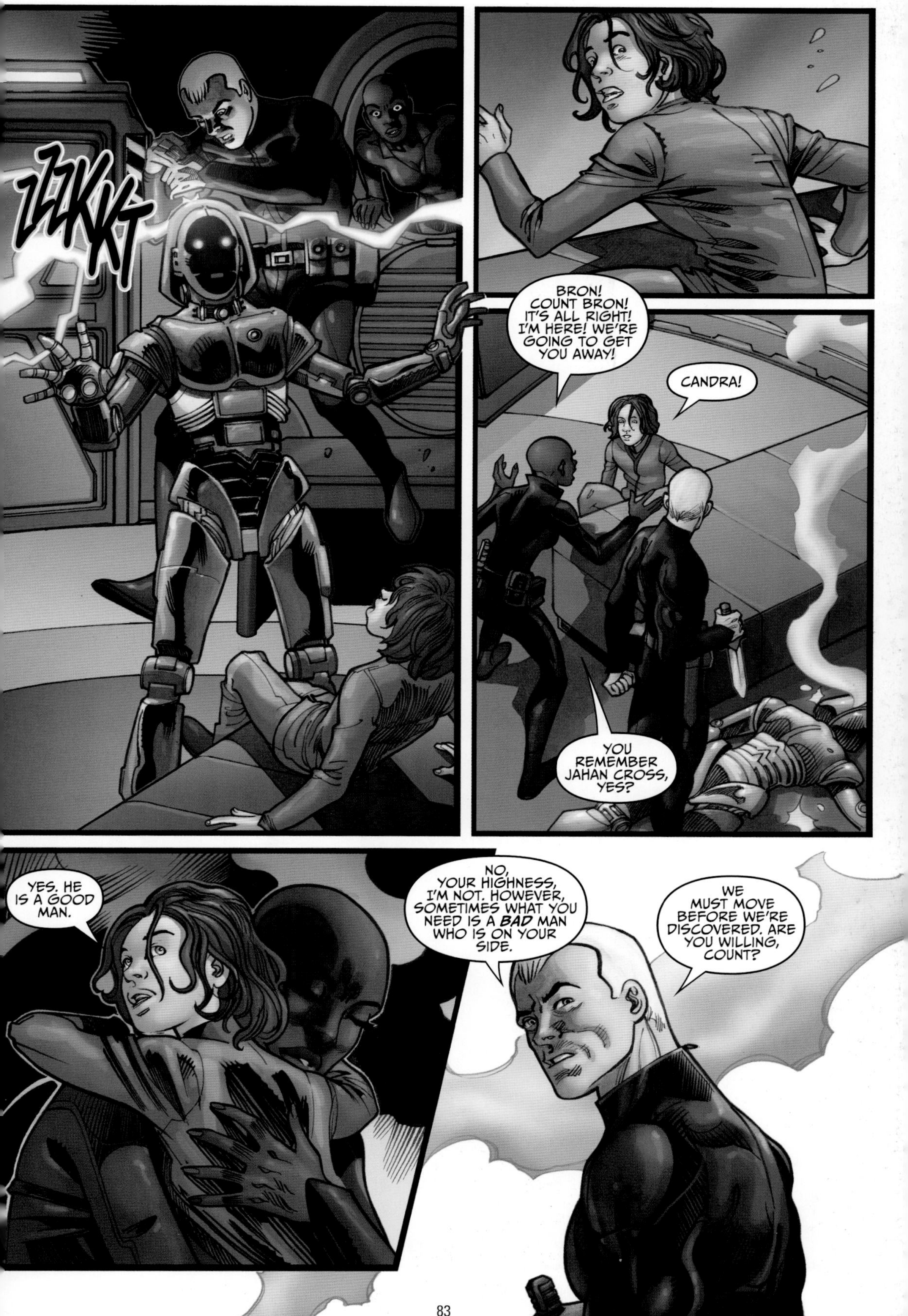
ZZZKKT
BRON! COUNT BRON! IT'S ALL RIGHT! I'M HERE! WE'RE GOING TO GET YOU AWAY!
CANDRA!
YOU REMEMBER JAHAN CROSS, YES?
YES. HE IS A GOOD MAN.
NO, YOUR HIGHNESS, I'M NOT. HOWEVER, SOMETIMES WHAT YOU NEED IS A *BAD* MAN WHO IS ON YOUR SIDE.
WE MUST MOVE BEFORE WE'RE DISCOVERED. ARE YOU WILLING, COUNT?

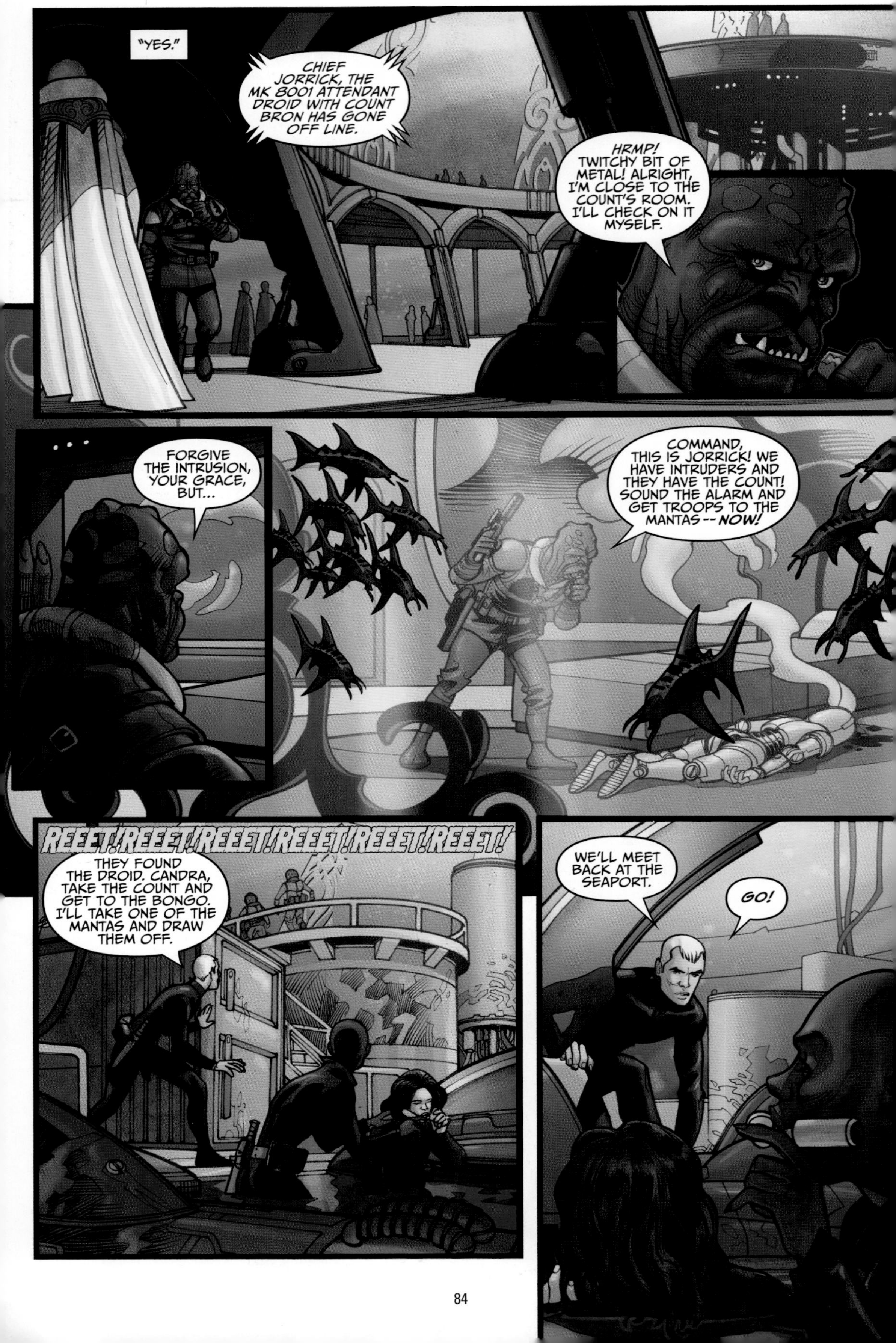
"YES."
CHIEF JORRICK, THE MK 8001 ATTENDANT DROID WITH COUNT BRON HAS GONE OFF LINE.
HRMP! TWITCHY BIT OF METAL! ALRIGHT, I'M CLOSE TO THE COUNT'S ROOM. I'LL CHECK ON IT MYSELF.
FORGIVE THE INTRUSION, YOUR GRACE, BUT...
COMMAND, THIS IS JORRICK! WE HAVE INTRUDERS AND THEY HAVE THE COUNT! SOUND THE ALARM AND GET TROOPS TO THE MANTAS--NOW!
REEET! REEET! REEET! REEET! REEET! REEET!
THEY FOUND THE DROID. CANDRA, TAKE THE COUNT AND GET TO THE BONGO. I'LL TAKE ONE OF THE MANTAS AND DRAW THEM OFF.
WE'LL MEET BACK AT THE SEAPORT.
GO!

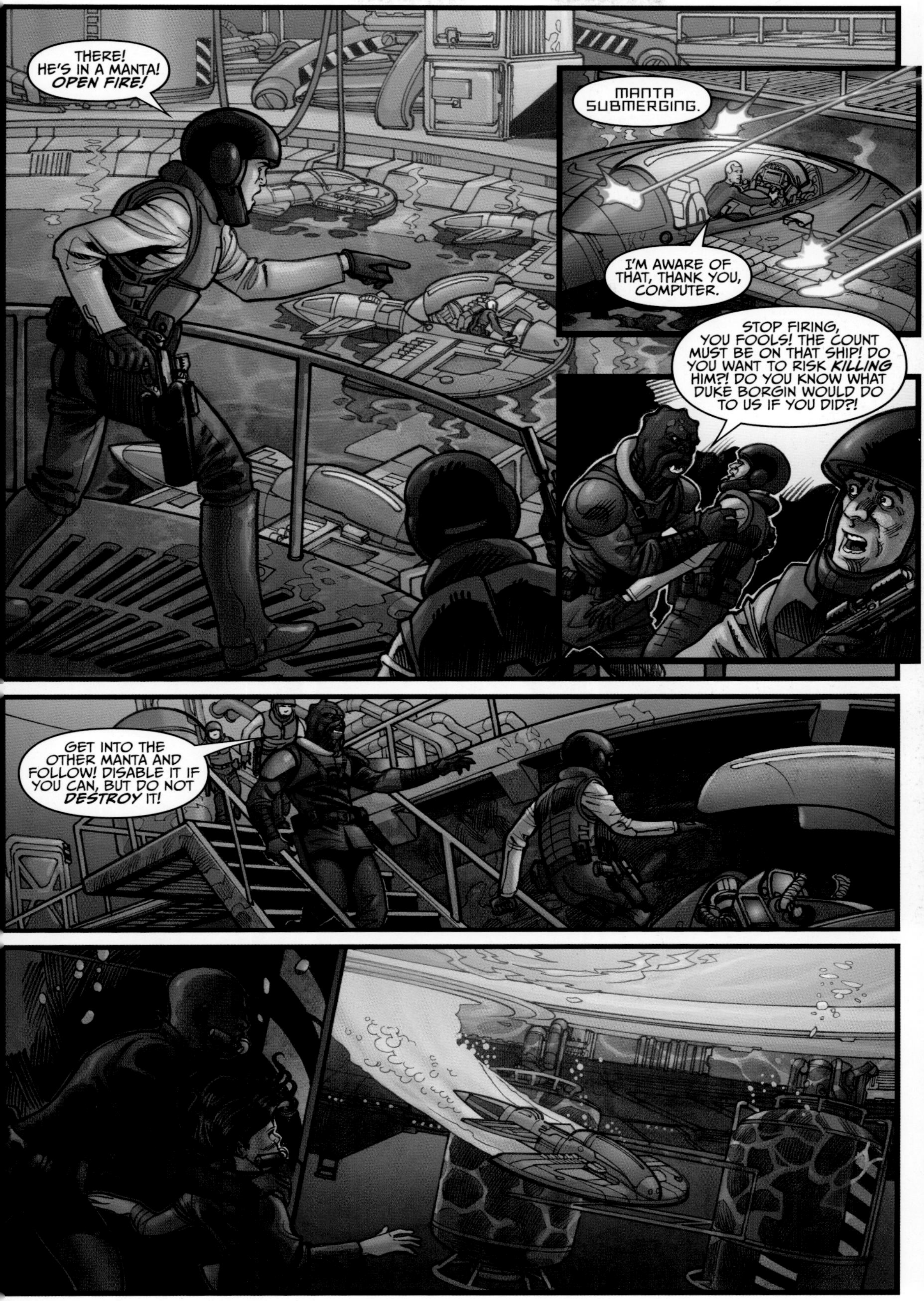
THERE! HE'S IN A MANTA! *OPEN FIRE!*
MANTA SUBMERGING.
I'M AWARE OF THAT, THANK YOU, COMPUTER.
STOP FIRING, YOU FOOLS! THE COUNT MUST BE ON THAT SHIP! DO YOU WANT TO RISK *KILLING* HIM?! DO YOU KNOW WHAT DUKE BORGIN WOULD DO TO US IF YOU DID?!
GET INTO THE OTHER MANTA AND FOLLOW! DISABLE IT IF YOU CAN, BUT DO NOT *DESTROY* IT!

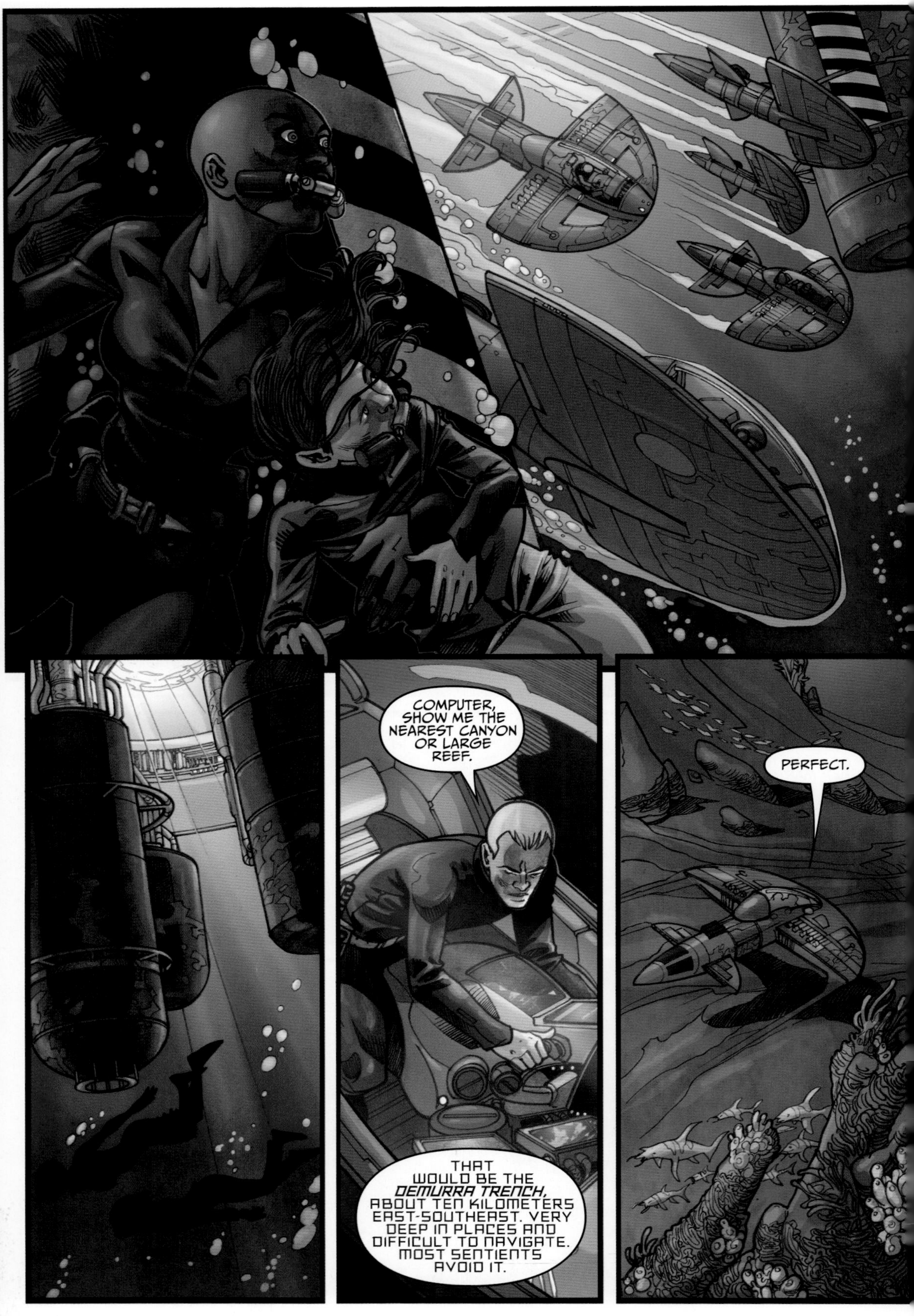
COMPUTER, SHOW ME THE NEAREST CANYON OR LARGE REEF.
THAT WOULD BE THE *DEMURRA TRENCH*, ABOUT TEN KILOMETERS EAST-SOUTHEAST. VERY DEEP IN PLACES AND DIFFICULT TO NAVIGATE. MOST SENTIENTS AVOID IT.
PERFECT.

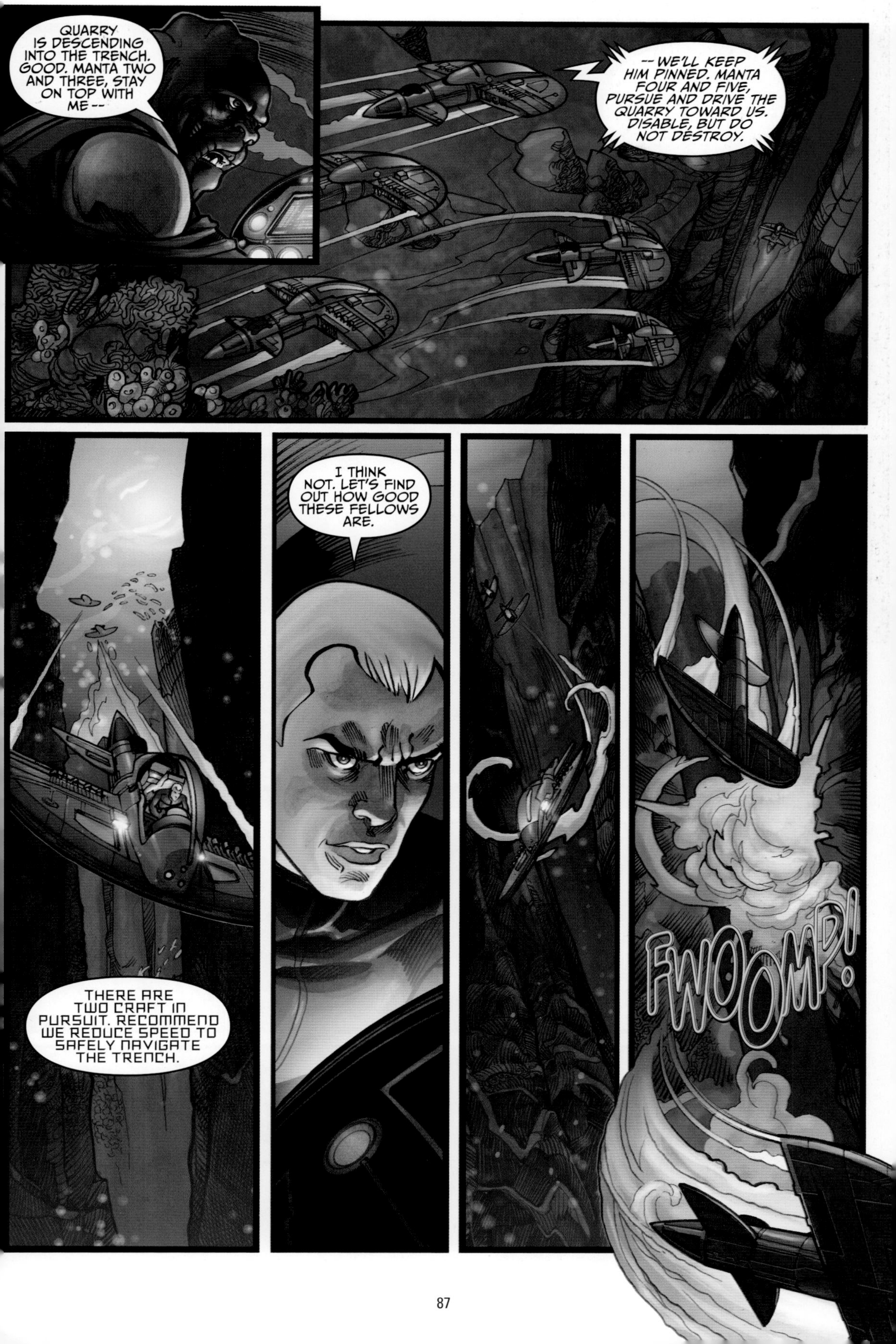
QUARRY IS DESCENDING INTO THE TRENCH. GOOD. MANTA TWO AND THREE, STAY ON TOP WITH ME --
-- WE'LL KEEP HIM PINNED. MANTA FOUR AND FIVE, PURSUE AND DRIVE THE QUARRY TOWARD US. DISABLE, BUT DO NOT DESTROY.
THERE ARE TWO CRAFT IN PURSUIT. RECOMMEND WE REDUCE SPEED TO SAFELY NAVIGATE THE TRENCH.
I THINK NOT. LET'S FIND OUT HOW GOOD THESE FELLOWS ARE.
FWOOMP!

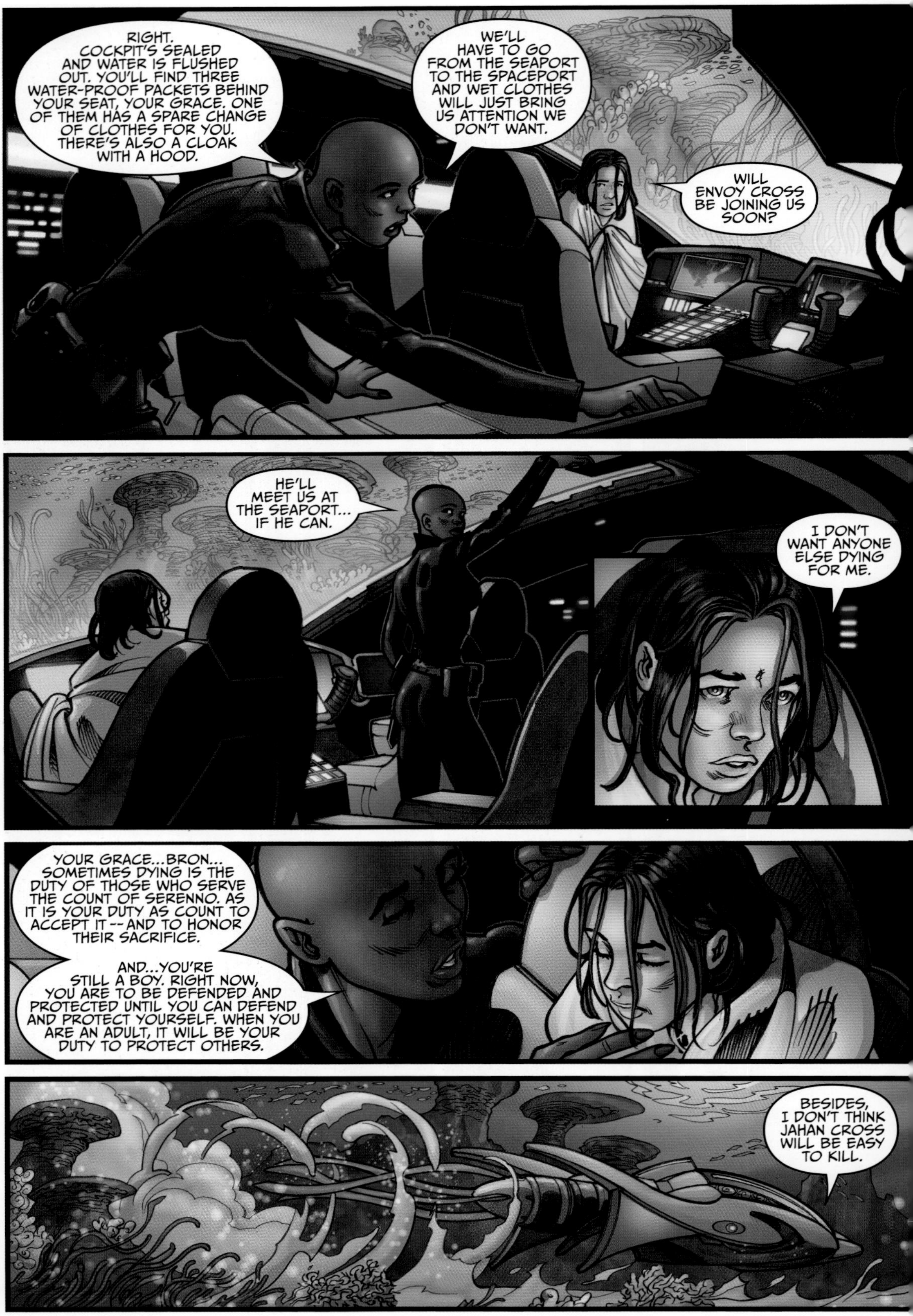
RIGHT. COCKPIT'S SEALED AND WATER IS FLUSHED OUT. YOU'LL FIND THREE WATER-PROOF PACKETS BEHIND YOUR SEAT, YOUR GRACE. ONE OF THEM HAS A SPARE CHANGE OF CLOTHES FOR YOU. THERE'S ALSO A CLOAK WITH A HOOD.
WE'LL HAVE TO GO FROM THE SEAPORT TO THE SPACEPORT AND WET CLOTHES WILL JUST BRING US ATTENTION WE DON'T WANT.
WILL ENVOY CROSS BE JOINING US SOON?
HE'LL MEET US AT THE SEAPORT... IF HE CAN.
I DON'T WANT ANYONE ELSE DYING FOR ME.
YOUR GRACE...BRON... SOMETIMES DYING IS THE DUTY OF THOSE WHO SERVE THE COUNT OF SERENNO. AS IT IS YOUR DUTY AS COUNT TO ACCEPT IT--AND TO HONOR THEIR SACRIFICE.
AND...YOU'RE STILL A BOY. RIGHT NOW, YOU ARE TO BE DEFENDED AND PROTECTED UNTIL YOU CAN DEFEND AND PROTECT YOURSELF. WHEN YOU ARE AN ADULT, IT WILL BE YOUR DUTY TO PROTECT OTHERS.
BESIDES, I DON'T THINK JAHAN CROSS WILL BE EASY TO KILL.

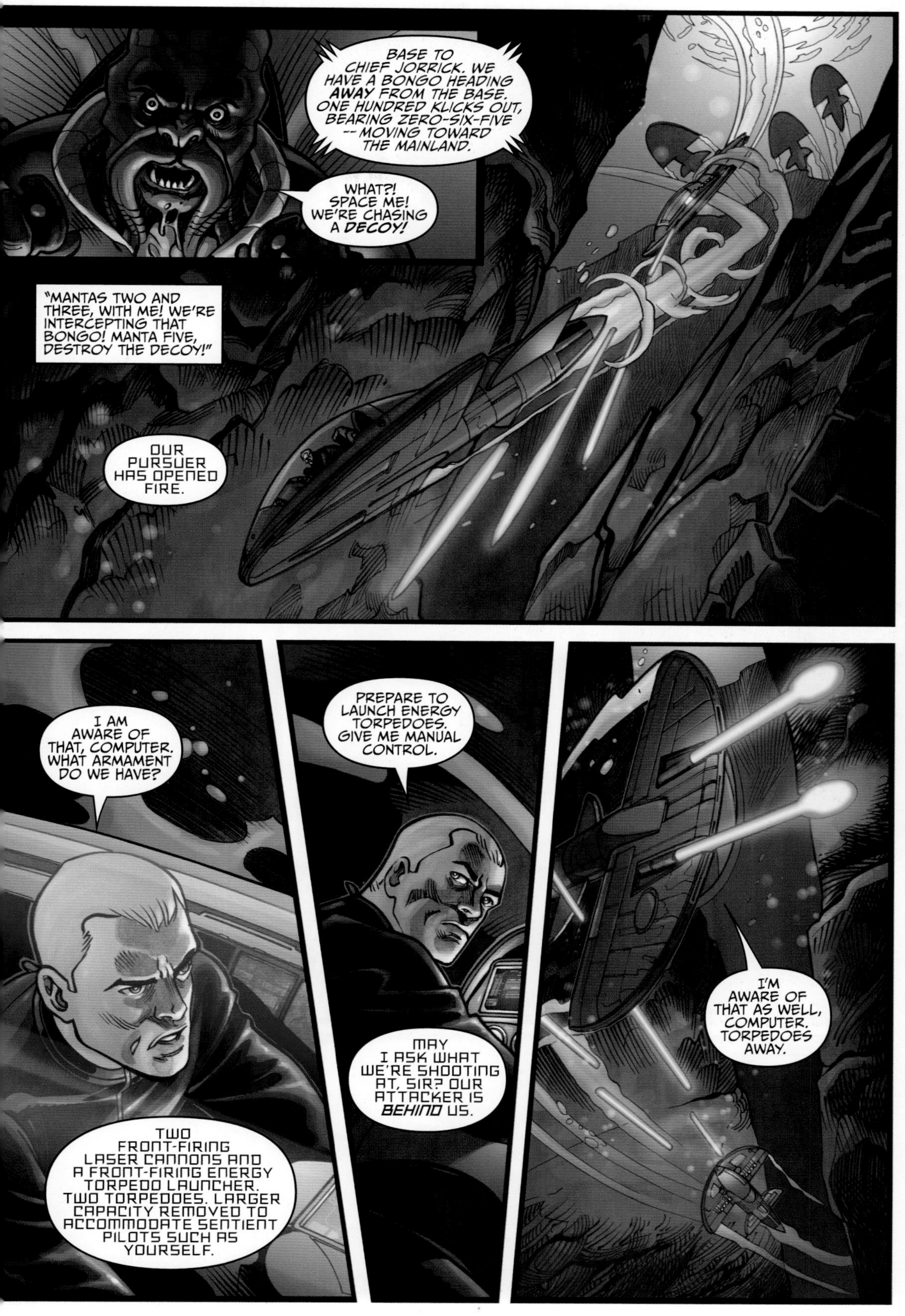
BASE TO CHIEF JORRICK. WE HAVE A BONGO HEADING AWAY FROM THE BASE. ONE HUNDRED KLICKS OUT, BEARING ZERO-SIX-FIVE --MOVING TOWARD THE MAINLAND.
WHAT?! SPACE ME! WE'RE CHASING A DECOY!
"MANTAS TWO AND THREE, WITH ME! WE'RE INTERCEPTING THAT BONGO! MANTA FIVE, DESTROY THE DECOY!"
OUR PURSUER HAS OPENED FIRE.
I AM AWARE OF THAT, COMPUTER. WHAT ARMAMENT DO WE HAVE?
TWO FRONT-FIRING LASER CANNONS AND A FRONT-FIRING ENERGY TORPEDO LAUNCHER. TWO TORPEDOES. LARGER CAPACITY REMOVED TO ACCOMMODATE SENTIENT PILOTS SUCH AS YOURSELF.
PREPARE TO LAUNCH ENERGY TORPEDOES. GIVE ME MANUAL CONTROL.
MAY I ASK WHAT WE'RE SHOOTING AT, SIR? OUR ATTACKER IS BEHIND US.
I'M AWARE OF THAT AS WELL, COMPUTER. TORPEDOES AWAY.

BARROOMPH!

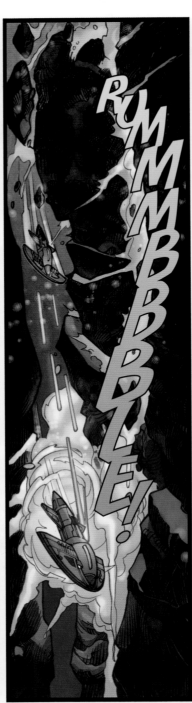

RUMMMMBBBLE!

KRUNK!

PURSUER DESTROYED. MANTAS ABOVE ARE DEPARTING.

MM. THEY'VE SPOTTED THE BONGO.

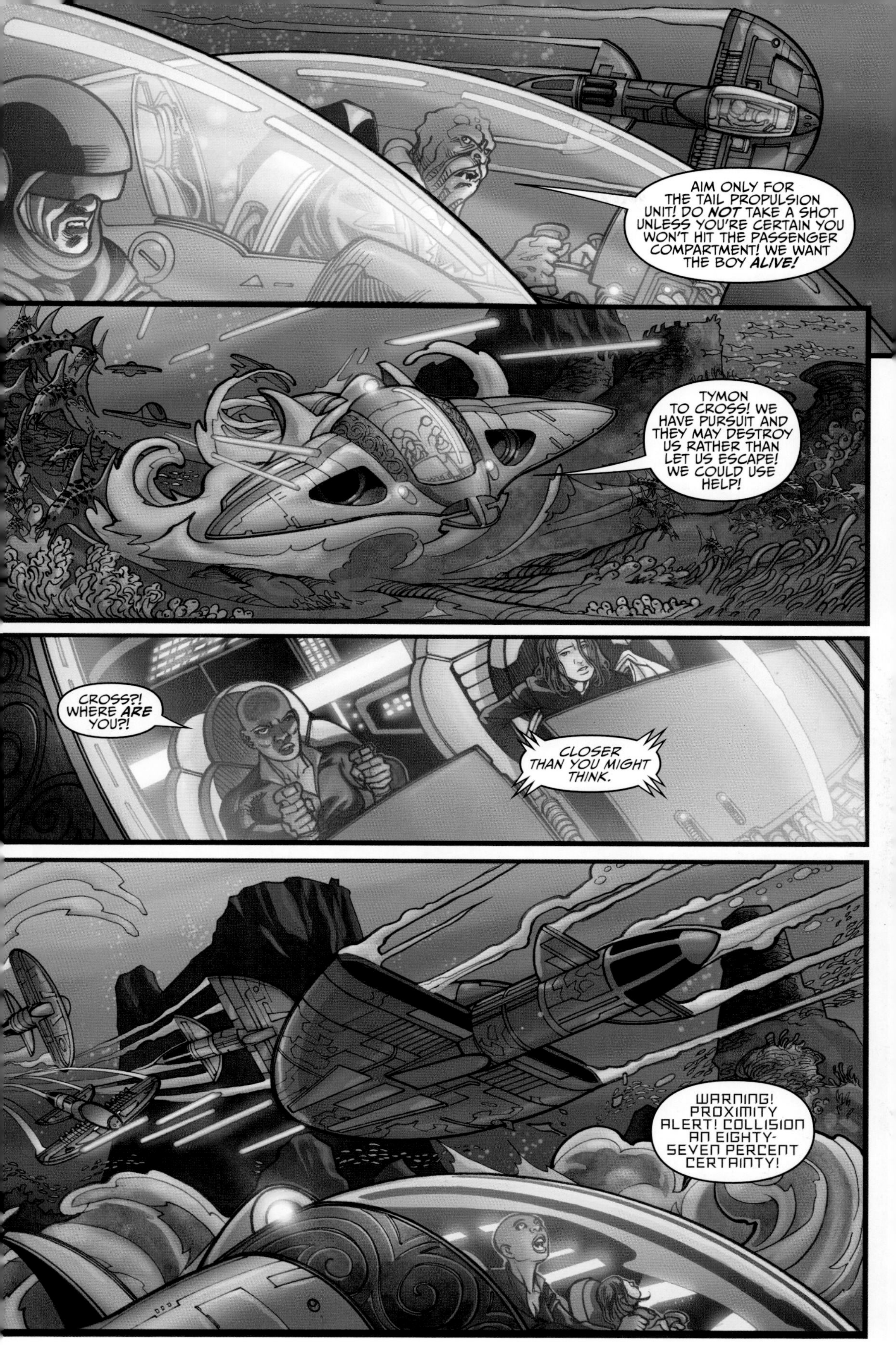
AIM ONLY FOR THE TAIL PROPULSION UNIT! DO NOT TAKE A SHOT UNLESS YOU'RE CERTAIN YOU WON'T HIT THE PASSENGER COMPARTMENT! WE WANT THE BOY ALIVE!
TYMON TO CROSS! WE HAVE PURSUIT AND THEY MAY DESTROY US RATHER THAN LET US ESCAPE! WE COULD USE HELP!
CROSS?! WHERE ARE YOU?!
CLOSER THAN YOU MIGHT THINK.
WARNING! PROXIMITY ALERT! COLLISION AN EIGHTY-SEVEN PERCENT CERTAINTY!

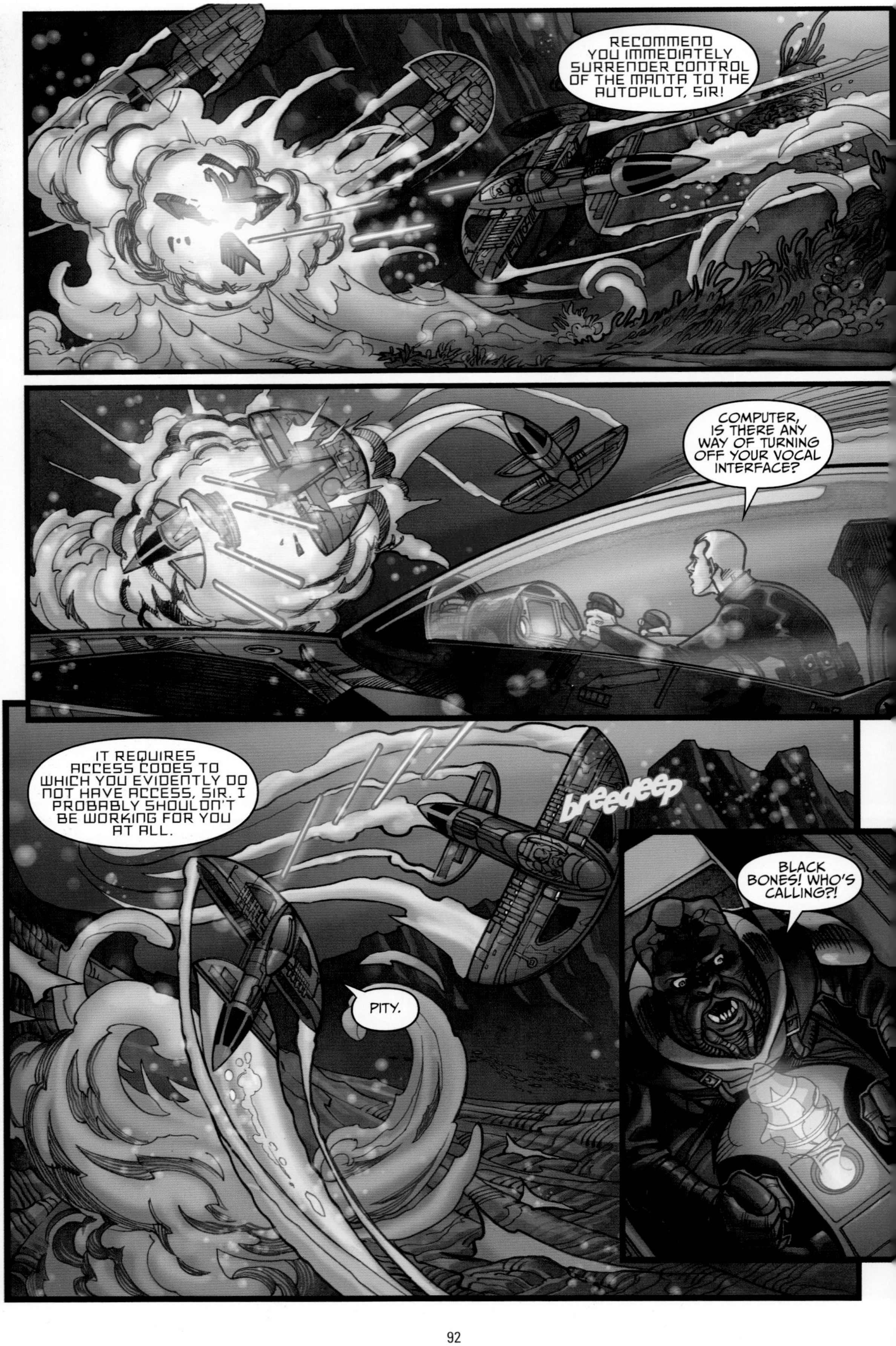
RECOMMEND YOU IMMEDIATELY SURRENDER CONTROL OF THE MANTA TO THE AUTOPILOT, SIR!
COMPUTER, IS THERE ANY WAY OF TURNING OFF YOUR VOCAL INTERFACE?
IT REQUIRES ACCESS CODES TO WHICH YOU EVIDENTLY DO NOT HAVE ACCESS, SIR. I PROBABLY SHOULDN'T BE WORKING FOR YOU AT ALL.
PITY.
breedeep
BLACK BONES! WHO'S CALLING?!

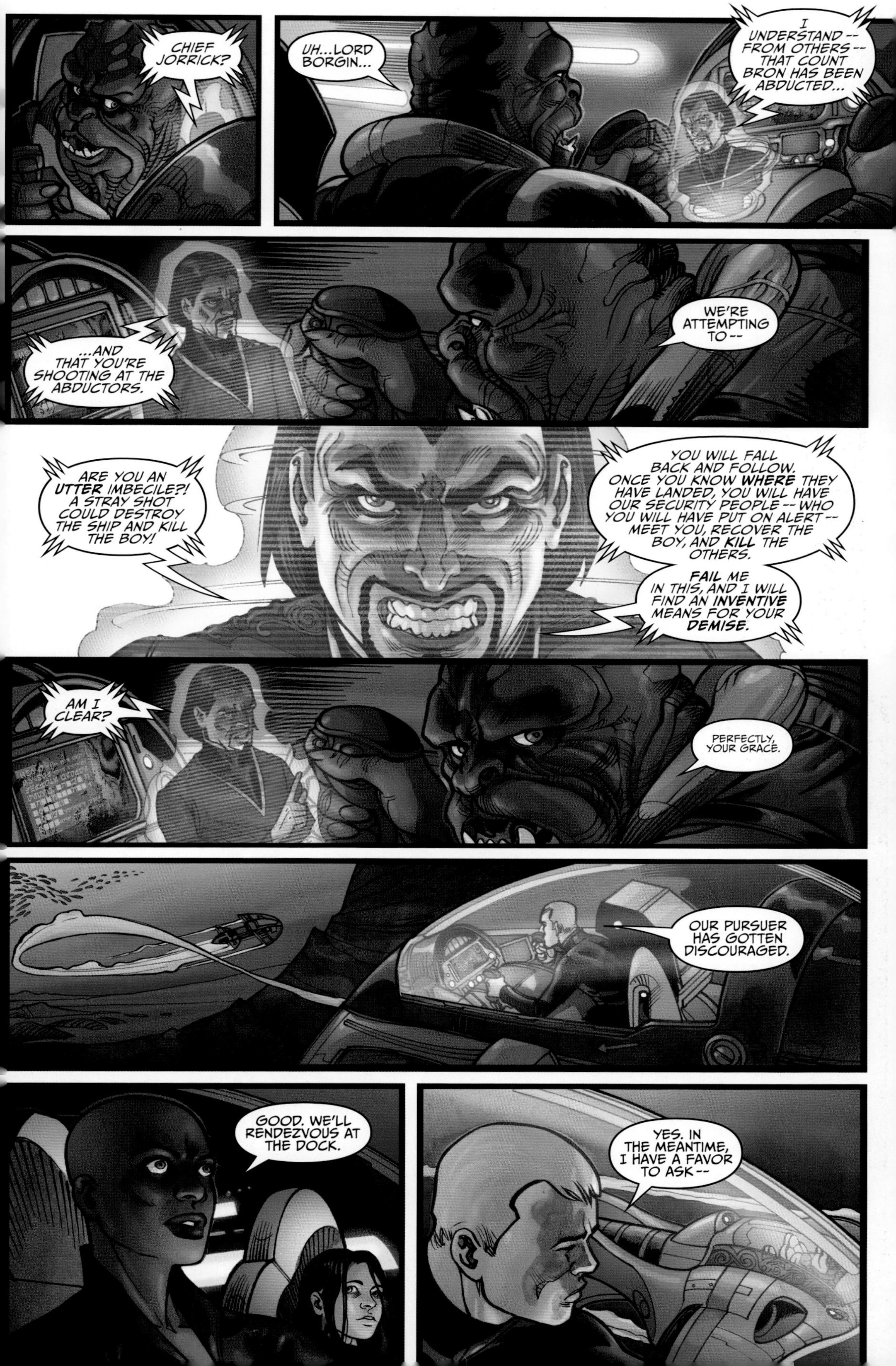
CHIEF JORRICK?
UH...LORD BORGIN...
I UNDERSTAND -- FROM OTHERS -- THAT COUNT BRON HAS BEEN ABDUCTED...
...AND THAT YOU'RE SHOOTING AT THE ABDUCTORS.
WE'RE ATTEMPTING TO --
ARE YOU AN UTTER IMBECILE?! A STRAY SHOT COULD DESTROY THE SHIP AND KILL THE BOY!
YOU WILL FALL BACK AND FOLLOW. ONCE YOU KNOW WHERE THEY HAVE LANDED, YOU WILL HAVE OUR SECURITY PEOPLE -- WHO YOU WILL HAVE PUT ON ALERT -- MEET YOU, RECOVER THE BOY, AND KILL THE OTHERS.
FAIL ME IN THIS, AND I WILL FIND AN INVENTIVE MEANS FOR YOUR DEMISE.
AM I CLEAR?
PERFECTLY, YOUR GRACE.
OUR PURSUER HAS GOTTEN DISCOURAGED.
GOOD. WE'LL RENDEZVOUS AT THE DOCK.
YES. IN THE MEANTIME, I HAVE A FAVOR TO ASK --

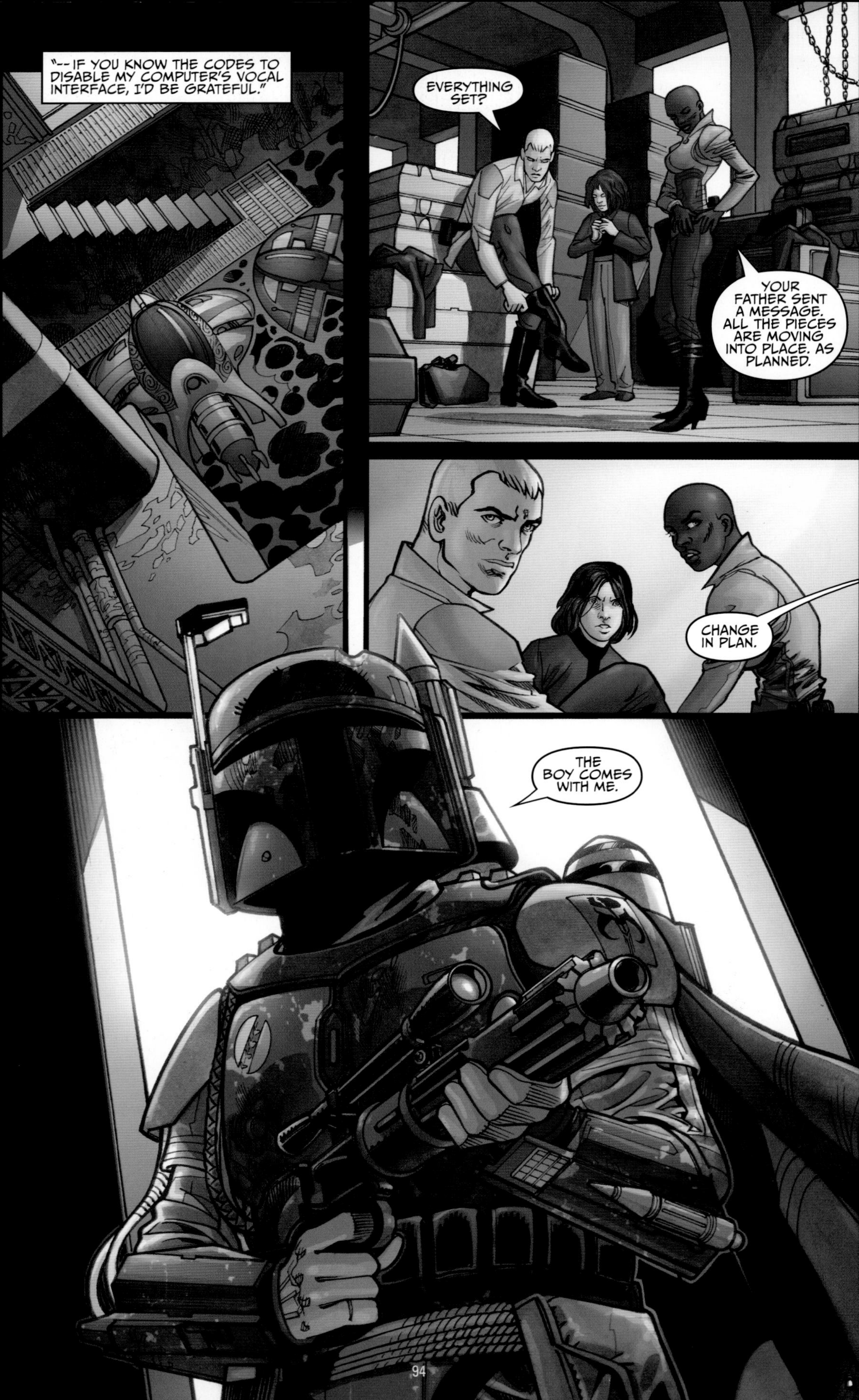
"--IF YOU KNOW THE CODES TO DISABLE MY COMPUTER'S VOCAL INTERFACE, I'D BE GRATEFUL."
EVERYTHING SET?
YOUR FATHER SENT A MESSAGE. ALL THE PIECES ARE MOVING INTO PLACE. AS PLANNED.
CHANGE IN PLAN.
THE BOY COMES WITH ME.

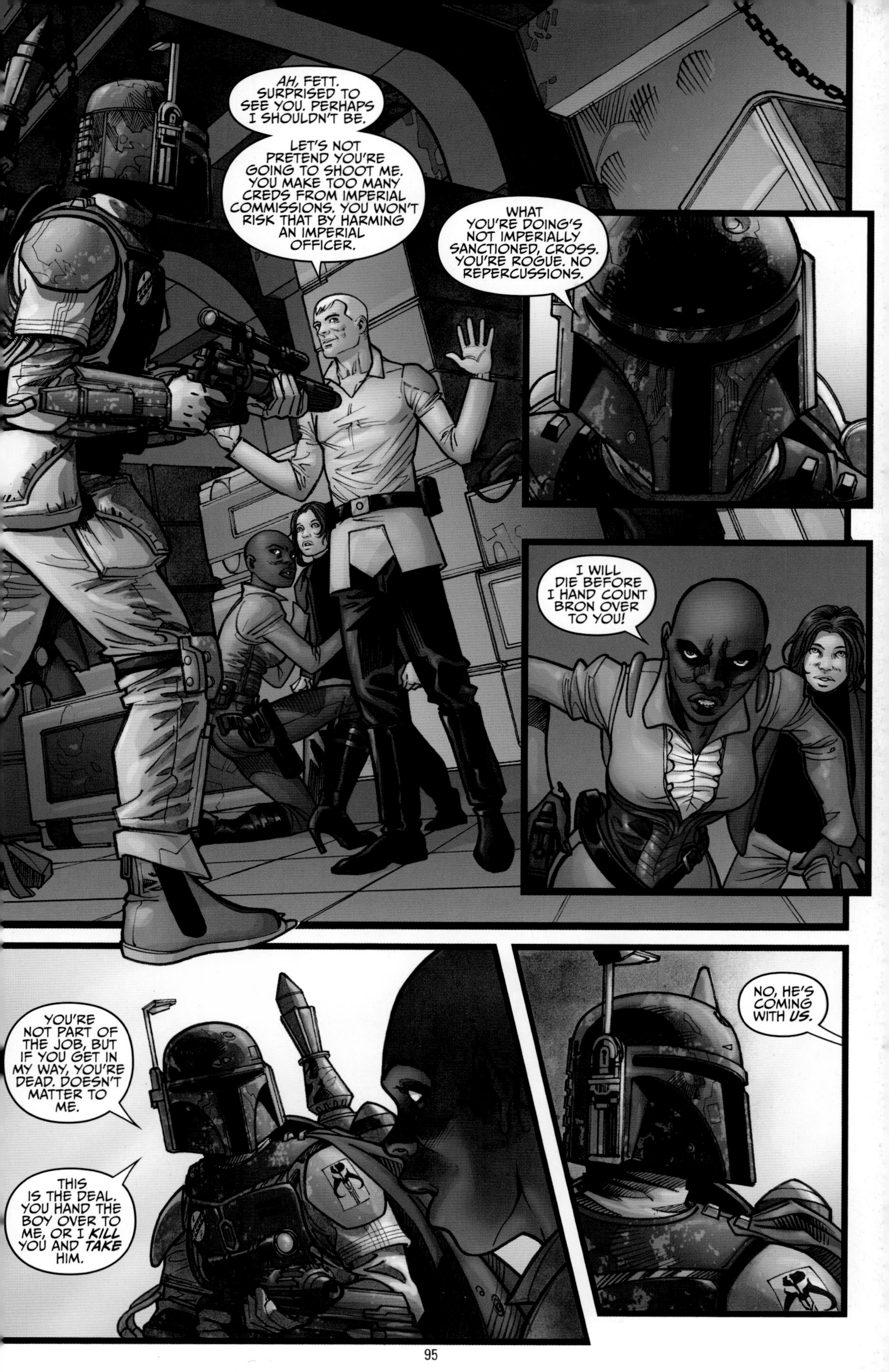
AH, FETT. SURPRISED TO SEE YOU. PERHAPS I SHOULDN'T BE.
LET'S NOT PRETEND YOU'RE GOING TO SHOOT ME. YOU MAKE TOO MANY CREDS FROM IMPERIAL COMMISSIONS. YOU WON'T RISK THAT BY HARMING AN IMPERIAL OFFICER.
WHAT YOU'RE DOING'S NOT IMPERIALLY SANCTIONED, CROSS. YOU'RE ROGUE. NO REPERCUSSIONS.
I WILL DIE BEFORE I HAND COUNT BRON OVER TO YOU!
YOU'RE NOT PART OF THE JOB, BUT IF YOU GET IN MY WAY, YOU'RE DEAD. DOESN'T MATTER TO ME.
THIS IS THE DEAL. YOU HAND THE BOY OVER TO ME, OR I *KILL* YOU AND *TAKE* HIM.
NO, HE'S COMING WITH *US*.

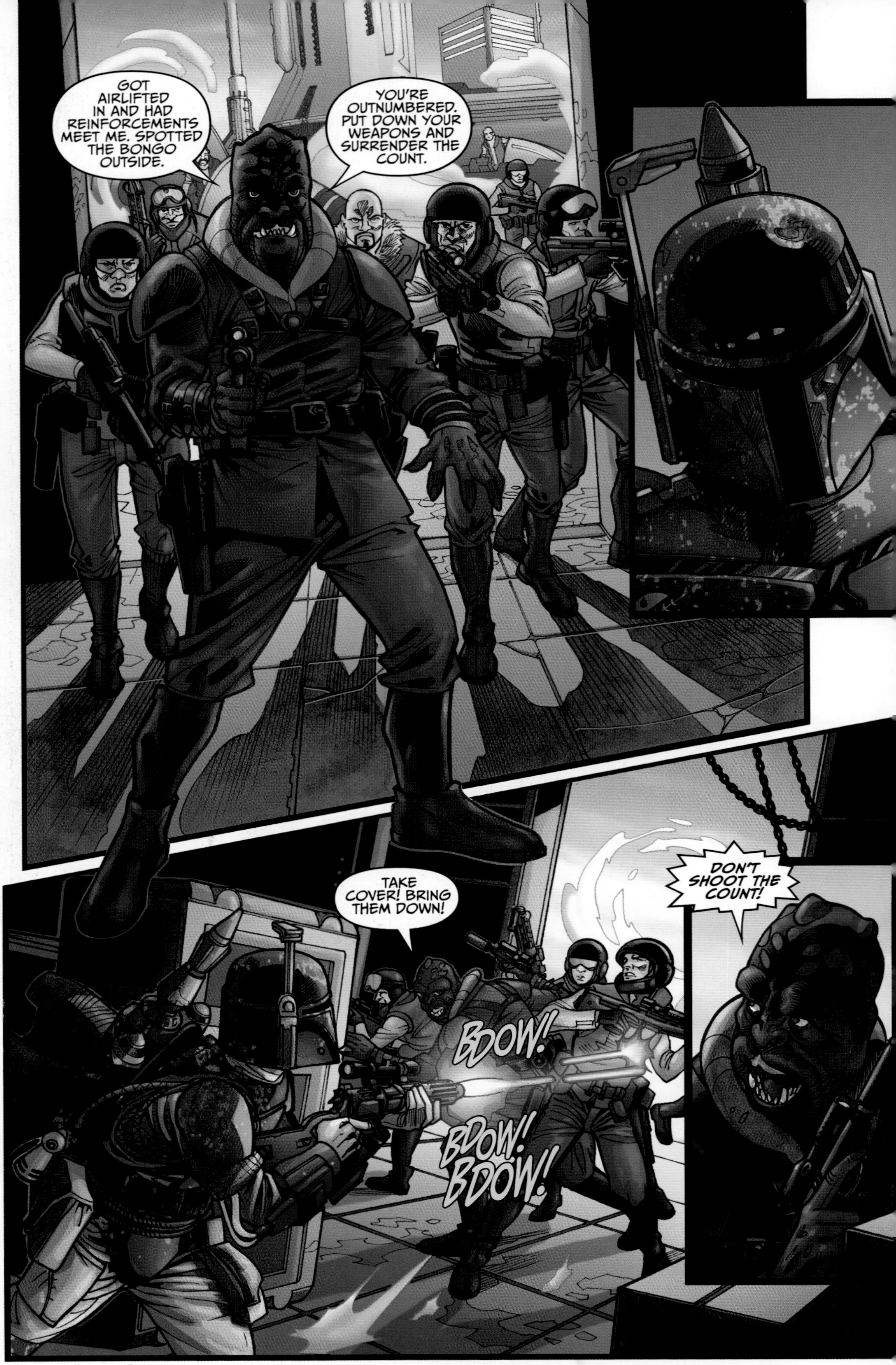
GOT AIRLIFTED IN AND HAD REINFORCEMENTS MEET ME. SPOTTED THE BONGO OUTSIDE.
YOU'RE OUTNUMBERED. PUT DOWN YOUR WEAPONS AND SURRENDER THE COUNT.
TAKE COVER! BRING THEM DOWN!
DON'T SHOOT THE COUNT!
BDOW!
BDOW! BDOW!

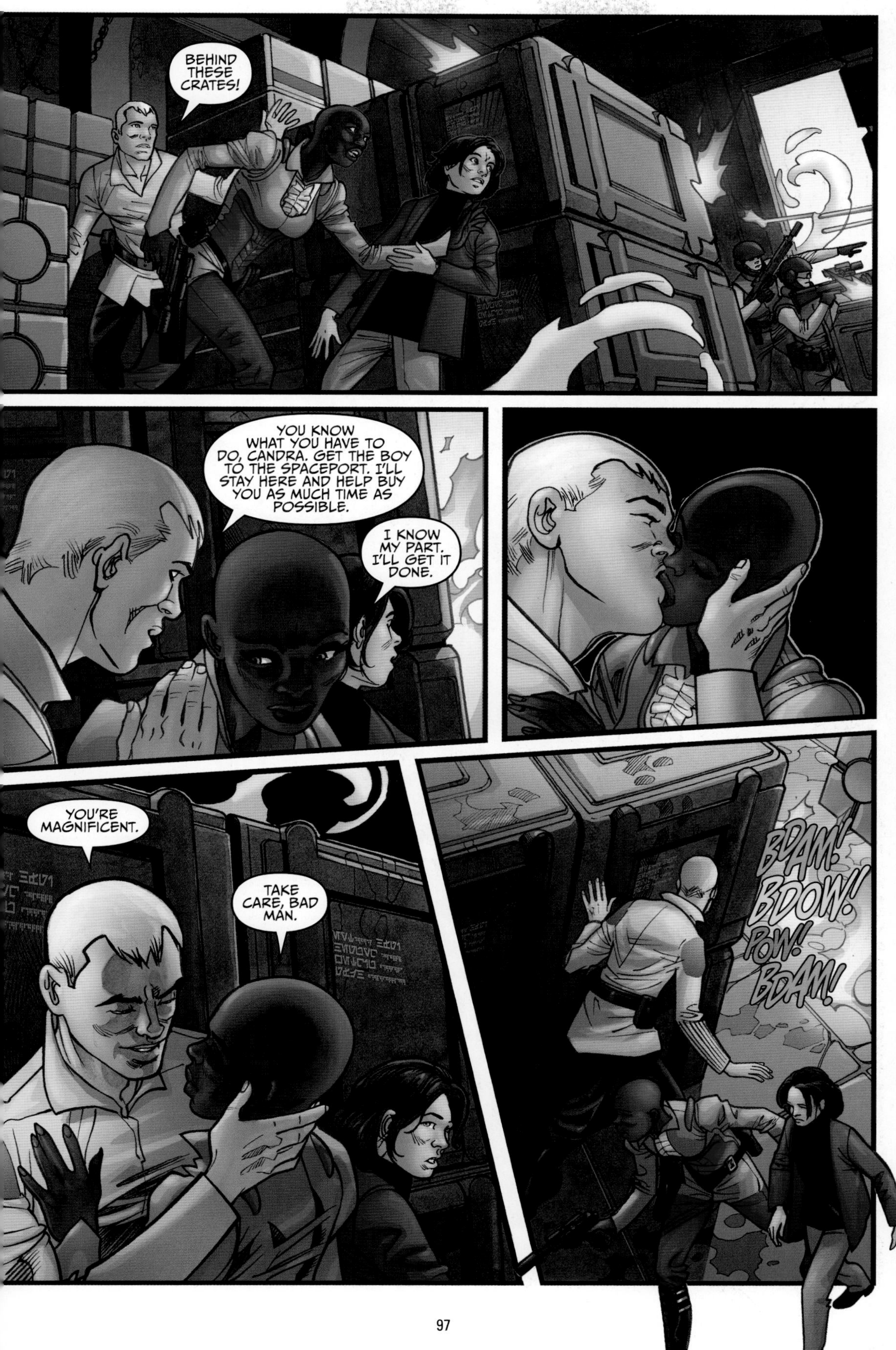
BEHIND THESE CRATES!
YOU KNOW WHAT YOU HAVE TO DO, CANDRA. GET THE BOY TO THE SPACEPORT. I'LL STAY HERE AND HELP BUY YOU AS MUCH TIME AS POSSIBLE.
I KNOW MY PART. I'LL GET IT DONE.
YOU'RE MAGNIFICENT.
TAKE CARE, BAD MAN.
BDAM! BDOW! POW! BDAM!

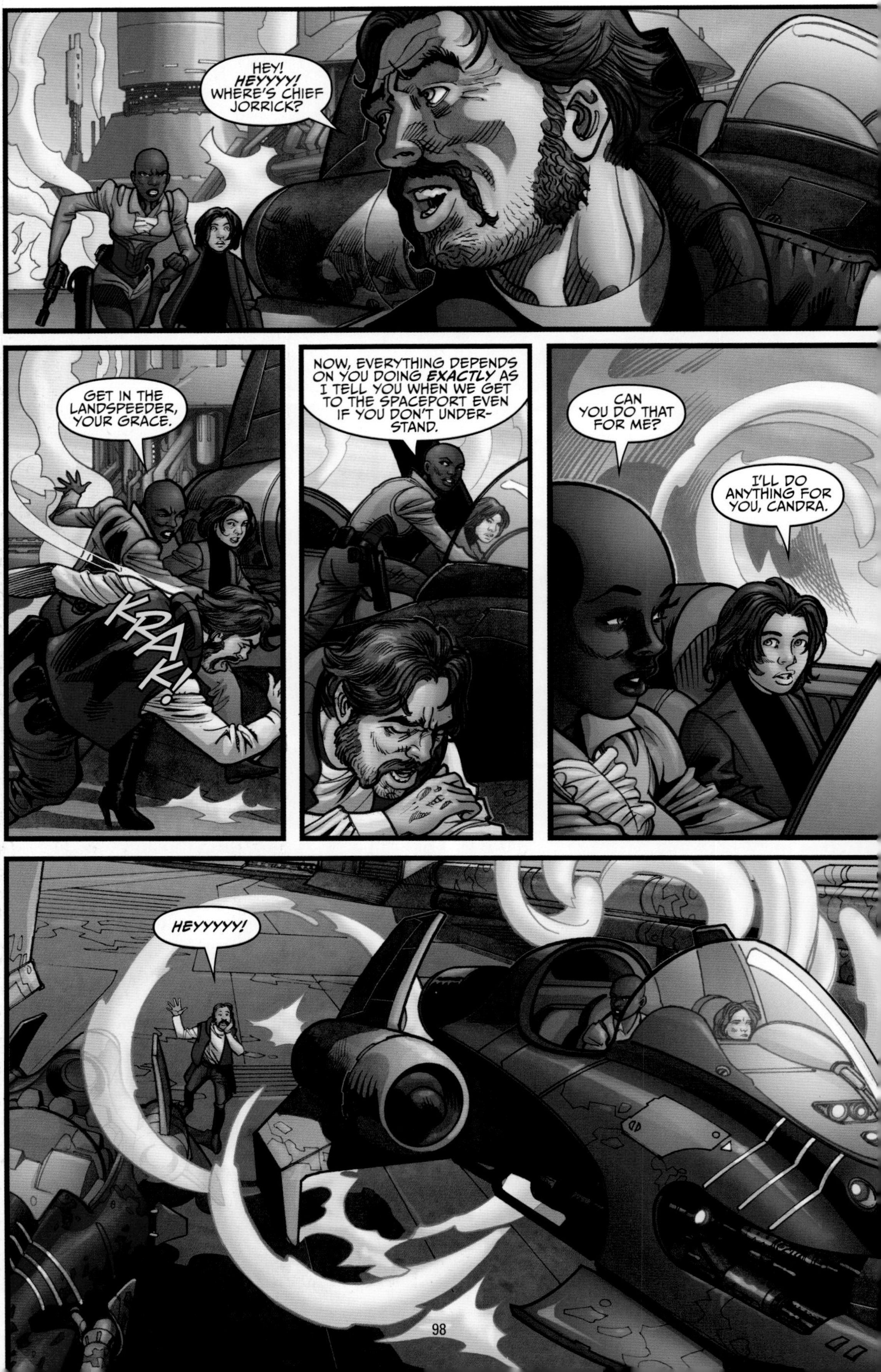
HEY! HEYYYY! WHERE'S CHIEF JORRICK?
GET IN THE LANDSPEEDER, YOUR GRACE.
KRAK!
NOW, EVERYTHING DEPENDS ON YOU DOING EXACTLY AS I TELL YOU WHEN WE GET TO THE SPACEPORT EVEN IF YOU DON'T UNDER-STAND.
CAN YOU DO THAT FOR ME?
I'LL DO ANYTHING FOR YOU, CANDRA.
HEYYYYY!

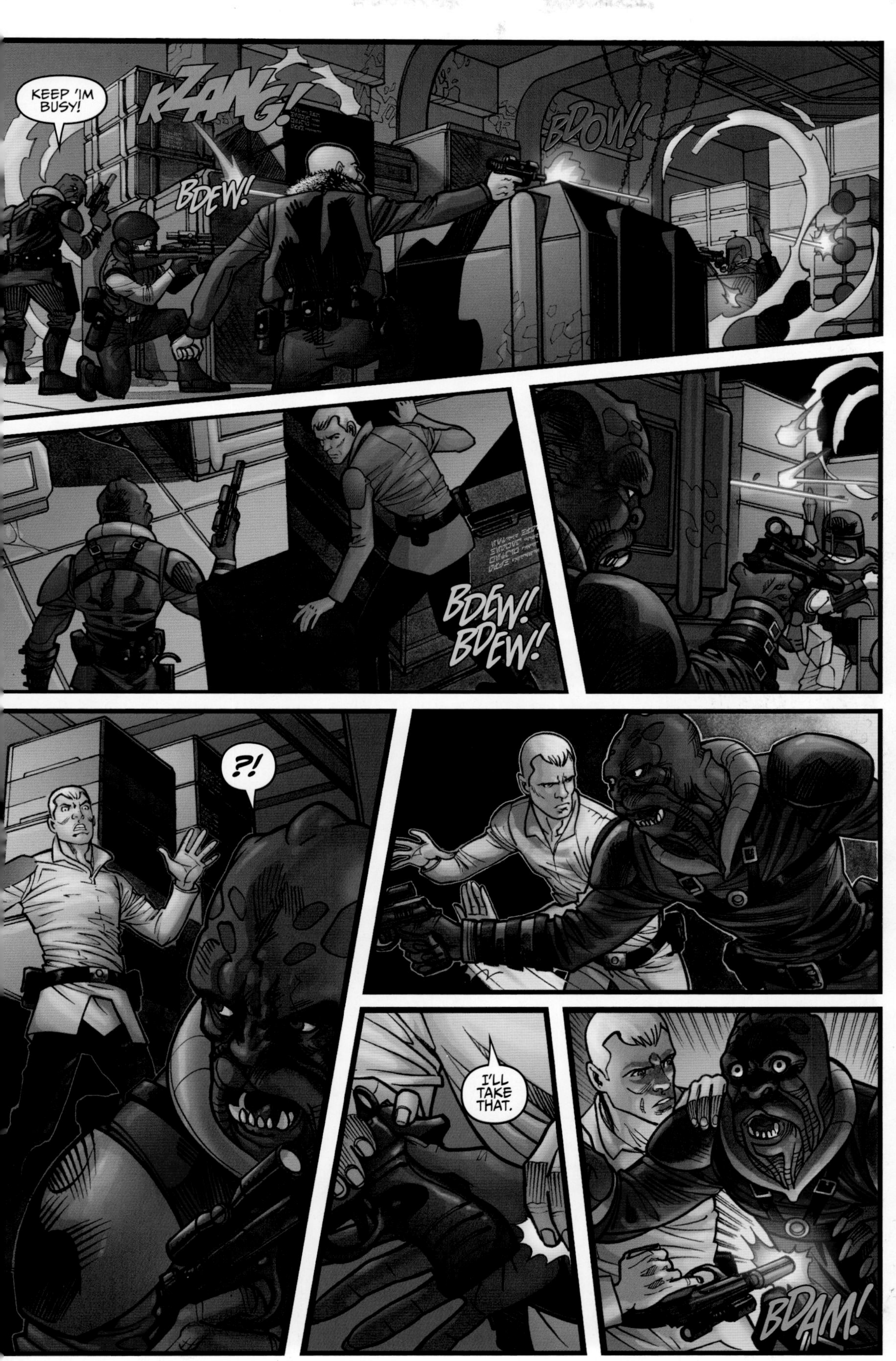
KEEP 'IM BUSY!
KZANG!
BDOW!
BDEW!
BDEW! BDEW!
?!
I'LL TAKE THAT.
BDAM!

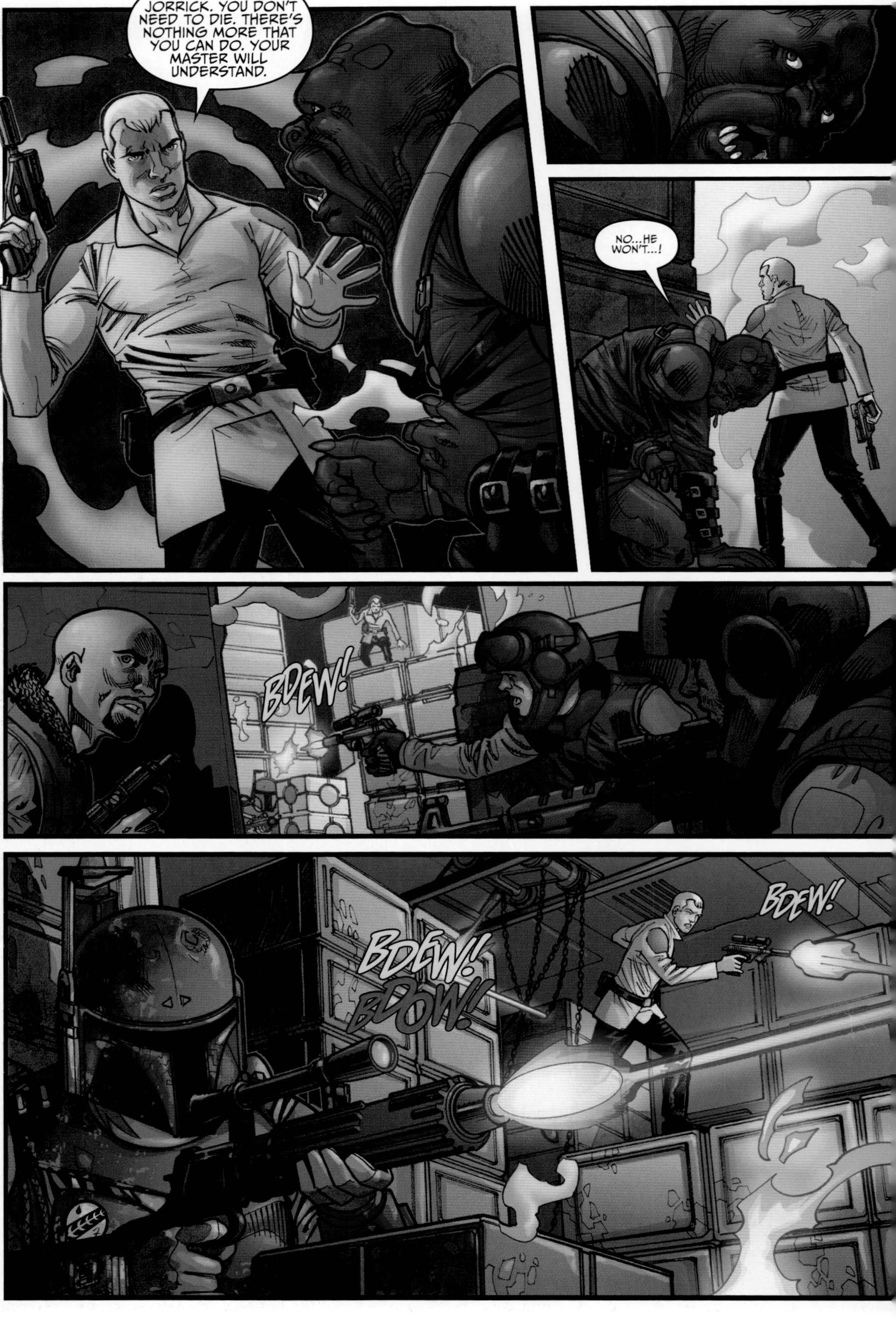
STAY DOWN, JORRICK. YOU DON'T NEED TO DIE. THERE'S NOTHING MORE THAT YOU CAN DO. YOUR MASTER WILL UNDERSTAND.
NO...HE WON'T...!
BDEW!
BDEW!
BDOW!
BDEW!

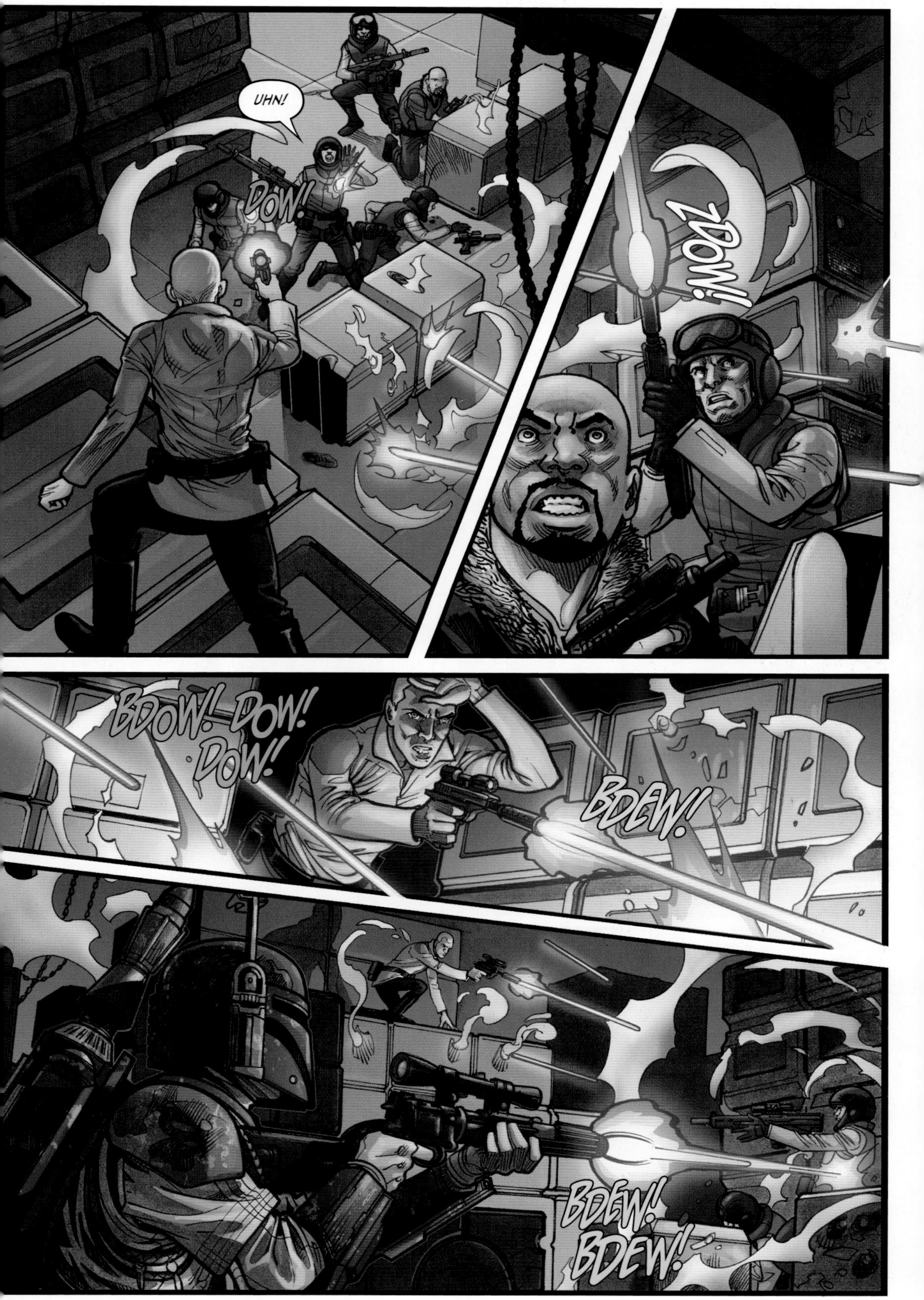
UHN!
DOW!
ZDOW!
BDOW! DOW! DOW!
BDEW!
BDEW! BDEW!

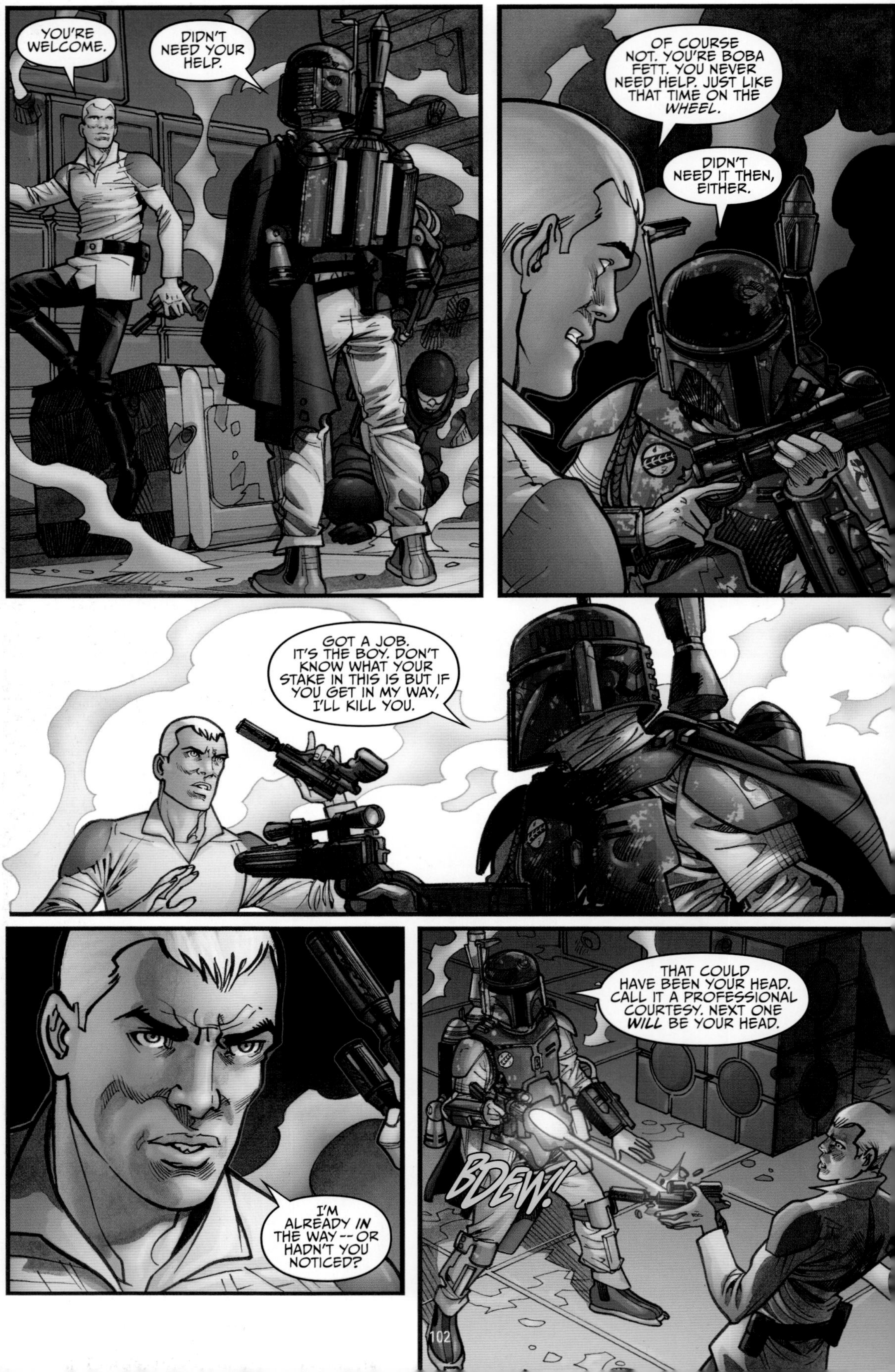

YOU'RE WELCOME.
DIDN'T NEED YOUR HELP.
OF COURSE NOT. YOU'RE BOBA FETT. YOU NEVER NEED HELP. JUST LIKE THAT TIME ON THE *WHEEL*.
DIDN'T NEED IT THEN, EITHER.
GOT A JOB. IT'S THE BOY. DON'T KNOW WHAT YOUR STAKE IN THIS IS BUT IF YOU GET IN MY WAY, I'LL KILL YOU.
I'M ALREADY *IN* THE WAY-- OR HADN'T YOU NOTICED?
THAT COULD HAVE BEEN YOUR HEAD. CALL IT A PROFESSIONAL COURTESY. NEXT ONE ***WILL*** BE YOUR HEAD.
BDEW!

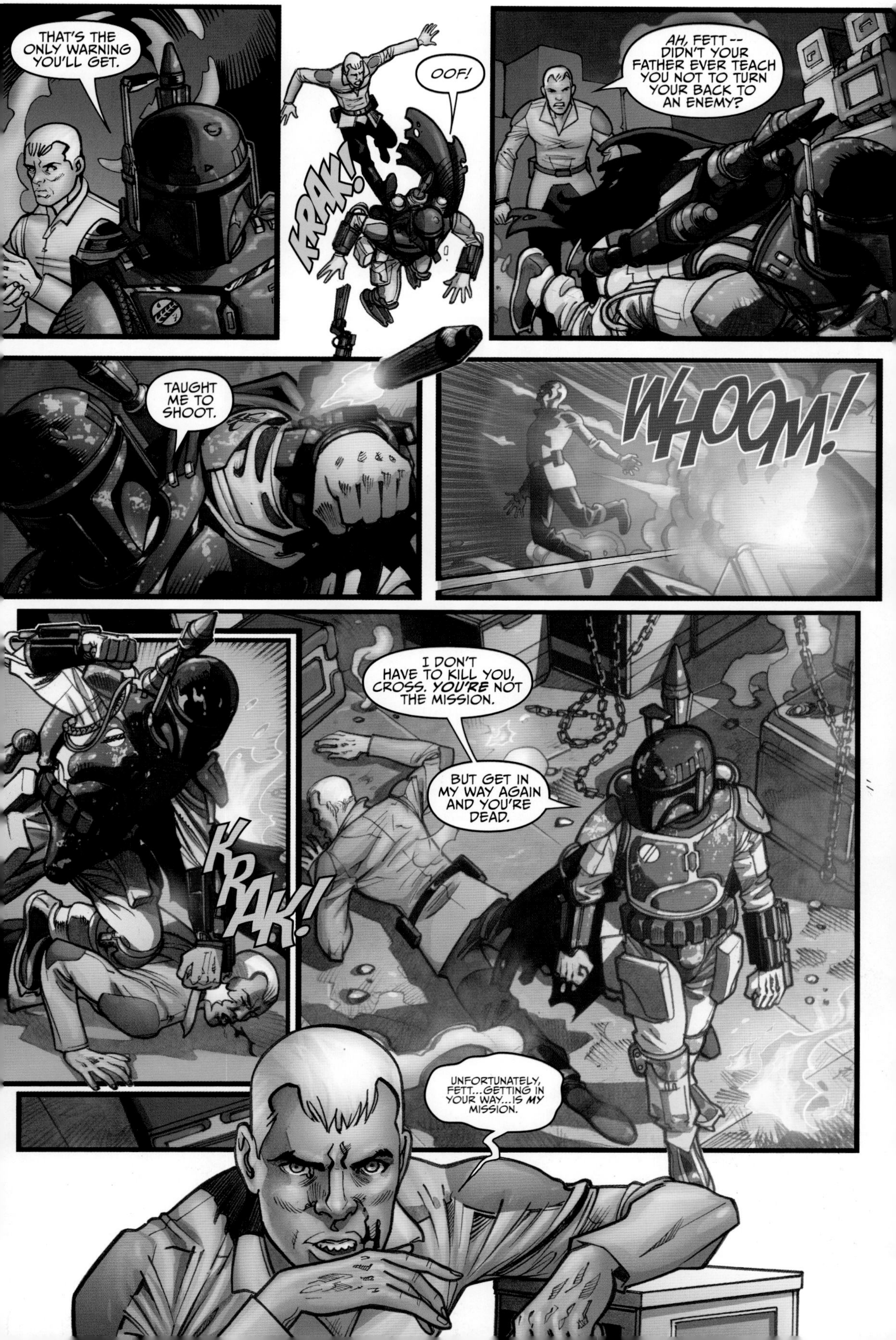
THAT'S THE ONLY WARNING YOU'LL GET.
OOF!
KRAK!
AH, FETT -- DIDN'T YOUR FATHER EVER TEACH YOU NOT TO TURN YOUR BACK TO AN ENEMY?
TAUGHT ME TO SHOOT.
WHOOM!
KRAK!
I DON'T HAVE TO KILL YOU, CROSS. YOU'RE NOT THE MISSION.
BUT GET IN MY WAY AGAIN AND YOU'RE DEAD.
UNFORTUNATELY, FETT...GETTING IN YOUR WAY...IS MY MISSION.

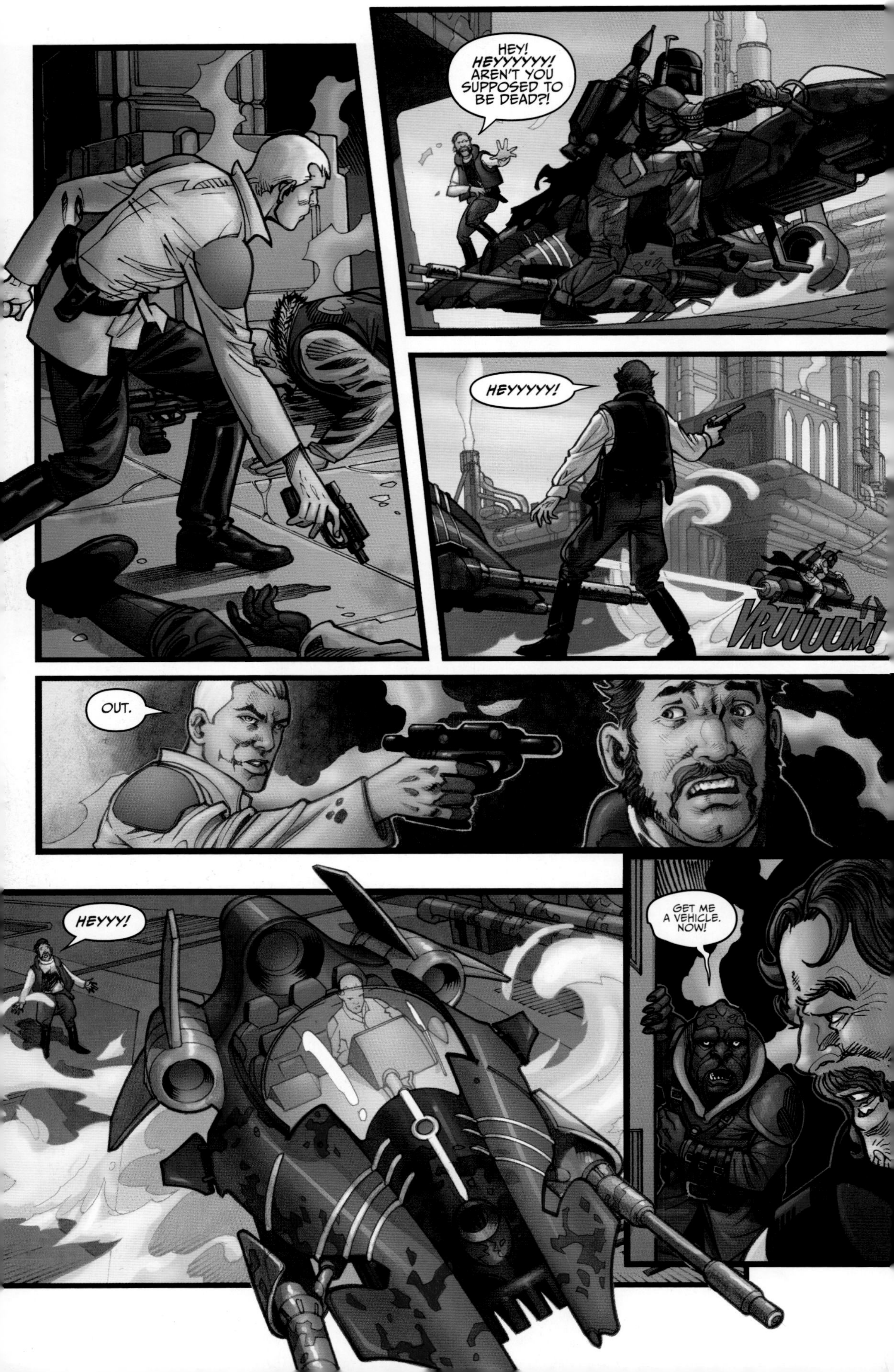
HEY! HEYYYYYY! AREN'T YOU SUPPOSED TO BE DEAD?!
HEYYYYY!
VRUUUUUM!
OUT.
GET ME A VEHICLE. NOW!
HEYYY!

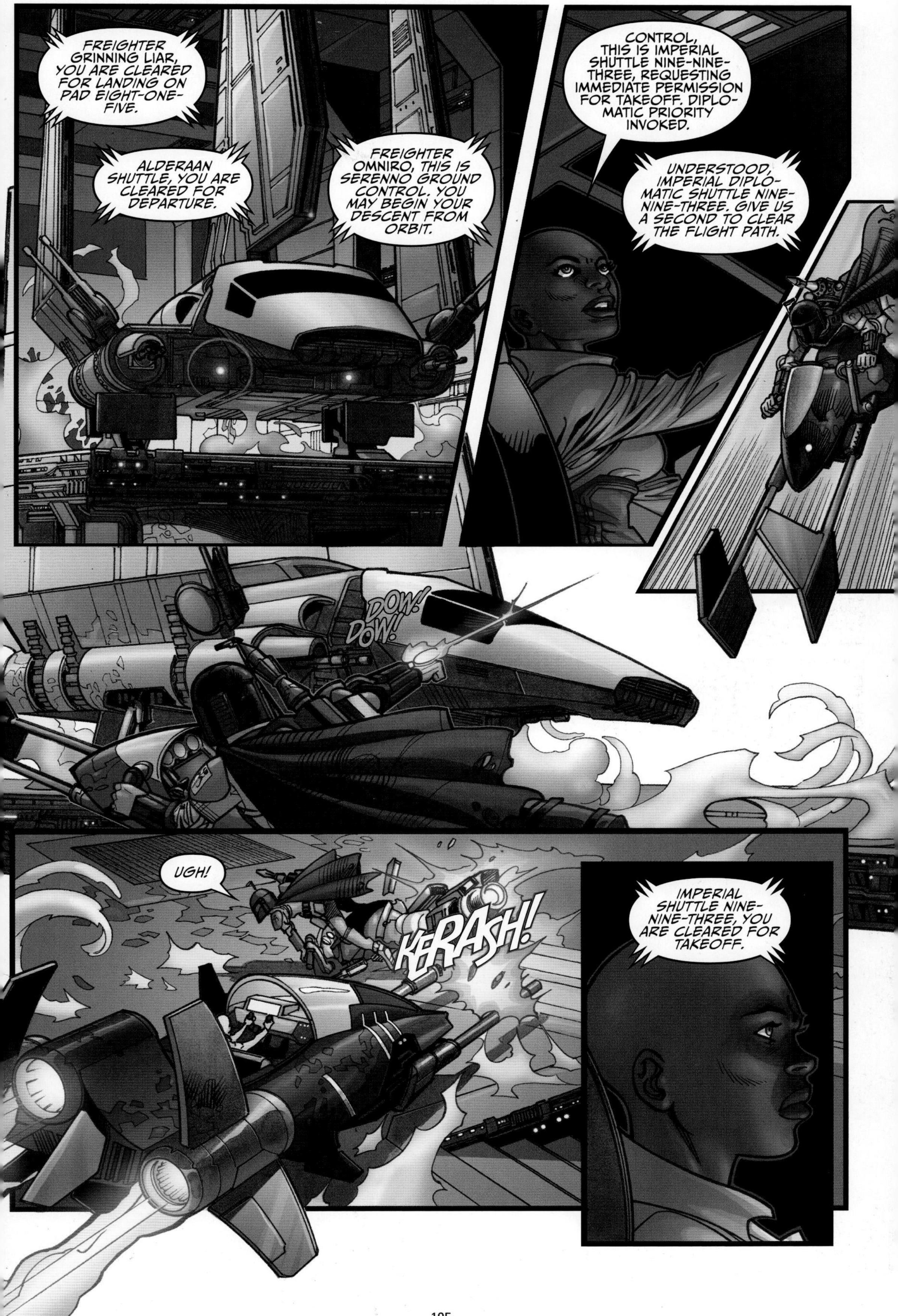
FREIGHTER GRINNING LIAR, YOU ARE CLEARED FOR LANDING ON PAD EIGHT-ONE-FIVE.
ALDERAAN SHUTTLE, YOU ARE CLEARED FOR DEPARTURE.
FREIGHTER OMNIRO, THIS IS SERENNO GROUND CONTROL. YOU MAY BEGIN YOUR DESCENT FROM ORBIT.
CONTROL, THIS IS IMPERIAL SHUTTLE NINE-NINE-THREE, REQUESTING IMMEDIATE PERMISSION FOR TAKEOFF. DIPLOMATIC PRIORITY INVOKED.
UNDERSTOOD, IMPERIAL DIPLOMATIC SHUTTLE NINE-NINE-THREE. GIVE US A SECOND TO CLEAR THE FLIGHT PATH.
DOW! DOW!
UGH!
KERASH!
IMPERIAL SHUTTLE NINE-NINE-THREE, YOU ARE CLEARED FOR TAKEOFF.

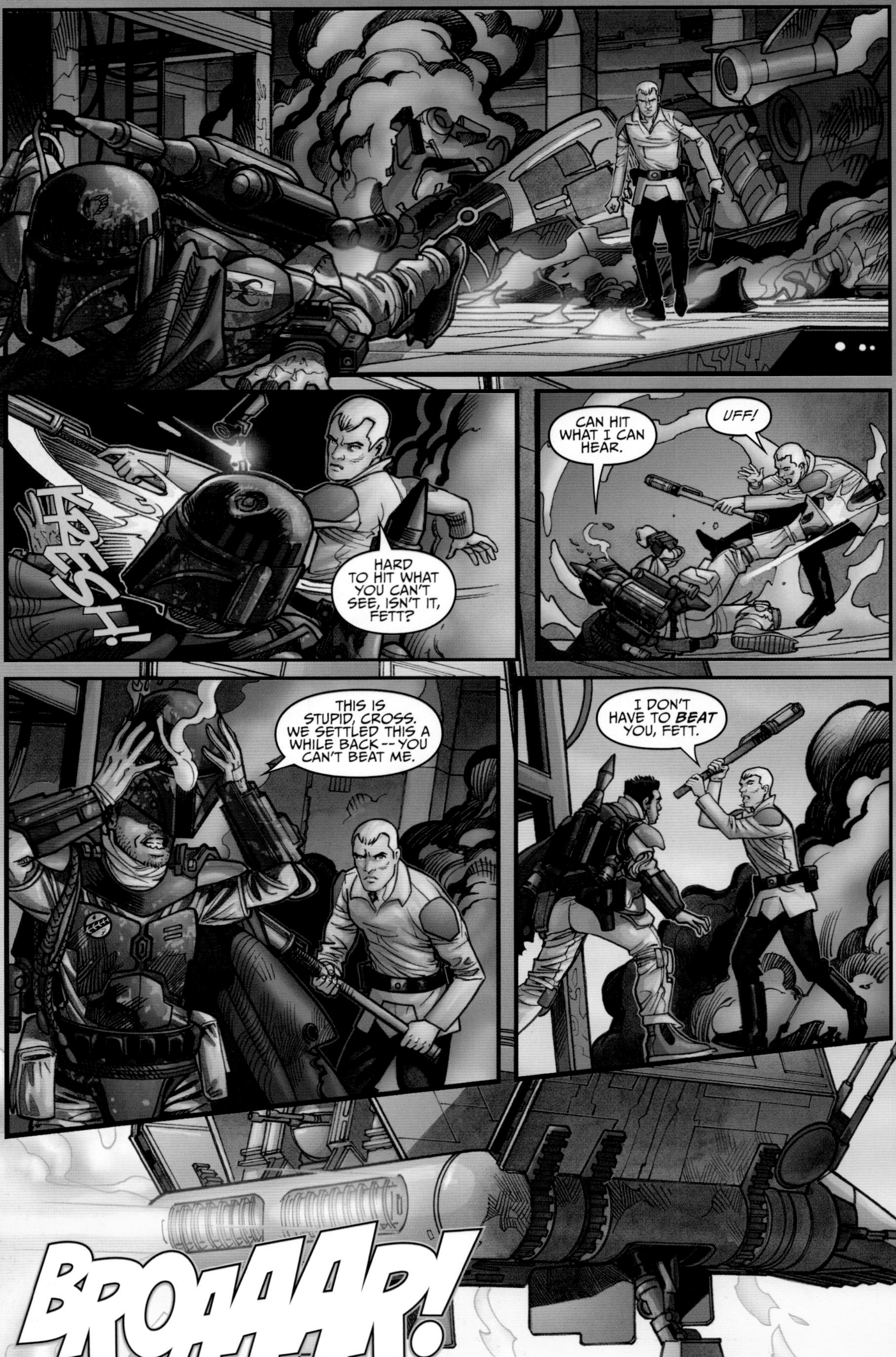
KRESH!
HARD TO HIT WHAT YOU CAN'T SEE, ISN'T IT, FETT?
CAN HIT WHAT I CAN HEAR.
UFF!
THIS IS STUPID, CROSS. WE SETTLED THIS A WHILE BACK -- YOU CAN'T BEAT ME.
I DON'T HAVE TO BEAT YOU, FETT.
BROAAAR!

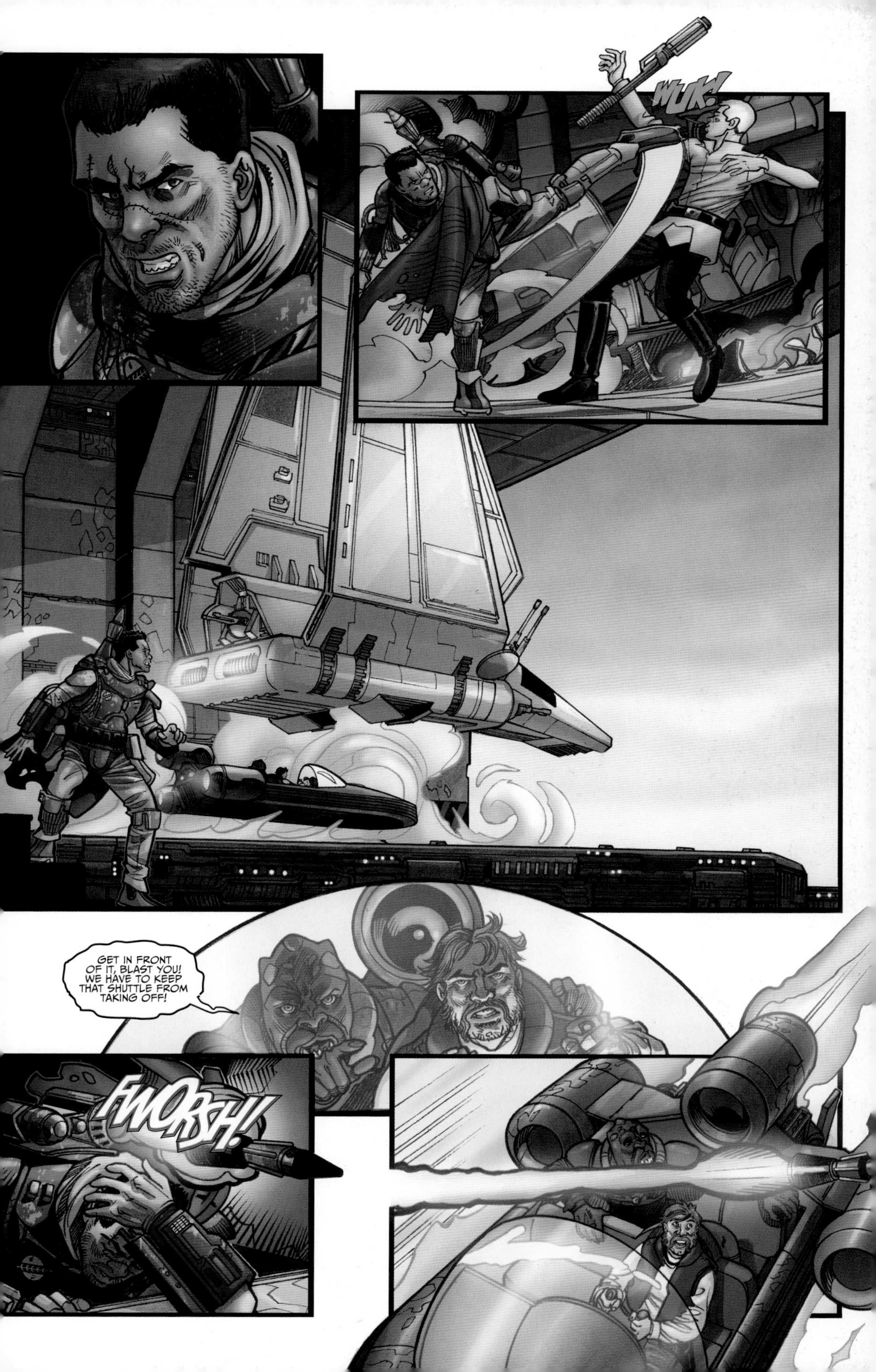
WUK!
GET IN FRONT OF IT, BLAST YOU! WE HAVE TO KEEP THAT SHUTTLE FROM TAKING OFF!
FWORSH!

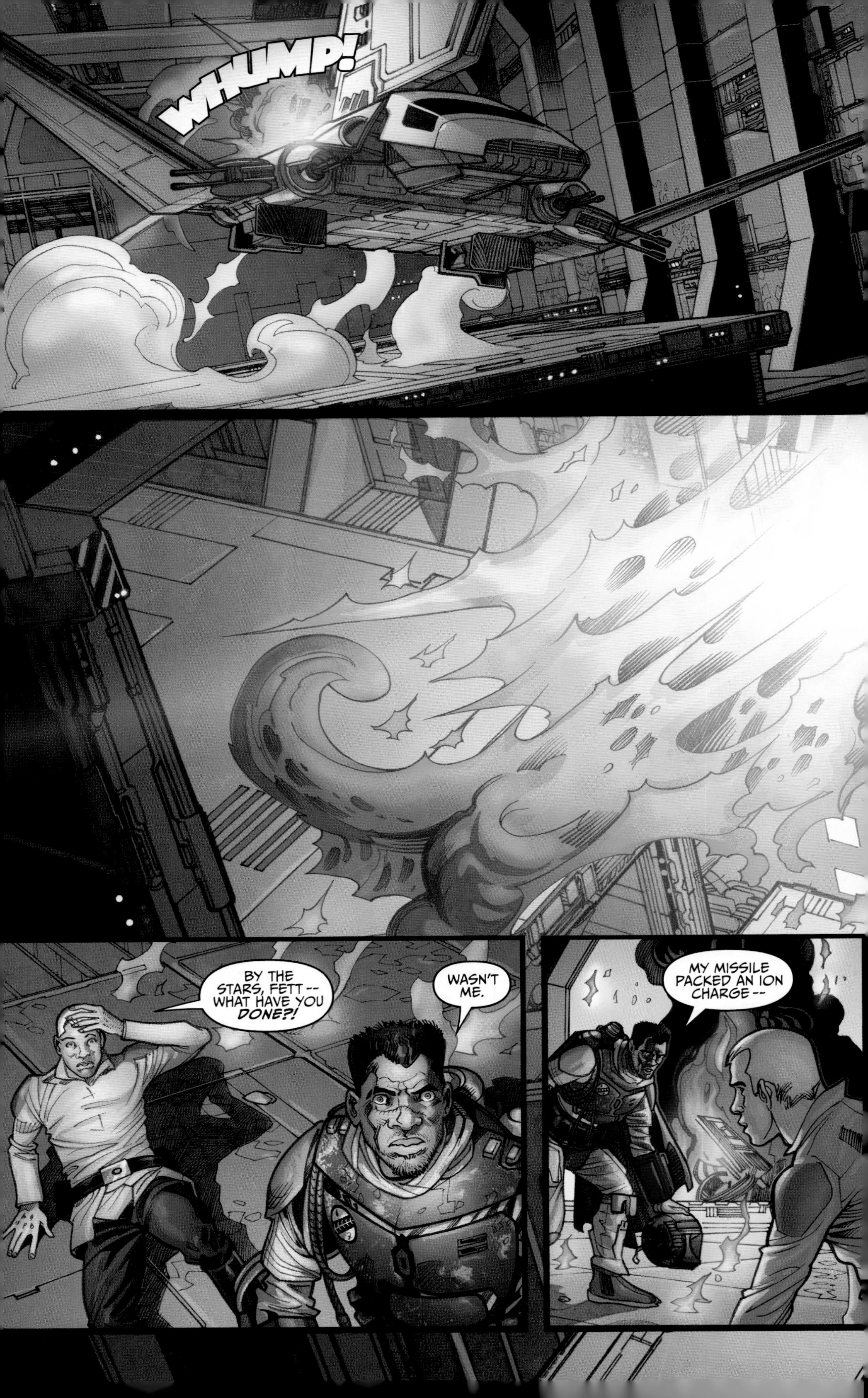
WHUMP!
BY THE STARS, FETT -- WHAT HAVE YOU DONE?!
WASN'T ME.
MY MISSILE PACKED AN ION CHARGE --

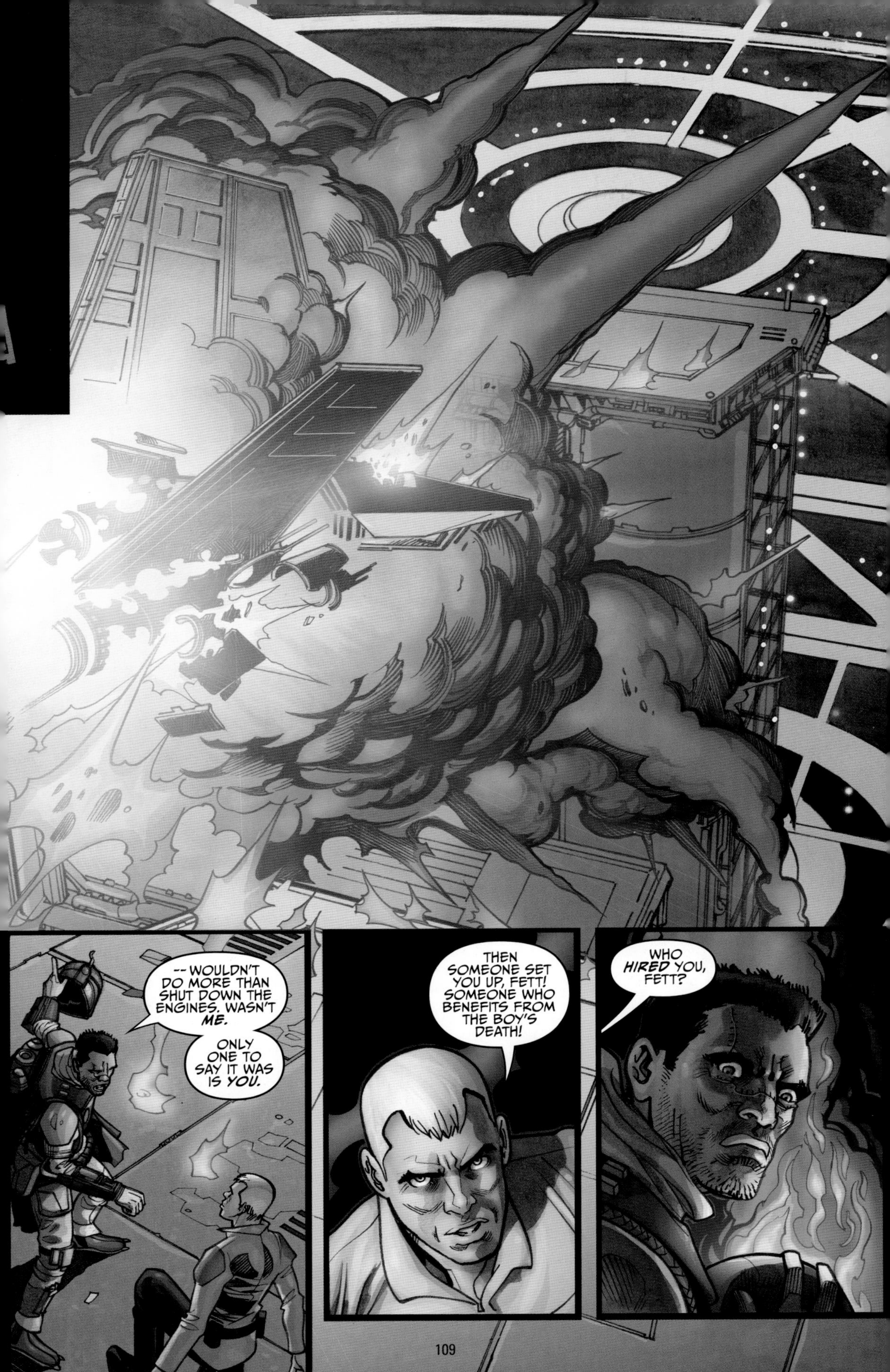

--WOULDN'T DO MORE THAN SHUT DOWN THE ENGINES. WASN'T *ME.*
ONLY ONE TO SAY IT WAS IS *YOU.*
THEN SOMEONE SET YOU UP, FETT! SOMEONE WHO BENEFITS FROM THE BOY'S DEATH!
WHO *HIRED* YOU, FETT?

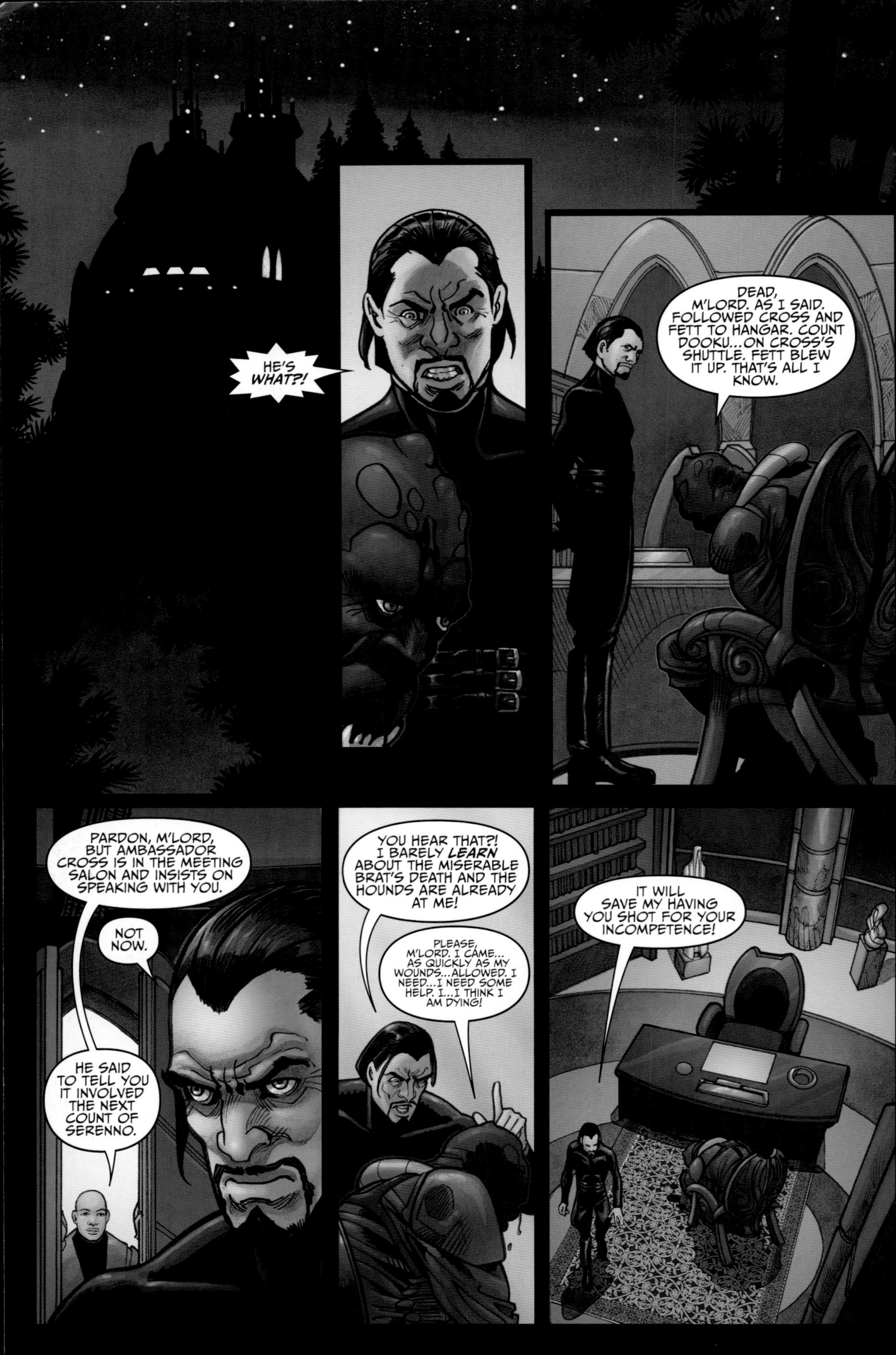
HE'S *WHAT?!*
DEAD, M'LORD. AS I SAID. FOLLOWED CROSS AND FETT TO HANGAR. COUNT DOOKU...ON CROSS'S SHUTTLE. FETT BLEW IT UP. THAT'S ALL I KNOW.
PARDON, M'LORD, BUT AMBASSADOR CROSS IS IN THE MEETING SALON AND INSISTS ON SPEAKING WITH YOU.
NOT NOW.
HE SAID TO TELL YOU IT INVOLVED THE NEXT COUNT OF SERENNO.
YOU HEAR THAT?! I BARELY *LEARN* ABOUT THE MISERABLE BRAT'S DEATH AND THE HOUNDS ARE ALREADY AT ME!
PLEASE, M'LORD. I CAME... AS QUICKLY AS MY WOUNDS...ALLOWED. I NEED...I NEED SOME HELP. I...I THINK I AM DYING!
IT WILL SAVE MY HAVING YOU SHOT FOR YOUR INCOMPETENCE!

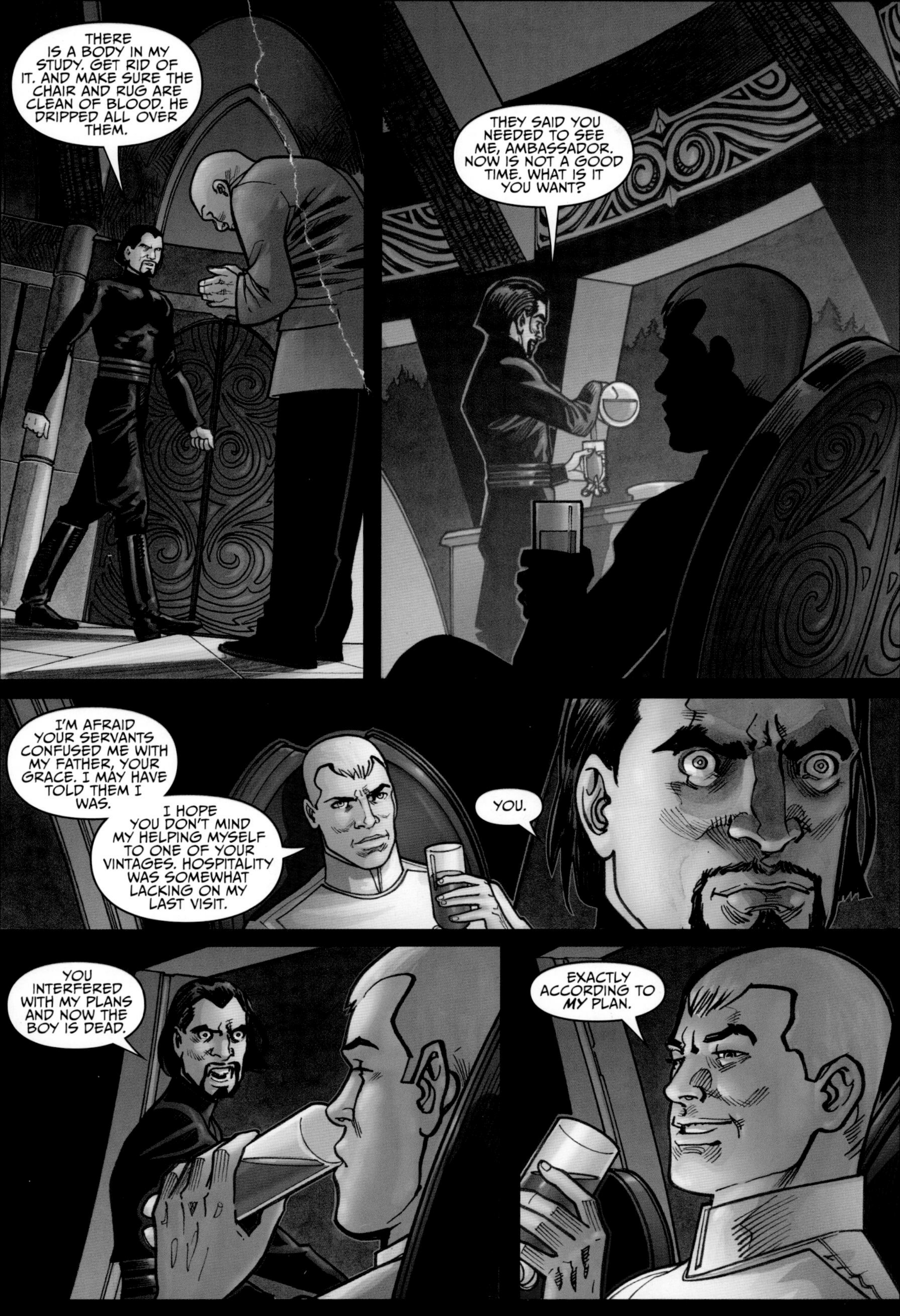
THERE IS A BODY IN MY STUDY. GET RID OF IT. AND MAKE SURE THE CHAIR AND RUG ARE CLEAN OF BLOOD. HE DRIPPED ALL OVER THEM.
THEY SAID YOU NEEDED TO SEE ME, AMBASSADOR. NOW IS NOT A GOOD TIME. WHAT IS IT YOU WANT?
I'M AFRAID YOUR SERVANTS CONFUSED ME WITH MY FATHER, YOUR GRACE. I MAY HAVE TOLD THEM I WAS.
I HOPE YOU DON'T MIND MY HELPING MYSELF TO ONE OF YOUR VINTAGES. HOSPITALITY WAS SOMEWHAT LACKING ON MY LAST VISIT.
YOU.
YOU INTERFERED WITH MY PLANS AND NOW THE BOY IS DEAD.
EXACTLY ACCORDING TO *MY* PLAN.

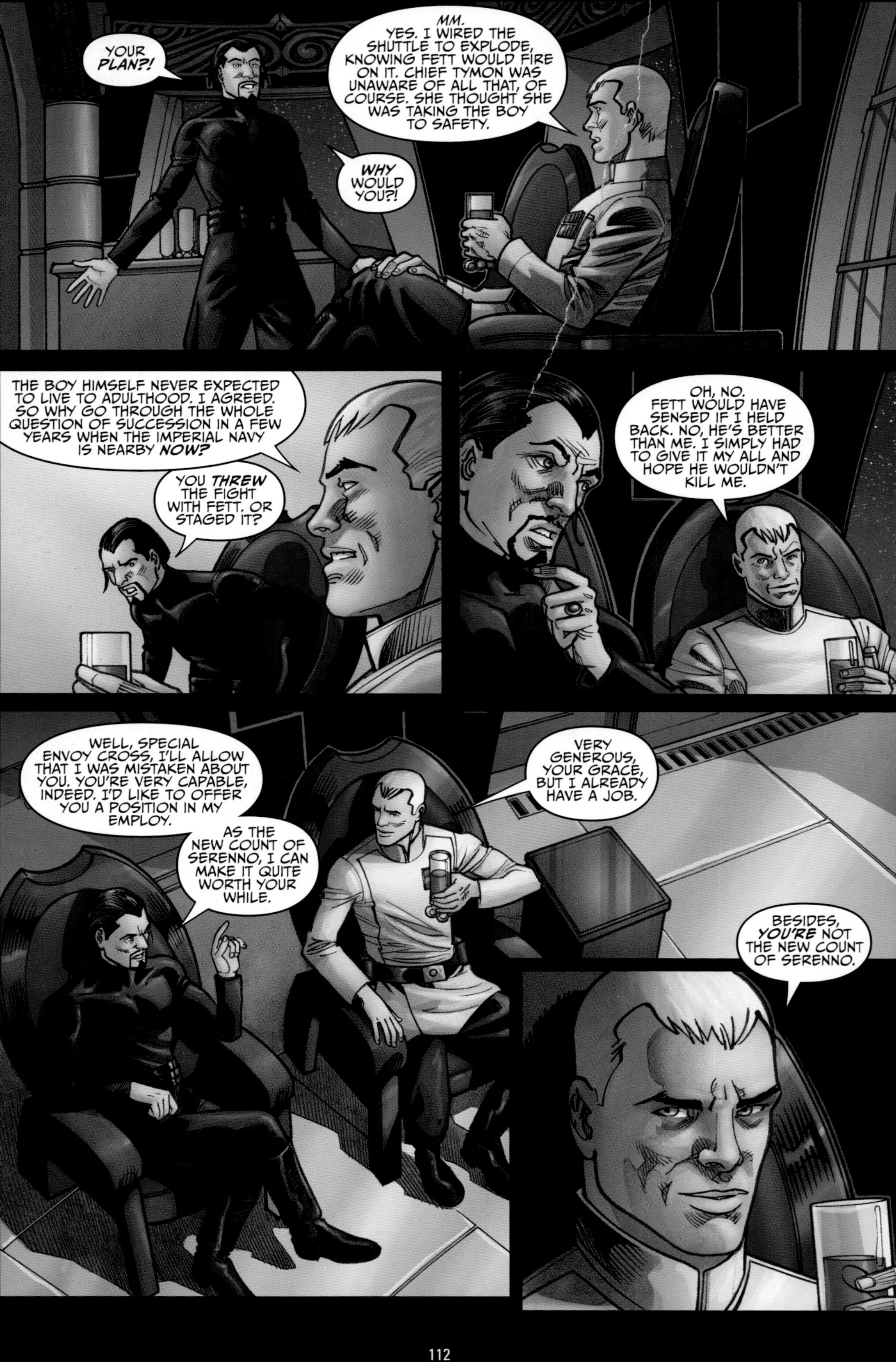
YOUR PLAN?!
MM. YES. I WIRED THE SHUTTLE TO EXPLODE, KNOWING FETT WOULD FIRE ON IT. CHIEF TYMON WAS UNAWARE OF ALL THAT, OF COURSE. SHE THOUGHT SHE WAS TAKING THE BOY TO SAFETY.
WHY WOULD YOU?!
THE BOY HIMSELF NEVER EXPECTED TO LIVE TO ADULTHOOD. I AGREED. SO WHY GO THROUGH THE WHOLE QUESTION OF SUCCESSION IN A FEW YEARS WHEN THE IMPERIAL NAVY IS NEARBY NOW?
YOU THREW THE FIGHT WITH FETT. OR STAGED IT?
OH, NO. FETT WOULD HAVE SENSED IF I HELD BACK. NO, HE'S BETTER THAN ME. I SIMPLY HAD TO GIVE IT MY ALL AND HOPE HE WOULDN'T KILL ME.
WELL, SPECIAL ENVOY CROSS, I'LL ALLOW THAT I WAS MISTAKEN ABOUT YOU. YOU'RE VERY CAPABLE, INDEED. I'D LIKE TO OFFER YOU A POSITION IN MY EMPLOY.
AS THE NEW COUNT OF SERENNO, I CAN MAKE IT QUITE WORTH YOUR WHILE.
VERY GENEROUS, YOUR GRACE, BUT I ALREADY HAVE A JOB.
BESIDES, YOU'RE NOT THE NEW COUNT OF SERENNO.

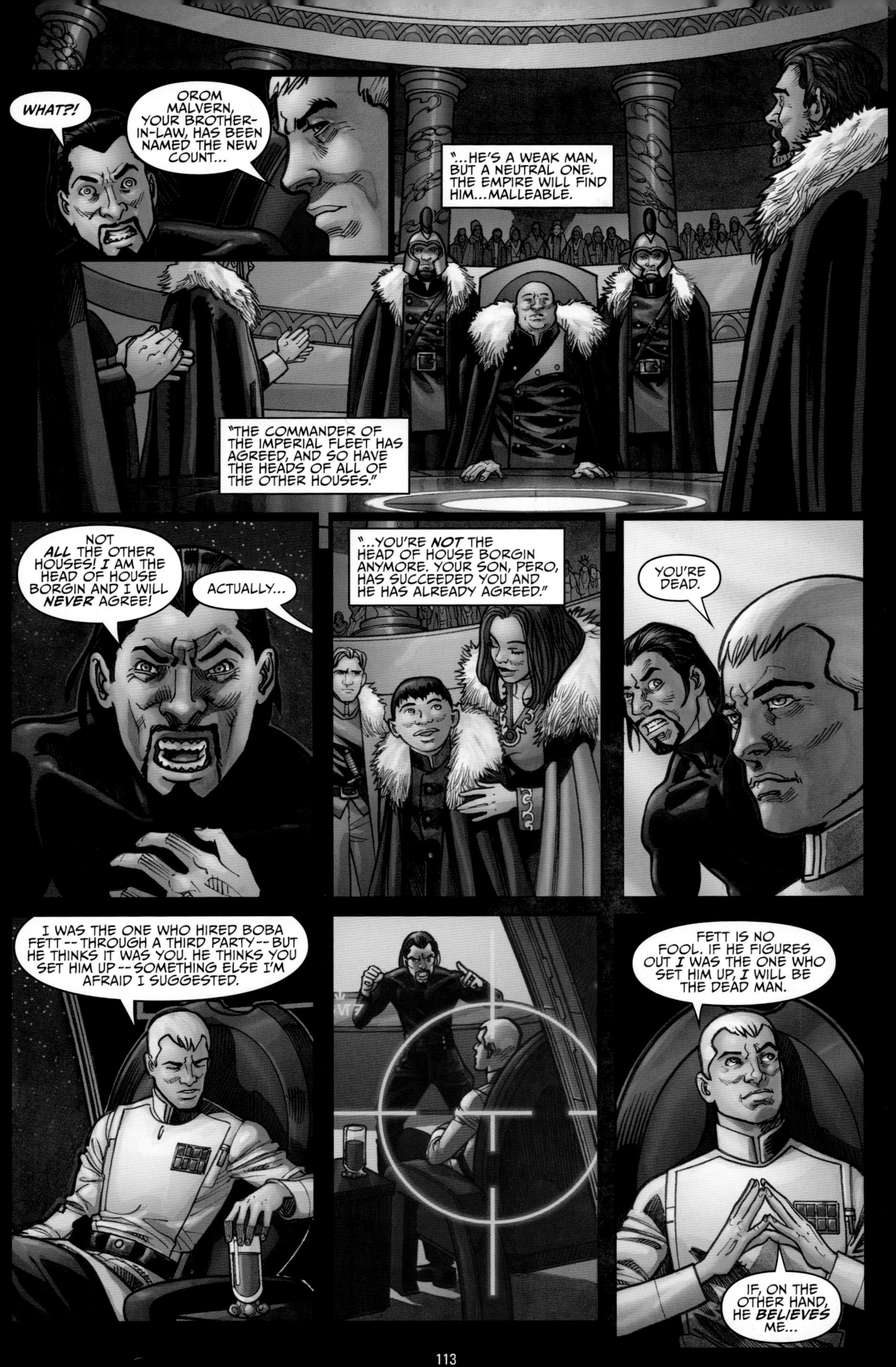
WHAT?!
OROM MALVERN, YOUR BROTHER-IN-LAW, HAS BEEN NAMED THE NEW COUNT...
"...HE'S A WEAK MAN, BUT A NEUTRAL ONE. THE EMPIRE WILL FIND HIM...MALLEABLE.
"THE COMMANDER OF THE IMPERIAL FLEET HAS AGREED, AND SO HAVE THE HEADS OF ALL OF THE OTHER HOUSES."
NOT ALL THE OTHER HOUSES! I AM THE HEAD OF HOUSE BORGIN AND I WILL NEVER AGREE!
ACTUALLY...
"...YOU'RE NOT THE HEAD OF HOUSE BORGIN ANYMORE. YOUR SON, PERO, HAS SUCCEEDED YOU AND HE HAS ALREADY AGREED."
YOU'RE DEAD.
I WAS THE ONE WHO HIRED BOBA FETT--THROUGH A THIRD PARTY--BUT HE THINKS IT WAS YOU. HE THINKS YOU SET HIM UP--SOMETHING ELSE I'M AFRAID I SUGGESTED.
FETT IS NO FOOL. IF HE FIGURES OUT I WAS THE ONE WHO SET HIM UP, I WILL BE THE DEAD MAN.
IF, ON THE OTHER HAND, HE BELIEVES ME...

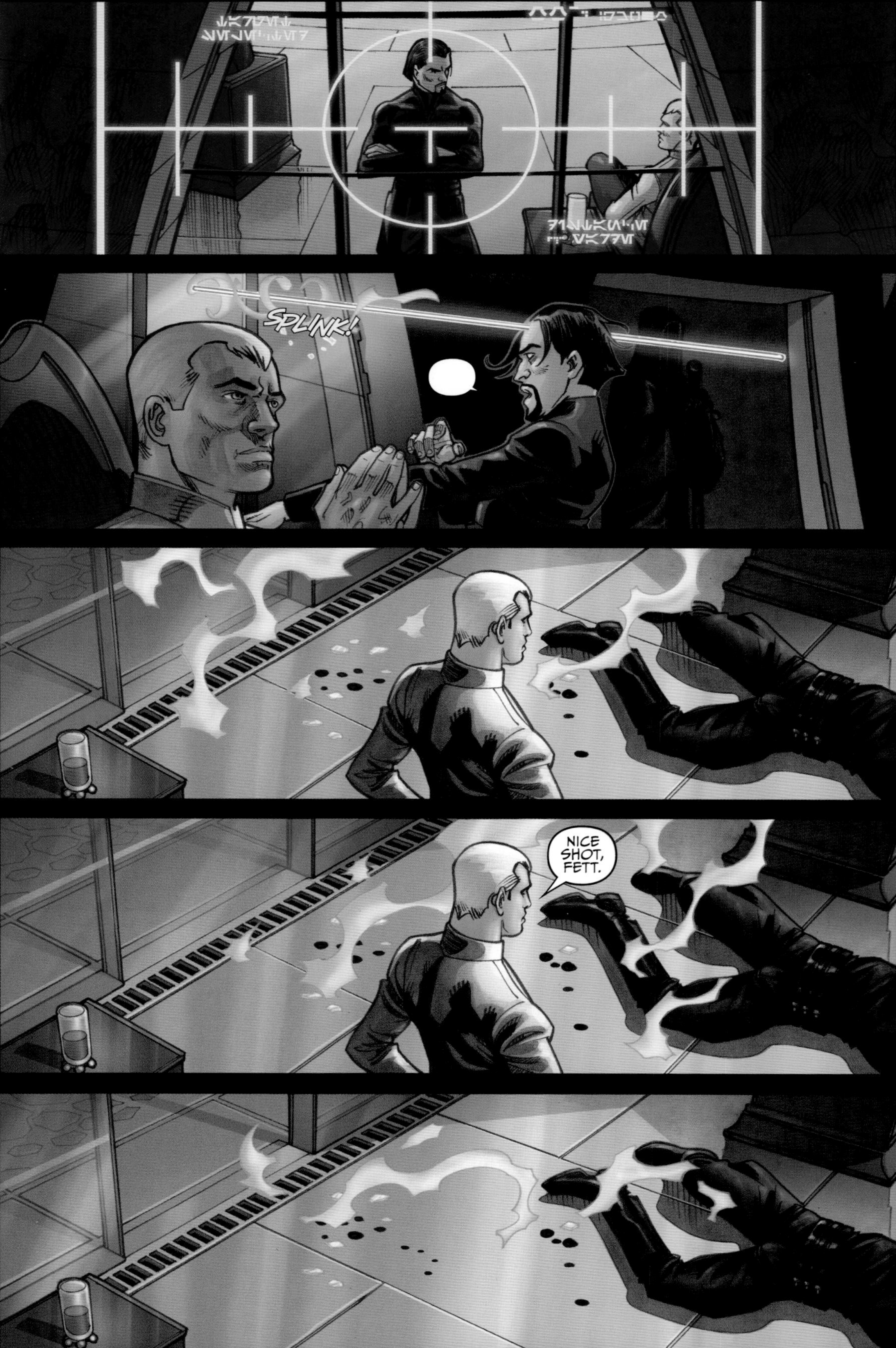
SPLINK!
NICE SHOT, FETT.

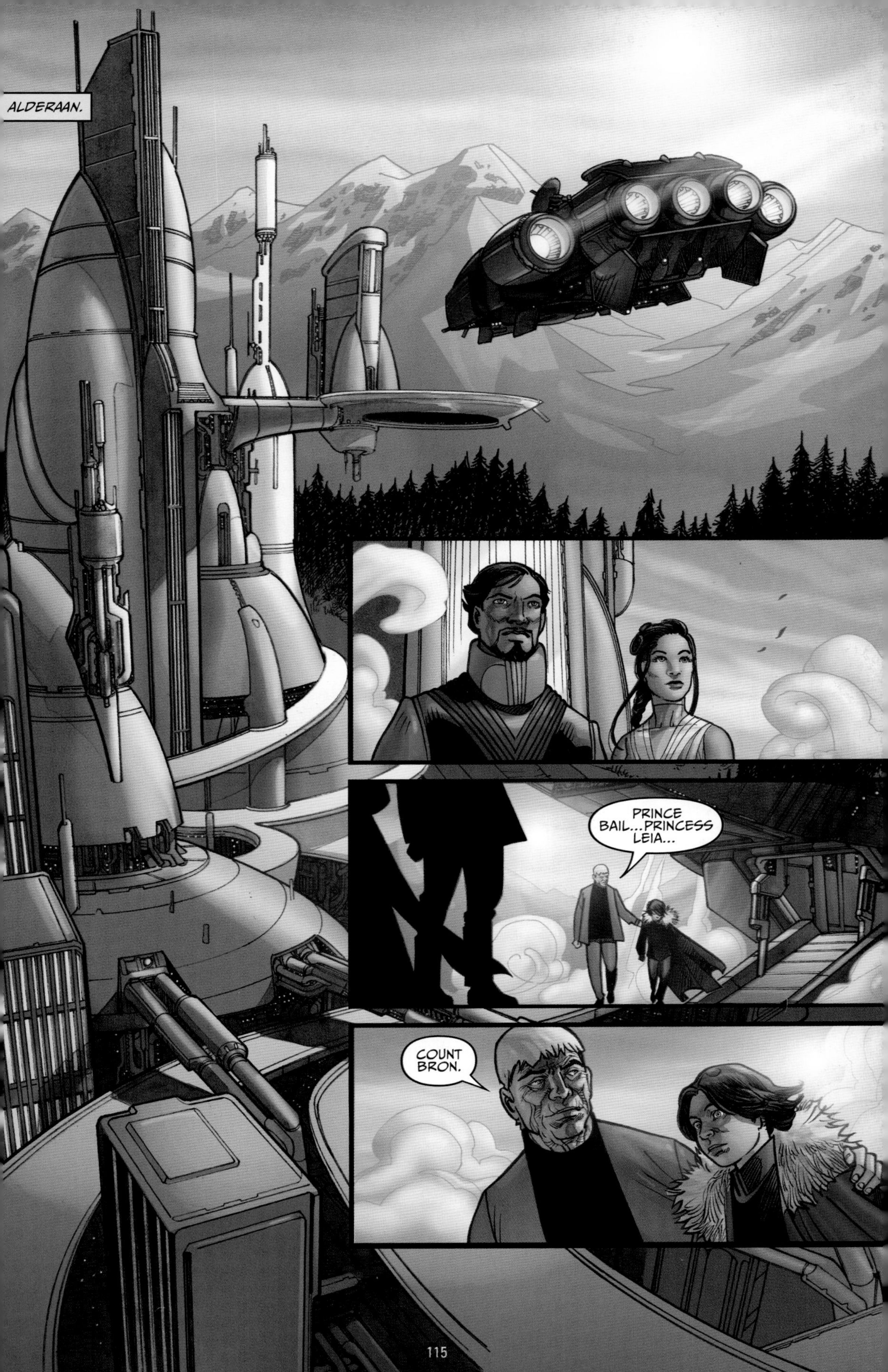

ALDERAAN.
PRINCE BAIL...PRINCESS LEIA...
COUNT BRON.

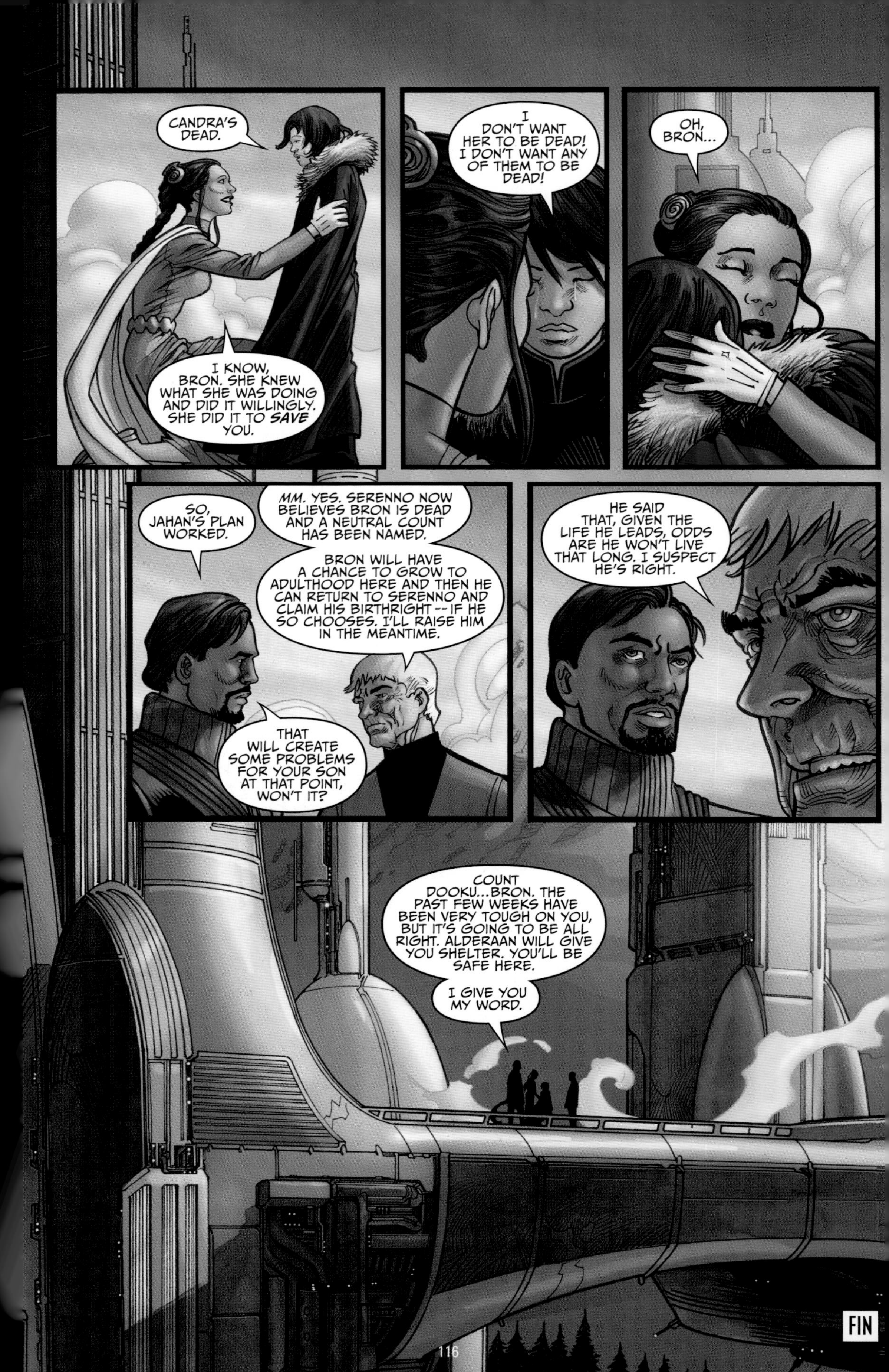
CANDRA'S DEAD.
I KNOW, BRON. SHE KNEW WHAT SHE WAS DOING AND DID IT WILLINGLY. SHE DID IT TO ***SAVE*** YOU.
I DON'T WANT HER TO BE DEAD! I DON'T WANT ANY OF THEM TO BE DEAD!
OH, BRON...
SO, JAHAN'S PLAN WORKED.
MM. YES. SERENNO NOW BELIEVES BRON IS DEAD AND A NEUTRAL COUNT HAS BEEN NAMED.
BRON WILL HAVE A CHANCE TO GROW TO ADULTHOOD HERE AND THEN HE CAN RETURN TO SERENNO AND CLAIM HIS BIRTHRIGHT -- IF HE SO CHOOSES. I'LL RAISE HIM IN THE MEANTIME.
THAT WILL CREATE SOME PROBLEMS FOR YOUR SON AT THAT POINT, WON'T IT?
HE SAID THAT, GIVEN THE LIFE HE LEADS, ODDS ARE HE WON'T LIVE THAT LONG. I SUSPECT HE'S RIGHT.
COUNT DOOKU...BRON. THE PAST FEW WEEKS HAVE BEEN VERY TOUGH ON YOU, BUT IT'S GOING TO BE ALL RIGHT. ALDERAAN WILL GIVE YOU SHELTER. YOU'LL BE SAFE HERE.
I GIVE YOU MY WORD.
FIN

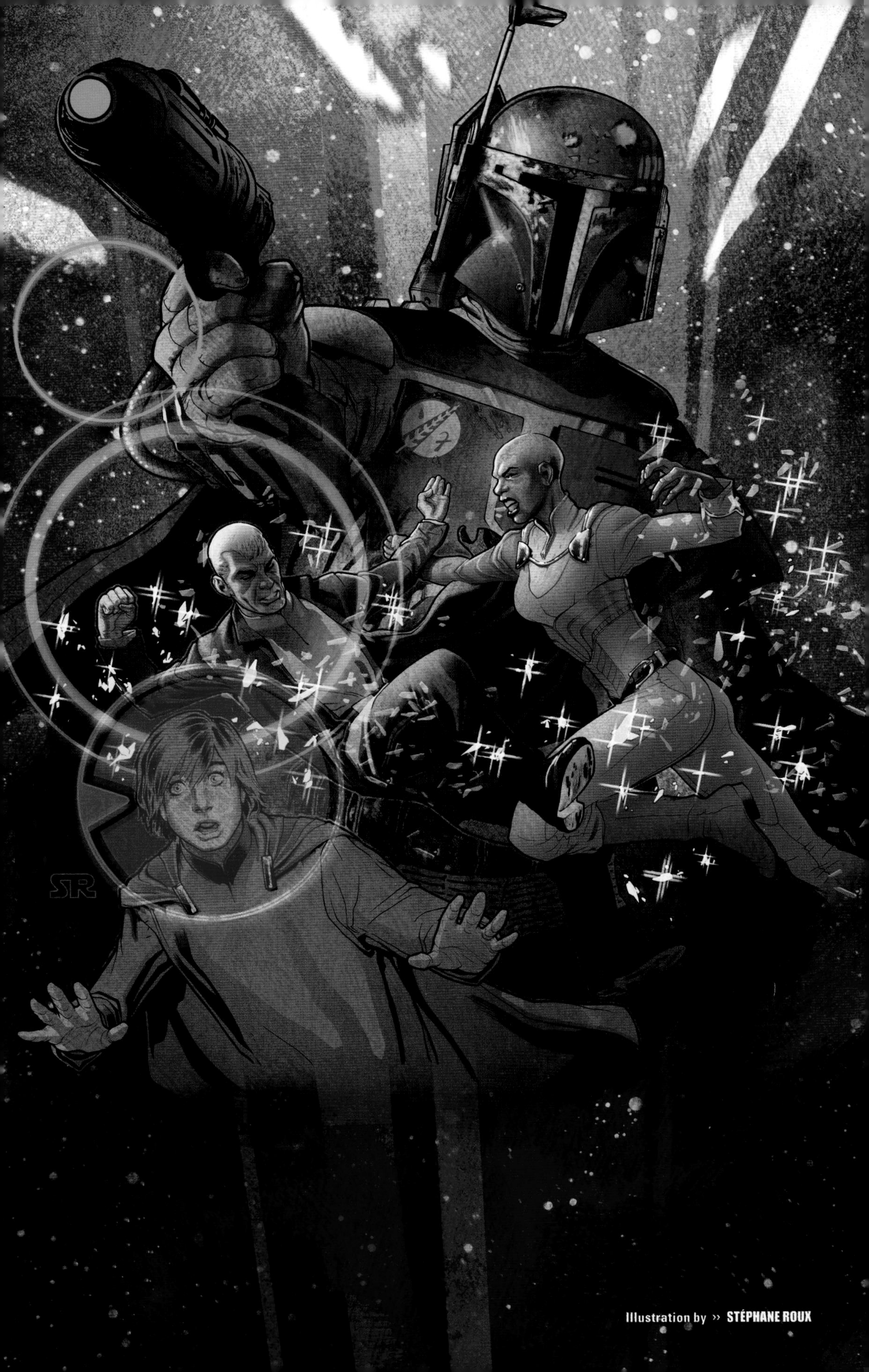
SR

Illustration by ›› **STÉPHANE ROUX**

STAR WARS GRAPHIC NOVEL TIMELINE (IN YEARS)

Dawn of the Jedi—36,000 BSW4

Omnibus: Tales of the Jedi—5,000–3,986 BSW4

Knights of the Old Republic—3,964–3,963 BSW4

The Old Republic—3678, 3653, 3600 BSW4

Lost Tribe of the Sith—2974 BSW4

Knight Errant—1,032 BSW4

Jedi vs. Sith—1,000 BSW4

Jedi: The Dark Side—53 BSW4

Omnibus: Rise of the Sith—33 BSW4

Episode I: The Phantom Menace—32 BSW4

Omnibus: Emissaries and Assassins—32 BSW4

Omnibus: Quinlan Vos—Jedi in Darkness—31–30 BSW4

Omnibus: Menace Revealed—31–22 BSW4

Honor and Duty—22 BSW4

Blood Ties—22 BSW4

Episode II: Attack of the Clones—22 BSW4

Clone Wars—22–19 BSW4

Omnibus: Clone Wars—22–19 BSW4

Clone Wars Adventures—22–19 BSW4

Darth Maul: Death Sentence—20 BSW4

Episode III: Revenge of the Sith—19 BSW4

Purge—19 BSW4

Dark Times—19 BSW4

Omnibus: Droids—5.5 BSW4

Omnibus: Boba Fett—3 BSW4–10 ASW4

Agent of the Empire—3 BSW4

The Force Unleashed—2 BSW4

Omnibus: At War with the Empire—1 BSW4

Episode IV: A New Hope—SW4

Star Wars—0 ASW4

Classic Star Wars—0–3 ASW4

Omnibus: A Long Time Ago. . . .—0–4 ASW4

Empire—0 ASW4

Omnibus: The Other Sons of Tatooine—0 ASW4

Omnibus: Early Victories—0–3 ASW4

Jabba the Hutt: The Art of the Deal—1 ASW4

Episode V: The Empire Strikes Back—3 ASW4

Omnibus: Shadows of the Empire—3.5–4.5 ASW4

Episode VI: Return of the Jedi—4 ASW4

Omnibus: X-Wing Rogue Squadron—4–5 ASW4

The Thrawn Trilogy—9 ASW4

Dark Empire—10 ASW4

Crimson Empire—11 ASW4

Jedi Academy: Leviathan—12 ASW4

Union—19 ASW4

Chewbacca—25 ASW4

Invasion—25 ASW4

Legacy—130–138 ASW4

Dawn of the Jedi
36,000 years before
Star Wars: A New Hope

Old Republic Era
25,000–1000 years before
Star Wars: A New Hope

Rise of the Empire Era
1000–0 years before Star
Wars: A New Hope

Rebellion Era
0–5 years after
Star Wars: A New Hope

New Republic Era
5–25 years after
Star Wars: A New Hope

New Jedi Order Era
25+ years after
Star Wars: A New Hope

Legacy Era
130+ years after
Star Wars: A New Hope

Vector
Crosses four eras in timeline

Volume 1 contains:
Knights of the Old Republic Volume 5
Dark Times Volume 3
Volume 2 contains:
Rebellion Volume 4
Legacy Volume 6

Infinities
Does not apply to timeline

Sergio Aragones Stomps Star Wars
Star Wars Tales
Omnibus: Infinities
Tag and Bink
Star Wars Visionaries

BSW4 = before *Episode IV: A New Hope*. ASW4 = after *Episode IV: A New Hope*.

STAR WARS®
DARK TIMES

In the wake of the Clone Wars and the destruction of the Jedi Order, the dark times have begun; this is the beginning of the era of Darth Vader and Emperor Palpatine. The future is grim, evil is on the rise, and there are no more safe places in the galaxy.

Dark Times Volume 1:
The Path to Nowhere
ISBN 978-1-59307-792-1 | $17.95

Dark Times Volume 2:
Parallels
ISBN 978-1-59307-945-1 | $17.95

Dark Times Volume 3:
Vector Volume 1
ISBN 978-1-59582-226-0 | $17.99

Dark Times Volume 4:
Blue Harvest
ISBN 978-1-59582-264-2 | $17.99

Dark Times Volume 5:
Out of the Wilderness
ISBN 978-1-59582-926-9 | $17.99

DARK
HORSE
BOOKS
DarkHorse.com

AVAILABLE AT YOUR LOCAL COMICS SHOP OR BOOKSTORE

STAR WARS®
LEGACY

More than one hundred years have passed since the events in *Return of the Jedi* and the days of the New Jedi Order. There is new evil gripping the galaxy, shattering a resurgent Empire, and seeking to destroy the last of the Jedi. Even as their power is failing, the Jedi hold onto one final hope . . . the last remaining heir to the Skywalker legacy.

AVAILABLE AT YOUR LOCAL COMICS SHOP OR BOOKSTORE

TO FIND A COMICS SHOP IN YOUR AREA, CALL 1-888-266-4226.
For more information or to order direct: *On the web: DarkHorse.com *E-mail: mailorder@DarkHorse.com
*Phone: 1-800-862-0052 Mon.-Fri. 9 A.M. to 5 P.M. Pacific Time.

STAR WARS © Lucasfilm Ltd. & ™ (BL 8015)